AF539985

STRUCTURE OF ENGLISH LANGUAGE

STRUCTURE OF ENGLISH LANGUAGE

[For B.A./M.A. (English) Courses of All Universities]

By
B.D. SHARMA

ANMOL PUBLICATIONS PVT. LTD.
NEW DELHI - 110 002 (INDIA)

ANMOL PUBLICATIONS PVT. LTD.
4374/4B, Ansari Road, Daryaganj
New Delhi - 110 002
Ph.: 23261597, 23278000
Visit us at: www.anmolpublications.com

Structure of English Language

First Published, 2005

ISBN 81-261-2122-X

PRINTED IN INDIA

Published by J.L. Kumar for Anmol Publications Pvt. Ltd., New Delhi - 110 002 and Printed at Mehra Offset Press, Delhi.

Contents

Preface *vii*

1. History of Language 1
2. Types of Changes in Present Day Situation 46
3. Family of Languages and Descent of English 90
4. Landmarks in the History of English 103
5. Foreign Influence on Language 154
6. Spelling and Pronunciation 213
7. English Grammer 230
8. Makers of Words 249

Preface

Structure of English Language as a paper is being taught at the graduate and post graduate level in M.A. (English) syllabus in almost all the Indian Universities. This book is a simple and easy introduction about the language history, family of languages, spelling and pronunciation, english grammer and influence of foreign language. Thus the matter presented here would be of interest as well as great use to the students of graduate and post graduate level.

The major topics dealt in this book are—History of Language; Types of Changes in Present Day Situation; Family of Languages and Descent of English; Landmarks in the History of English; Foreign Influence on Language; Spelling and Pronunciation; English Grammer; Makers of Words.

B.D. Sharma

1

History of Language

The English language as a separate idiom came into existence when the Teutonic Tribes had made themselves masters of the greater part of South Britain. The settlers spoke dialects which were very much allied, and from a fusion of their dialects resulted the English language. But the historical records of Englísh do not go so far back as this, the oldest written text in the English language date from 700 A.D. and from this time onwards, inspite of the loss of many manuscripts, there is an adequate evidence for the language in use at that time. The history of English from the earliest days to the present time has been one of the continuous development. But the language has been undergoing constant change ever since it was a language, and it is changing still, but the transition from the one period to another has been quite gradual, though in some periods changes have taken place more rapidly than in other periods. English is now divided, both in its language and literature, into three divisions, Old, Middle and Modern English.

The English language in common with all other languages existing today has an eventful history in the past. It was not always as what we know it now. It is at present effort to enumerate briefly those external historical events which have left a definite impress upon the English language.

Historians of the English language distinguish three great periods of its development. The following may serve as a brief introduction to each of the periods of its growth:

(i) **The Old English Period (600-1100).** The first is the old English Period sometimes also called the Anglo-Saxon

Period. This period was full inflexions because during this period the endings of the noun the adjective and the verb were preserved almost unimpaired. Earlier the inhabitants of English were called the Britans or Celts and their language was called Celtic. Probably Celtic language was spoken in England throughout the period of Roman occupation from 55 B.C. to 410 A.D. Soon after the withdrawal of Romans from England, the 'English' tribes called Anglo, Saxon and Jute descended with their hordes and began to settle and fight their way up the rivers and along the coasts from about the first half of the fifth century. The Superior Celtic civilization, their spiritual and intellectual supremacy came rapidly to an end. The English tribes drove them westwards. Coming of the two races into contact brought a number of Celtic words and with them some Latin words into the English language. But many of the celts fled into the hills of Wales, Cornwall and Scotland and there, their language was perpetuated, and the language of the invading tribes became the language of England and came to be known as old English or Anglo Saxon.

(ii) The Middle English Period (1100-1500). The conquest of England in 1066 by William of Normandy is another most important landmark in the history of English. In the course of its history, English language was much effected by the event so called. The immediate results of the Norman conquest were that Government passed out of the hands of English men into those of the Normans. Norman bishops, Norman knights and Norman barons flooded the country. The English language had come into contact with the French even before the Norman Conquest. After this Norman Conquest for some years there were two languages spoken, English by the Saxon Nobility and French by the Norman barons and official classes. But the Norman French enjoyed greater prestige and higher social status, because it was the language of court, of the nobility, of the law courts and of learned professions. But the English men naturally clung to their own speech and about 90 percent of people still spoke English. The result of such enteraction of the two languages was the emergence of what is called Middle English. Gradually a change came over and English replaced French as the language of law courts in 1362. Therefore we can say that the Middle English period is one of the series of momentus changes in life of the nation and in the history of the language.

(iii) The Modern English Period (1500 Onwards). It should not be imagined that these three are sharply marked periods and that between the close of one period and beginning of another were a complete and sudden change. With the closing years of the fifteenth century the New learning spread to England from Italy, with the introduction of Greek into Oxford and Cambridge, a new era began in the culture of England. Another important event in the history of English Language was the invention of printing. Printing discredited dialect and contributed to the establishment of 'standard' to the language. Printing also made it possible and convenient to bring books with in the reach of all. Thus, it proved a powerful force for promoting a standard uniform language and to spread it all over the country. There was a great increase in the number of schools, and journalism came into existence and the novel was beginning to grow popular.

CHARACTERISTICS OF ENGLISH

The English language is spoken and read by the largest number of people in the world. It is like a mighty tree which today spreads its branches over so many people. But the land on which it has grown like such a mighty tree was for many centuries unconscious of any English footfall. English is spoken by more native speakers than any other language except presumably. North Chinese, if we count the important factor of foreign speakers, English is the most widespread of languages. The number of native speakers of English was estimated for 1920 at about 170 millions. Atmost all of these speakers use **Standard English.**

The wide appeal of the language is not merely due to **historical, political** and **economic reasons** as some people seem to believe. The significance of English is also due to certain inherent qualities and characteristic features which outstand in making it what it is today. It is worth labouring to know what they are. Long before the Teotonic people settled in Britain it formed part of a continent stretching far into the Northern and Western seas. The inhabitants lived in caves or in the huts made of the branches of trees. The climate was cold and wet, and a short summer was followed by a long dull and severe winter. But the land had the charm of its own.

It is of course difficult to characterise a language in general terms. Languages are not always amenable to such description. Nevertheless, it can be said that the English Language is the most receptive and heterogeneous tongue. From almost every language of the world it has taken to itself, the vocabulary, grammatical use and habits of spelling and pronounciation. The historical study of the language shows that in the fifth and sixth centuries when the Angelo Saxons, and Jutes conquered England, it was a 'pure' unmixed language with an extraordinary flexibility to make compound words from its elements, to express new ideas. But througthout its history it has received foreign words with readiness and ease and has assimilated the alien elements to its own character. Hence the copiousness and rich variety of its vocabulary.

The another important characteristic features of English is its extraordinary simplicity of inflexions. Old English was a highly inflected language but modern English has evolved through progressive simplification of inflexions. As a result of dropping out inflexional endings, the relationships of words in a sentence is indicated, unlike in some European languages, by word-order. This is the important feature of English. In inflected languages like Latin, German, the inflexions indicate the relationship of words in the sentence and the word-order can be fairly free. But in English, word-order is fixed in relation to meaning in the sentence like "the dog bit the man" without making it a startling news.

Among three Teotonic tribes the Angels were the last to arrive on the scene. But they were more influential than the other two tribes and their name observed that of Jute and Saxon and stamped itself on the land they won. From their name the nation as well as the language was called English. The word English is derived from the name of the Angles but is used without destruction for the language of all the three Teotonic tribes and for all the people living in the island. The form of the word was first **English,** from **Angletisc.**

One anther characteristic which gives English an exceptional advantage is natural gender in place of grammatical gender of other European languages. In learning English, the student does not have to labour under the burden of memorizing, along with the meaning of every noun, its gender. In Roman language, as in Hindi, there are only two genders. Everything on the earth is either Masculine or feminine. Though in Germanic languages there are three genders, the way the gender is attributed to the noun is arbitrary to the point of being irrational. Thus in German, sun is femimine, moon is masculine while child, woman and maiden are neuter. In English, Gender is determined by the sex of living creatures, while determinate nouns are called neuter. This is undoubtedly a great advantage in facilitating the acquisition of English by foreigners.

An other characteristic is that in its phonetic structure, English presents an impression of precision and neatness. The two groups of consonants, the voiced and the voiceless are well defined and present a picture of symmetry. They are so precisely pronounced that there is no scope for ambiguity in sound. Fortunately English is free from indistinct or half slurred consonants, excepting that r, when not followed by a vowal sound is indistinct. But then has been gradually giving up its claims to the rank of a consonant. In English, modification of consonant by the surrounding vowels is less frequent than in some other European languages. The vowel sounds, too are clear precise and relatively independent of their surroundings.

The another feature of the English Language is that in great many ways it is particularly suited to tense and vigorous ways of expression. English sentences are amenable to abbreviations which render the language business–like and convenient. By avoiding hyperbolic expressions which do not mean what they say, English has acquired a kind of balance and sobriety. Judged from the standard of logic there is no other language so high as English. It has a tense system that is superior to any other of European language while we find the time divided into present, past and future in many languages, further division of each of those tenses into simple perfect, perfect continuous and progressive is nowhere seen so consistently and precisely as in English. The distinction subtle and difficult as it is, is superior to any one found in other language. English Grammar, difficult as it is for a foreigner allows certain freedom as, for instance, in the use of a number of words like family, clergy, committee, club are of plural number from the logic of facts, and singular from the grammatical point of view. But there are no rigorous rules in the uses of them either as singular or plural or depending on the meaning to be conveyed.

According to **Otto Jespersons**, "The English Language is a methodical, energetic, business-like and sober language, that does not care much for finery and elegance but does care for logical consistency and is opposed to any attempt to narrow-in life by police regulations and strict rules either of grammer or of lexicon".

In this way we can say that the language reveals the soul of the nation. The English language, it will be evident, is very humble and obscure in its origin. It is in no sense native to England. The original speakers of the tongue from which English was born were the three Teotonic tribes conquered the island in the fifth and sixth centuries. The English language is not the result of any human design. It is the sum total of a series of historical incidents.

WRITTEN FORMS AND BASIC FUNCTIONS OF LANGUAGE

The spoken form of any given language is liable to undergo change and development in the course of its history. The development undrgone by the English language in the last one thousand years can be understood by comparing a passage of old writing English with a passage from Modern English. Written language always come later than the spoken form and spoken form of any word is a symbol of the thing referred to by that word. The written form is the symbol of that symbol; and so it is twice removed from the referred thing. The primitive form of writing meant carving, painting or drawing of the symbolic elements or the visible features of an experience. When the association between the written symbol and the spoken word becomes fixed, the symbol may come to lose original pictorial value and to deviate from its older form. At this stage the association has come to be one of written symbol and spoken sound regardless of the meaning borne by the sound. Later the symbol are only used in phonetics and the number of symbols are reduced. The alphabets of many Indian languages as well as the national alphabets of Japanese consists of such syllabaries. Syllabaries is a further simplification of writing when these characters are used to represent not whole syllables but single sounds of the language as in Greek, Latin and derived alphabets, including in English. Writing is an outgrowth of drawing. Probably all peoples make pictures by painting drawing scratching or carving. These pictures aside from other uses sometimes serve as messages or reminders that is they modify the conduct of the beholder and they may be persistently used in this way. The Indians of North America are skilful draftmen and in older times made extensive practical use of pictures.

The records and messages, like writing, have the advantage of being permanent and transportable, but they fall short of writing in accuracy since they bear no fixed relation of linguistic forms and accordingly do not share in the delicate adjustment of the latter. In the use of pictures we can often see the beginnings of the transition, and traces of it remain in the actual systems of writing.

Real writing uses a limited number of conventional symbols we must therefore suppose that in the transition the pictures become conventionalized. The way of outlining each animals for instance, becomes so fixed that even a very imperfect sketch leaves us doubt as to the species of animal. To some degree it is true of the pictures of **American Indians**. In actual system of writing we often find symbols which still betray this origin. When the picture has become rigidly conventionalised we may call it a character. A character is a uniform mark or set of marks which people produce under certain conditions and to which accordingly, they respond in a certain way. Once this habit is established, the resemblance of the character to any particular object is of secondary importance, and may be obliterated by changes in the convention of forming the character. The other more important place of the transition from the use of picture to real writing is the association of the characters with linguistic froms. Most situations contain features that do not lead themselves to picturing; the picture-user resorts to all sorts of devices that will elicit the proper response.Thus we saw the Indian drawing twenty nine strokes above his beaver to represent the number of beaver-pelts. Instead of depicting the process of exchange by a series of pictures, he represented it by two crossed lines with the sets of traded objects at either side.

When a picture user was confronted by a problem of this kind, we may suppose that he actually spoke to himself and tried out various wordings of the troublesome message. Language, after all is our one way of communicating the kind of things that do not lend themselves to drawing. If we make this supposition we can understand that the picture-users might in time arrange the characters in the order of the spoken words of their language, and that they might develop a convention of represening every part say every word, of the spoken utterance by some character.

In real writing some characters have a twofold value. For which they represent both a picturable object and a phonetic or linguistic form; other characters having lost their pictorial value, represent only phonetic or linguistic form, purely pictoral characters that are not associated with speech-forms sink into subsidary use. The linguistic value predominates more and more especially as the characters because conventionalized in shape, losing their resemblance to pictured objects. The characters become symbol that is marks or groups of marks that conventionally represent some linguistic form and respond to the symbol as they respond to the hearing of the linguistic form. Actually the writer utters the speech from before or during the act of writing and the hearer utters it in the act of reading, only after considerable practise. Do we succced in making these speech-movements inaudible and inconspicuous? It is different that languages is used to serve a multiplicity of purposes. In accordance with the different purposes to be served, language is used in different ways and we respond differently to each particular use of language. For example, there is the language of science, journalism, advertising, political oratory, political effusion and prayer and worship. In these instances language is used as if it were a multipurpose tool which could be put to a variety of uses as and when required. Many people fail to understand the subtle and complicated nature of language.

One of the basic functions of languages is to communicate information of some kind or another. Information here can include propaganda of all kinds. All informative discourse is used to describe the world around us and to reason about it.

Besides informative there are two other basic functions of language. There are the expressive and the directive functions. Science provides us with instances of the best informative discourse. Poetry gives us the finest examples of the expressive function of language. The poetry cannot be communicated whereas in information it needs expression of language. All poets attempt to communicate their own feelings and attitude. When the poet Robert Burns compares his love to a red rose, which is newly sprung in June, or to melody that is sweetly played in tune, he is trying to express the emotion which he feels keenly and trying to arouse similar feelings in the readers. Not only poets but other people also use expressive language to express their tender feelings. The lover uses the expressive language to convey his passions and tenderness to his beloved. While dealing with expressive language we are not to apply the common standard of truth or falsehood, correctness or incorrectness. We must bear in mind the fact that the purpose of the poet in writing his poetry is not to convey information but to express emotion and to arouse it in the reader. There is no doubt that some poems have informative contents which cannot be denied while dealing their total effect.,

The third basic function of language is to cause some overt action. The common examples of directive function of language are commands and requests. Commands are distinguished from request in a very subtle way and any command can be turned into a request by adding "please" at the beginning or by a suitable change in the tone of the voice or in the expression of the face. As directive discourse has no truth, value, it cannot be described as true or false.

The examples of informative, expressive and directive language have been compared by giving M. Copi to chemically pure specimens. This three fold division cannot be applied to all languages mechanically because very often we find in the most ordinary use of language, a combination of all three functions. For example a poem may be both informative and directive. A sermon at the same time is both directive and expressive. The serman preached may also contain some facts which are conveyed through the informative use of language. A treatise on science, though primarily informative can also convey to the reader something of the writers enthusiasm and thus serve the expressive function of language. In addition to this, it may also be directive in function in as much as it bids the reader to check for himself whether the conclusions arrived at by the author are correct. Thus we find that most ordinary uses of language involve all the three basic functions of conveying information, evincing emotion and inducing action.

The scholars stated that the grammatical features of language in philosoplical terms took no account of the structural difference between languages, but obscured it by forcing their descriptions into the scheme of Latin Grammar. They had not observed the sounds of speech and confused them with the written symbols of the alphabets. This fails to distinguish between actual speech and the use of writing distorted also their motions about the history of language. They saw that in medieval and wisdom times highly cultivated persons wrote and also spoke good Latin, while less educated or carden scribes made many mistakes; failing to see that this Latin-writing was an artificial and academic exercise, they concluded that languages are preserved by the usage of educated and careful people and changed by the corruptions of the vulgar. In the case of the modern languages like English they believed, accordingly that the speech forms of books and of upperclass conversation represented an older and purer level from which the vulgarism of the common people had braunched off as "corruptions" by a process of **"linguistic decay"**. The Grammarions felt free, therefore to prescribe fanciful rules which they derived from consideration of logic.

Outside the tradition of Europe, several nations had developed linguistic doctrines chiefly on an antiquarian basis. The Arabs had worked out a grammar of the classical form of their languages, as it appears in the Koran, on the model of this the Jews in **Mohammedan** countries constructed a **Hebrew grammar.** At the Renaissance, European scholars became acquainted with the tradition, the term root, for the central part of a word comes from Hebrew grammer. In the far East, the Chinies had gained a great deal of antiquarian linguistic knowledge, especially in the way of lexicography.

It was in India, however, that there arose a body of knowledge which was destined to revolutionize European ideas about language. The Brahmin religion guarded as sacred tests some very ancient collections of hymns, the oldest of these collections, the Rig-Veda, dates in parts at a conservative estimate from about 1200 B.C. As the languages of these text grew antiquated, the proper way of pronouncing them, and their correct interpretation became the task of a special class of learned men. The **antiquarian** interest in language which arose in this way, was carried over into a more practical sphere. Among the Hindus, as among us, different classes of society differed in speech. Apparently these were forces at work which led upperclass speakers to adopt lower class forms of speech. We find the Hindu grammarians extending their interest from the scriptures to the upper-caste language and making rules and lists of forms descriptive of the correct type of speech, which they called **Sanskrit**. In time they worked out a systematic arrangement of grammar and lexicon. Generations of such labours must have preceded the writing of the oldest treatise that has come down to us, the grammar of "Panini". This grammar, which dates from somewhere round 350 to 250 B.C. is one of the greatest movements of human intelligence. It describes with the minutest detail, every inflection, derivation, and composition and every syntactic usage of its author's speech. No other language to this day has been so perfectly described. It may have been due in part, to this excellent codification that Sanskrit became, in time, the official and literary language of all of Brahmin India. Long after it had ceased to be spoken as anyone's native language it remained the artificial medium for all writing on learned or religious topics. Some knowledge of Sanskrit and of the Hindu Grammar had reached Europe, through missionaries.

MOMENTOUS CHANGES IN THE ENGLISH LANGUAGE

Professor Scherillo, in his history of the origins of Italian literature, commenting upon the statement frequently made that Dante created the Italian language, reminds his readers that this is claiming for the Italian poet a function like that of Adam in Eden, when he gave names to all the beasts of the field and the fowls of the air! A similar reminder might appropriately have been addressed to those writers who have called Chaucer the creator of English. Such a statement of course totally misrepresents the development of the language. Chaucer employed the London speech of his time, and a minute comparison of his usage with that of the contemporary London archives. At least Mr. Henry Bradley, in the light of his experience in editing the New English Dictionary, was very cautious about attributing such contributions to the poet. It is even doubtful if Chaucer had any important part in making the East Midland the dominant dialect. The speech of the capital would have become standard English if he had never written a line. But he did add greatly to its prestige and distinction. The very fact that he wrote in English instead of French was significant. He developed the resources of the language for literary use, and set an example which was followed by a long line of poets.

Chaucer's language, then, is late Middle English of the South East Midland type. As compared with Anglo-Saxon or some of the other dialects of Middle English, its inflections are simple and offer little difficulty to the reader to today. But many words retained a syllabic *-e,* either final or in the ending *-es* or *en,* which afterwards ceased to be pronounced, and the vowels had in general their present continental rather than their English sound. For metrical purposes, consequently, Chaucer's language was very different from ours, and it is impossible to read his verse properly—to say nothing of appreciation it—without having some knowledge of the older pronunciation and grammatical forms. It is because this knowledge was lost from the fifteenth century down to the middle of the nineteenth that many of Chaucer's most enthusiastic admirers among English poets and critics has regarded his meter as irregular and rough.

The brief grammatical outline that follows is intended to supply the reader or student with such knowledge of Chaucer's sounds and inflections as is necessary for the intelligent reading of the verse. To save space, certain inflectional forms, such as the principal parts of strong verbs, which are registered in the Glossary, are not repeated here. The Glossary also records exceptional forms, like the contracted third singular present indicative of verbs or "petrified" datives of nouns, and it shows the nominative forms of nouns and adjectives when they are likely to gave any trouble because of their unlikeness of modern English.

PRONUNCIATION

Vowels and Diphthongs. There is considerable inconsistency in the spelling of the vowels and diphthongs. Vowels are commonly, but not regularly, doubled to indicate length—not only *e*, as in modern English *e.g.* "deed" but also *a* and *o,* and rarely *i.*

Sound	*Pronunciation*	*Spelling*	*Examples*
ā	like *a* in "father"	a, aa	names, caas.
ă	like *a* in Ger. "Mann"		acan, that,
ā (close)	like *a* in "fate"	e, ee	sweete.
ē (open)	like *e* in "there"	e, ee	heeth.
ĕ	like *e* in "set"	e	tendre.
e (the neutral vowel	like *a* in "about"	e	yonge, sonne.
Ī	like *i* in "machine"	i, y	ryden, shires.
Ĭ	like *i* in "sit"	i, y	this, thyng.
ō (close)	like *o* in "note"	o, oo	good, bote.
ō (open)	like *oa* in "broad"	o, oo	holy, rood (vb.)
ŏ	like *o* in "hot"	o	oft, lot.
ū	like *oo* in "bloot"	ou, ow, ogh	fowles, droghte.
ŭ	like *u* in "full"	u, o	but, yong, songen pt. pl.).
iū	like *u* in "mute"	u, eu, ew	Pruce, vertu, salewe.
ēi	like ē in + *i*	ai, ay, ei, ey	sayle, day, wey.
au	like *ou* in "house"	au, aw	cause, draughte.
ēu	like ē + *u*	eu, ew	knew.
ēu	like ē + *u*	eu, ew	lewed.
oi	like *oy* in "boy"	oi, oy	coy, joye.
ōu	like ō + *u*	ou, ow	growen.
ōu	like õ + *u*	ou, ow	knowen, sowle.
ou	like A + *u*	o (u), before gh	fo (u) ghte, tho (u) ght.

Some of the pronunications indicated in the accompanying table are only approximate, and others are doubtful. Chaucer's close ē and ō did not quite correspond to the vowels now heard in "name" and "note", which are really diphthongal (ē + a transitional i, ō + u). It is hard to judge in how many cases Chaucer's ã preserved the sound of a in German "Mann", and when it had the sound of æ, as in modern English "that" (and AS. "pæt"). The combinations eu, ew, represented not only the descending diphthong ē*u, ew* (as in knew, from AS. cnéow; lewed, As. læwed), but also the ascending diphthong iu (as probably in salewen, Fr. "saluer"). The first sound ultimately developed into the second (as in modern English "knew", "lewd"), and it is uncertain just what Chaucer's pronunciation was in individual cases. Similarly, in the combinations ou, ow, the original distinction between ōu (with close ō) and ōu (with open ō) was apparently breaking down, and the two classes of words are not kept apart in rime. But the diphthong ou (or various origins) before gh had a different sound, which developed into the modern long vowel in "thought" and "fought". The pronunciation of the diphthongs variously spelled ai, ay, ei, ey is a matter of disagreement. The sounds concerned are of different origins, some coming, from e + i or e + g (as in selyen, we, counseil), others from ee + g (as in day, fayn), and others from a + i (as in batayle, fayle). They had all fallen together so as to rime acceptably one with another. It is doubtful whether the pronunciation was ãi (as in "aisle") or æi (approaching the modern pronunciation of "way", "day"). But a sound intermediate between the two seems probable.

The distinction between open and close ē and ō does not appear in Chaucer's spelling, and no simple rule can be given which will guide the reader in all cases. The modern spellings ea and oa ("heath", "boat") usually point to the broad pronunciation in Middle English, but there are many exceptions. The modern pronunciation—ō for Chaucer's ō (as in "rode") and oo (*i.e.*, long u) for his ō (as in "noon")—is a better test in the case of ō, but it fails with ē, where the two classes of sounds have fallen together (as in "seek" and "heath"). Even the evidence of etymology is not always decisive, for special conditions sometimes affected the development of words. But as a general rule ē (close) corresponds to AS. (or Old Mercian) ē,ēo, ON. ē and o, OF. (and Anglo-Norman) ē (close) ē (open), to AS. æe, ēa, and ĕ (when lengthened in Middle English), ON æe, and OF. (or Anglo-Norman) ē; ō (close), to AS. ō or ō lengthened before consonantal combinations, ON. ō, and OF. (or Anglo-Norman) ō (close); ō (open), to AS. or ON. ā and ŏ (when lengthened before a nasal or in open syllables and OF. ŏ (when lengthened in open syllables). For the assistance of readers who find it difficulty to apply these tests, cases of open ē and ō have been marked (ē and ō) in the Glossary of the present edition. Full treatment of the history of the sounds will of course be found in the Middle English grammars listed in the Bibliography, especially those of Luick and Jordan.

Consonants. Chaucer's consonants are pronounced for the most part as in Modern Enlgish. But there were no silent consonants, except h in French words like honour and g in French gn, which had the sound of single n (as in resigne, riming with medicyne). Ordinarily in the combinations gn (in native English words), kn (or cn), and wr, g, k and w were pronounced, and l was pronounced before f, k and m (as in half, folk, palmer). The sound of ng is held to have been regularly that of ng in "finger". Double g had sometimes the sound of dg (as in juggen), sometimes that of gg in "bigger" (as in frogges). The modern pronunciation is a safe guide. ch had the English sound (as in "church"), not the French ("as in "machine"). The spirant gh, which became silent in later English, had the sound of the German ch in "Ech" and "doch" (palatal after a front vowel, and guttural after a back vowel). R was trilled. S and th ought regularly to have been unvoiced (*i.e.*, with the sound of s in "sit" and th in "thin"), except when between vowels. Between vowels they were voiced (sounded as in Mod. Eng. "those"). But the distinction may not have been observed consistently, and the later voicing in many words (th in "these", "those", and s in "is", "was") may have begun in Chaucer's period. The suffix-cion (Mod. Eng. tion) had two syllables, and could rime with words in -on or in -oun. The spellings of the ending in the MSS are very inconsistent.

INFLECTIONS

The inflectional endings in Chaucer's language which differ from those in modern English can be briefly indicated for the various parts of speech. In many cases they consist simply of a final-e which in later English ceased to be pronounced.

Nouns. Many nouns have in the nominative case a final -e which is lost in modern English. It is not strictly an inflectional ending, but usually represents a final vowel in the language from which the word descends or is derived. Examples: ende, from AS. "ende"; name, from AS. "nama"; sone, from AS. "sunu"; entente, from OF. "entente." When the -e does not have a corresponding vowel in the source (as in carte, from AS. "cræy"), it is called unhistoric or inorganic. In a number of nouns Chaucer had two forms, one with the one without final –e. Such words are entered in the Glossary with an -e in parenthesis—as, for example, bliss (e).

The regular inflectional endings in the great majority of Chaucerian nouns are the same as in the Modern English—s or es in the genitive (or possessive) singular and in the plural. But there are a few exceptional forms to be noted, all of them obvious survivals of older inflections. Of course some of them, like the um-, lauting plurals, are familiar in modern English.

Gen. sg. without ending: a) in nouns of the AS. n-declension (chirche, lady, herte); b) in nouns of the AS. r-declension (fader, brother); c) in nouns with final s (Venus sone).

Dat. sg. This is normally without ending in Chaucer (in the hous, in my lyf). But in certain stereotyped phrases the old dative ending survived. Examples: on lyse, a-lyse, Mod. Eng. "alive"; on fyre, "afire"; to bedde, to shippe, with childe. Many of the phrases in which 'this so-called "petrified" dative survives are recorded in the Glossary.

Plural without ending: a) in AS. neuter nouns, and others, which had no ending in the nom. acc. pl. (yeer, but also yeres, deer, sheep, freend), b) nouns in -s (caas, pass); c) in umlauting nouns, which still form their plural by a change of vowel (men, gees, feet).

Plural in en: now rare, but common in AS. and represented by a number of cases in Chaucer (asshen, eyen or yen, hosen, fon, pesen, been). Parallel forms in -es usually also occurred.

Adjectives. The adjective, like the noun, sometimes has a final -e in the nominative case (swete, grene, drave). Such forms are recorded in the Glossary.

The English of Chaucer's period still preserved the old Germanic distinction, since lost, between the strong and the weak declensions. The latter occurs: a) when the adjective follows the article, a demonstrative or possessive pronoun, or a noun in the genitive (the yonge sonne, his halve course, Epicurus owne sone); b) when it is used with a noun in the vocative (O stronge God); c) often when it is used with proper names (faire Venus); d) perhaps in a few other cases when the adjective is used substantially, though other explanations of the ending can usually be found (the beste, where the article precedes; by weste, perhaps a dative). The ending of the weak adjectives is -e, which is also the regular ending of the strong plural. The following paradigm represents Chaucer's regular usage:

	Strong	Weak	Strong	Weak
Singular	yong	yonge	swete	swete
Plural	yonge	yonge	swete	swete

The inflectional -e, whether of the weak from or the plural, is usually not found in predicate adjectives, which are underlined. It is also rarely pronounced, though often written, in adjectives of two syllables, where it does not fall in with the rhythm of the verse (or, probably, of prose speech). In trisyllabic adjectives, however, where it makes a fourth syllable, it is often preserved. Compare the holy blissful martir with the semelieste man, O wommanliche wyf.

In addition to the regular weak and plural endings, Chaucer's adjectives show some exceptional forms. The old strong ending of the genitive signular -es is preserved in alleskinnes, "of every kind", noskinnes, "of no kind." There appear to be a very few datives in -e, survivals of the old strong dative inflection, though in most of the cases concerned other explanations of the ending as possible. Examples: of olde tyme, with harde grace, of purpos grete, in salte see, by weste—some of which may be explained as extensions of the use of the weak inflection. An old accusative ending is preserved in the combination halvendel (AS. "halfne dæl"). The AS. strong genitive plural survives in one word aller (also aller, alder, in composition), from "ealra". There are a few examples of plural adjectives with the French ending -es (places delitables, houres inequales). These occur chiefly in the works translated from the French.

The regular suffixes for the comparison of adjectives are the same as in modern English, -er and -est. In Anglo-Saxon both the comparative and the superlative took the weak inflection, and the corresponding forms are often spelled with a final e (-ere, -este) in Chaucer. But the ending is seldom pronounced in the verse except where it constitutes a second or a fourth syllable (The semelieste man). A few forms show the umlaut of the root vowel, as in Anglo-Saxon (lenger, strenger, elder, etc.), or the doubling of a final consonant (gretter, sonner). A number of adjectives are irregularly compared: good, bettre, beste; bad, badder, or werse (worse), werste (worste); muche (1), more or mo, moste (meste); lytel, lasse (lesse), leeste; etc. Such exceptional forms are registered in the Glossary.

Adverbs. The regular endings of Chaucer's adverbs are -e and ly or liche (the last two coming from the adjectival ending lich with the adverbial ending). Examples: brighte, smerte, royalliche or royally. There are a few adverbs in -es or -en, which correspond to AS. ending in -es or wan. Examples: ones, tyes, hennes aboven, abuten. With the forms in -es, properly genitives in origin, may be compared the adverbial phrase his thanks, "willingly". The exceptional form whilom appears to correspond to the AS. dat. pl. hwflum, but is probably to be explained as a late modification of Middle English whilen, into which the AS. from normally developed.

Pronouns. The pronouns are mostly like those in modern English. Exceptional forms, which might give the reader trouble, are resistered in the Glossary. The following special cases may be noted here.

In the first person, ich (Northern Ik) occurs beside I. The possessive adjectives myn and thyn take the regular -e in the plural. In the third person singular, the neuter genitive is the same as the masculine—his (not "its"). The spelling hise ("his", "its") is often found, in the manuscripts, with plural nouns, but the -e appears not to have been pronounced and has been struck off in the present text. The plural forms of the personal pronoun in the third person were: nom. they, gen. hire, dat., acc. hem, (the forms "their" and "them" not having yet come into London English). In the plural possessives oure, youre, hire, the -e seems to have been regularly unpronounced.

In the demonstrative thise (these) the final -e was almost invariably silent, and usually in the plural forms some, swiche, and whiche, when used pronominally. When used adjectivally these words are more likely to show an inflectional -e.

Verbs. Chaucer's verbs show the characteristic Germanic distinction between the weak and the strong conjugations. Strong verbs, often called irregular, make their preterite tense by the change of the root vowel (ablaut), and weak verbs, by the addition of an ending (de to te). The principal parts of the strong verbs, which for

Present tense (strong and weak alike)

Indicative		Subjective	
Singular	1. singe	Singular	singe
	2. singest	Plural	singe (n)
	3. singeth		
Plural	singe (n)		

the most part resemble those in modern English so closely as to be easily recognizable, are fully registered in the Glossary, as are also the forms of weak verbs that present any peculiarities. The inflectional endings are shown in the followings tables. Parentheses are used to indicate alternative forms. Thus n may always be dropped in the verbal ending en, the prefix y- may or may not be used with participles.

A number of verbs have contracted forms in the second and the third singular: lixt (liest), bit biddeth), fint (findeth), set (setteth), stont (stondeth), worth (wortheth). Such forms, when not easily recognizable, are recorded in the Glossary.

Preterite Indicative

Strong

Singular	1. song, sang
	2. song (e)
	3. song, sang
Plural	songe (n)

Weak

Singular	1. wende	lovede
	2. wendest	lovedest
	3. wende	lovede
Plural	wende (n)	lovede (n)

The preterite subjunctive, like the present has -e in the singular and -e (n) in plural

Imperative

Strong

Singular	2. sing
Plural	2. singeth, -e

	Weak	
Singular	2. loke	her
Plural	2. loketh, -e	hereth, -e

Strong verbs and long-stemmed weak verbs of the first class in Anglo-Saxon have regularly no -e in the second singular; other weak verbs have -e. But -e is often written in the manuscripts, and sometimes pronounced in the verse, in forms not historically entitled to it. Example: As sende love and pees bitwixe hem two. Such forms, which appears in longstemmed weak verbs in late Anglo-Saxon, are perhaps sometimes to be regarded as jussive subjunctives.

Infinitive. The ending is -en or -e in strong and weak verbs alike: singe (n), wene (n). In a very few verbs there is preserved an old gerundive or inflected infinitive with a dative -e: to done, to sene, to seyne.

Participles. The present active participle of all verbs, weak and strong, ends in -ing or -inge: singing (e), loving (e). The preterite passive participle of strong verbs ends in -e(n), of weak verbs, in -d or -t. Examples (y) sunge (n), (y) loved, (y-) taught. The prefix y- (from AS. ge-) is frequent with both strong and weak verbs. The preterite participle is ordinarily uninflected, but in a few cases has the adjectival plural ending in -e. Examples: Sing they ben tolde; with eres spraddle.

Preterite-present (or strong weak) verbs. These is a small class of verbs in the Germanic languages in which, an old strong preterite came to be used as a present tense, and a new weak preterite was formed to express past time. For example:

	Present		Preterite
Singular	1. shal	Singular	1. shodle
	2. shalt		2. sholdest
	3. shal		3. sholde
Plural	shull (en), shal	Plural	sholde (n).

The other preterite-present verbs are can (pret, kouthe, koude); dar (pret. dorste); may (pret. mighte); most (pret, moste); owe (pret. oughte), thar (pret. thurfte, but confused with dorste); and woot (pret. wiste). The peculiar forms of all these verbs are entered in the Glossary.

Anomalous verbs. The following four verbs show exceptional irregularities.

Goon, pret. yede and wente.

Doon, pret. dide.

Wil (e), wol (e), 2 sg. wilt, wolt, 3 sg. wil (e), wol (e), pl., willen, wil, wollen, wol; pret wolde. The -e of the 1 and 3 sg. present indicative, though apparently always silent, is often found in the manuscripts, and is historically justified (AS. wile, originally subjective).

Been. Pres. ind. sg. am, art, is; pl. been, be, rarely are (n). Pres. sbj. sg. be; pl. been, be. Pret. ind. sg. was, were, was; pl. were (n). Pret. sbj. sg. were; pl. were (n). Imperative sg. be; pl. beeth.

VERSIFICATION

The various verse-forms used by Chaucer are discussed in the introductions and notes to the separate works. But a few general directions may be given here for the reading of his lines.

The most important difference between Chaucer's English and modern English, for the purpose of versification, lies in the numerous final -e's and other light inflectional endings described in the preceding pages. These endings are ordinarily pronounced in the verse, and indeed are essential to the rhythm. They are also pronounced in rime, and Chaucer with almost complete consistency avoided riming words in -e with words not etymologically or grammatically entitled to that ending. But within the verse final -e is regularly elided before an initial vowel or before an h which is either silent (as in honour) of slightly pronounced (as in he, his, her, him, hem, hadde, and a few other words). Before initial consonants -e is ordinarily sounded, though there are cases or almost every page where it must have been either slurred or entirely apocopated. These statements apply, of course, only to the light, unstressed final -e, and not the long e (often spelled ee) in words like majestee or charitee.

Most of Chaucer's lines, if read naturally and with a proper regard to grammatical endings, have an obvious rhythm. But there are many cases, apart from doubful textual readings, where there is uncertainty as to elision or apocopation, or even a responable choice between two ways of rendering a line. Probably no rules can ever be laid down to settle all such questions. Certain characteristics of Chaucer's versification may, however, be borne in mind. His lines—as contrasted, for example, with those of Gower—have great freedom and variety of movement. He constantly shifts the position of the caesural pause. He often reverses the rhythm of a foot, substituting a trochaic for an iambic movement. Like most English poets, he not infrequently has an extra light syllable in a line (a trisyllabic foot in place of the regular iambus), though in such cases it is often impossible to determine whether to resort to apocopation. The extra syllable seems to have been most frequent in the caesural pause. One other irregularity, which some critics have condemned and the scribes themselves sometimes tried to correct by emendation, Chaucer certainly allowed himself. He not infrequently omitted the unaccented syllable at the beginning of a line. These headless, or ninesyllable, lines—seven-syllable in the case of the octosyllabic meter—are by no means objectionable when the initial stress falls upon an important word. When a preposition or conjunction gets this initial accent, there is perhaps more reason for the objections of the critics, but the evidence of the manuscripts makes it necessary to admit many such lines to the text.

In the following short passage from the General Prologue, which will serve as a specimen of scansion, the metrical stresses are marked with an accent ('), syllabic lighte's have a diaeresis ("), and elided or apocopated e's are underdotted. It will be understood, of course, that the metrical accents varied in strength, unimportant words receiving only a secondary stress.

A CLÉRK ther wás of Óxenfórd alsó,

That únto lógyk háddë lónge yg.

As léenë wás his hórs as ís a rákë,

And hé was nát right fát, I úndertákë,

But lóoked hólwë, and thérto sóbrely'.

Ful thrédbare wás his óvereste coúrtepy';

For hé hadde géten hym yét no bénefíeë,

Ne wás so wórldly fór to háve offíeë.

For hy'm was bévere háve at his béddes héed

Twénty bóokës, clád in blák or réed,

Of Áristótle and his philósophíë,

Than róbes r'iche, fíthele, or gáy sautríë.

But ál be thát he wás a phílosóphrë,

Yet háddë hé but lítel góold in eófrë;

But ál that hé my'ght of his fréendës héntë,

On bóokës ánd on lérnynge hé it spéntë,

And bísily' gán for the sóulës préyë

Of hém that yáf hym whérewith tó scoléyë.

Of stúdie tóok he móost eure and móost héedë.

Noght ó word spák he móorë thán was néedë,

And thát was séyd in fórme and réveréncë,

And shórt and quy'k and fúl of hy' senténcë;

Sównynge in móral vértu wás his spéchë,

And gládly wódle he lérne and gládly téchë,

THE TEXT

As already explained in the Preface to the present revised edition, and for the reasons there given, the following general introduction on the text has been reprinted here in substantially its original form. It sets forth the principles followed by the editor in the construction of his text, and the same principles hold for the second edition. In most of the works, too, very few textual changes have been made in revision. But in the case of the Canterbury Tales the Manly-Rieckert edition, referred to expectantly in the original Preface and in the following pages, appeared in 1940. Since it was based upon all known manuscripts, over eighty in number, the classification of authorities there given completely supersedes the tentative one in this work, which is here reprinted simply to show the basis of the editor's decision. The variants recorded in the Textual Notes are reprinted for the same reason, and for fuller information on both matters the reader should consult the Manly-Rickert edition. But a considerable number of readings have been altered in the text in the light of the new evidence in Manly's apparatus, and a list of these will be found on pages 883-885 at the beginning of the Textual Notes.

In the Textual Notes on the separate works will be found lists of the manuscripts and other authorities for the text, together with references to previous studies in their classification. Special problems, also, are discussed in the notes on the works in connection with which they arise. But here, in the introduction, may properly be given some account of the general method of the present edition.

The entire text has been made afresh by the editor. It is based upon his examination of all the published manuscript materials and photographs or collations of some of the more important unpublished sources. Account has been taken of the numerous studies that hae been made of the character and relations of the manuscripts, and it has been the editor's intention to pay due regard to critical principles. In fact the text may be called a critical edition, with one reservation. In the case of some of the more important works, including the Canterbury Tales, the manuscript materials accessible to the editor have not been exhaustive. But the best copies of all the works have been available for use as the basis of the edition, and enough others have been compared to make possible, in the editor's belief, the establishment of trustworthy texts.

The Canterbury Tales, for example, are preserved in some ninety manuscripts and early prints, complete or fragmentary. Photographs of all these copies have recently been brought together at the University of Chicago by Professor Manly and his associates, who are preparing a great critical edition. Their work, which is eagerly awaited by all Chaucerians, will shed new light on doubtful readings, and will probably make it possible for the first time to reconstruct the successive stages in the compositions of the Canterbury Tales. But it does not appear likely that a text based upon the complete collation would be materially different from one that can be constructed from the eight published manuscripts, which include the best copy, the Ellesmere MS., and are so distributed as to represent all the important groups of authorities. For the Pardoner's Prologue and Tale, of course, the editor has used the specimens published by the Chaucer Society, representing in all over fifty copies, upon which Zupitza and Koch based their classification of the authorities; and for the Clerk's Tale he has had the published specimens from eight additional manucripts. He has been further aided by the numerous citations of the readings of special passages printed in such textual studies as Professor Tatlock's paper on the Harleian Manuscript and the late Professor Brusendorff's Chaucer Tradition. In addition to all this printed material, the editor has collated the Cardigan MS., a superior copy which was not represented among the specimens printed by the Chaucer Society, and the Morgan MS., which is classified with those of less authority.

In textual method the present editor does not belong to the severest critical school. When the readings of the "critical text" or of a superior archetype appeared unsatisfactory or manifestly inferior, he has accepted help from other authorities more often than the strict constructionists might approve. He has seen no way of avoiding the exercise of personal judgment. But he has not practiced mere eclecticism, and in making his decisions he has endeavored to give constant attention to the relation of the manuscripts and to all relevant consideration of language, meter, and usage. Some of the problems that have arisen and they vary considerably in the diffeent works of Chaucer—may be briefly described.

In the Canterbury Tales, for example, as is fully set forth in the Textual Notes below, the A Type of manuscripts, represnted by Ellesmere, Hengwrt, Cambridge Dd, and Cambridge Gg—whether or not they all go back to a single archetype below the original—is generally accepted as of superior authority to the B type, which includes Harleian 7334. Corpus, Petworth, and Lansdowne. They are the basis of the present text, as of all recent editions. In the Pardoner's Tale, for which nearly all the authorities have been printed and compared, there seems to be no case where the reading of the more numerous manuscripts of type B is preferable. But elsewhere in the tales there are a few passages where the B readings seem to the editor superior to the A readings, and he has not hesitated to adopt them. thus in the General Prologue, I, 510 (where, of course, only the eight published manuscripts and the Cardigan and Morgan copies were considered) chaunterie (B) clearly afford at better and more Chaucerian rhythm than chauntrye (A), which Professor Liddell, in his critical edition, retained in strict adherence to his archetype. Other examples of B readings acepted in the present text are ben (A leyn), PrT, VII, 676, Odenake (A Onedake). MkT, VII, 2072; out of the yerd (A into this yerd), NPT, VII, 3422; gilteless (A giltless), FrankIT, V, 1318; fayerye (A fairye), MerchT, IV 1743.

Although some editors would follow their archetype more strictly, the readings mentioned are of course entirely defensible from the point of view of critical method, since the original of the A manuscripts need not have been at all points superior to that of type B. More serious difficulties in adhering to critical procedure arise in connection with the baffling MS. Harl. 1334, the peculiar relations of which are said to have deterred Mr. Henry Bradshaw from editing the Conterbury Tales. Classified somewhat doubtfully by the textual critics among the manuscripts of type B, the Harleian copy shows evidence of contamination with the superior type A, and has many unique readings of great interest. Some editors, among them Professors Skeat and Mr. Pollard, have held it to contain Chaucerian revisions, and they have consequently felt free to draw upon any of its readings that seem intrinsically attractive. Other scholars have doubted the special authority of the manuscript, and, in the opinion of the present editor, it has been virtually disproved by Professor Tatlock in his study on the subject. Taking the more important passages where the Harleian readings are unique among the eight published manuscripts, Mr. Tatlock collated them with some thirty five other copies to discover how much support they might have, and then examined the readings themselves to determine their character and value. He showed that many which has been adopted by the editors were clearly scribal emendations, and in some cases very poor ones. The officious and entirely unnecessary substitution of cloysterlees for reccheless in the familiar passage of the General Prologue (I, 179) is typical of the procedure of this anonymous editor. Again, in KnT, I 1906. the Harleian reading And westward in the mynde and in memorye may safely be regarded as the scribe' emendation of the defective reading of most manuscripts, And on (or in) the westward in memory. Professor Tatlock in the study in which he discredited the Harleian text as a whole was inclined to accept its authority in this passage. But the reading, And on the gate westerward in memorye, which has been found in a few scattered manuscripts, is more likely to have been what Chaucer wrote, and would explain easily the corrupted forms which the line is preserved. Similarly the greater number of unique Harleian readings appear on examination to be emendtions, and many of them can be traced to the scribe's deslike of headless, or ninesyllable, lines There remain, however, a few pasages in which it is hard not to follow the Harleian text. In KnT, I, 2037, where all the printed manscripts have the obvious blunder sertres (or a varient thereof), the Harleian reads correctly sterres, which all editors adopt (except Koch, who emends to cercles). Again in Gen Prol, I 485, And swich he was ypreved afte sithes all the manuscripts except the Harleian read preved, to the decided impairment of the rhythm. In this case Professor Liddell, whose definitely announced policy was to "boycott the Harleian," adopted its reading, as he did also in KnT, I, 3104, And he hire serveth also gentilly (where all the other printed manuscripts read so). On the other hand in KnT, I, 2892, Mr Liddell read Upon thise stedes grete and white, rejecting the relief afforded by the Harleian text (that weren grete and white), though the other reading compels us to accent upon unnaturally on the first syllable and to pronounce the final -e of thise, which is usually silent. Possibly the correct reading of this line is Upon thise steedes grete and lilye whyte, which is found in MS. Cardigan. Again in KnT, I, 3071, Mr. Liddel reads I rede we make of sorwes two, with objectionable ryhthm and questionable haitus, and refuses to insert that on the sole authority of the Harleian. It is difficult for any editor to proceed consistently, and improbable that any two editors would always agree, in delaing with these readings. In the present edition they are accepted sparingly, and only when the alternative readings are so unsatisfactory, or those of the Harleian manuscript so intrinsically superior, as to justify the risk. In its wholesale correction of headless lines the editor has not followed the Harleian scribe, for there is abundant evidence that Chaucer wrote them in both his decasyllabic and his octosyllabic verse. But in lines where the rhythm is otherwise objectionable or open to question the help of the Harleian manuscript has sometimes been accepted, and special considerations have sometimes entered into the editors decision. Thu in Gen Prol, I, 752, the Harleian reading, For to have been a marchal in an halle, has been adopted in place of the shorter For to been of the other manuscripts, not simply because of the headless line, but because of the possibility that the Harleian reading preserves, or restores, the good old use of the perfect infinitive to express action contrary to fact. In the case of all doubtful readings the editor has tried to give special consideration to old grammatical forms or idioms which might have been lost or corrupted by the scribes.

The presence of correct unique readings in he Harleian copy may be explained either on the theory of emendation, or on that of contamination with some good lost manuscript, and there is other evidene that the Harleian text is derived in part from a source which belonged to type A. It is perhaps even possible that Harleian preserved some good readings which were coincidently corrupted in the A manuscripts and in the remaining manuscripts of type B. But of course the chances of this are slight.

The problem of unique readings arises sometimes with superior manuscripts, like the Elelsmere copy of the Canterbury Tales or the Cambridge Gg copy of the Parliament of Fowls. In the ease of Ellesmere the editor has had no such means of testing them as was afforded for the Harleian manuscript by Professor Tatlock's study. The Chicago collations, when published, will show just how much scattered support such readings may have. But from the evidence furnished by printed texts and the editor's collation of the Cardigan and Morgan manuscripts it does not appear that they are to be accepted without scrutiny on the bare authority off Ellesmere. That manuscript, though superior to all others, has its proportion of errors, some of which it shares with other manuscripts of the a group. It therefore cannot be regarded as an independent witness to the original text; nor do its peculiar readings look like revisions by the author. It does, however, preserve some lines, apparently genuine, and marginal glosses, very likely due to Chaucer, which are not found in any of the other published texts. These passages, at least, it seems to have derived from a good copy outside its immediate source and now unknown. There is consequently justification for considering its unique reading, and the editor has accepted them in a very few cases, especially where they preserve good old forms or idioms that might have been lost through scribal corruption. Examples of the cases where this consideraton has affected the decision are KnT, I, 1176, wistest; KnT, I, 1573, after he (rest, afterward he with variants); KnT, I, 1260, witen (rest, woot, wote, etc.); MLT, II, 336, hastifliche (rest, hastiliche, hastily). In mere matters of orthography, when verbal variants are not involved, the Ellesmere copy has been followed, as representing a good scribal tradition. But throughout all Chaucer's works, as explained below, the spellings of the manuscripts have been corrected for grammatical accuracy and for the adjustment of rimes.

The question of the authority of a superior manuscript arises again in connection with the Parliament of Fowls. The Combridge MS. Gg. 1.27, like the Ellesmere copy of the Canterbury Tales, belongs to the best group of authorities, and is commonly adopted as the basis of the text. But there are two opinions as to the value of its testimony when it stands alone or has very slight support from other manuscripts. It is not esay to decide this question. The present editor finds about twenty readings, either peculiar to Gg or having slight support in other manuscripts which clearly right or so strongly preferable to the critical text as practically to demand adoption. Some thirty-five more appear to deserve serious consideration, and a few of them have been hesitatingly adopted. Still other Gg readings would have a strong claim for adoption if the manuscript were known to be derived in any fashion from a source independent of all the rest. A few of its readings have been adopted for reasons connected with grammar or meter. Gg variant in mere phraselogy have been in nearly every case rejected, though some of them are tempting. The fact that the manuscript preserves the unique copy of the revised Prologue to the Legend of Good Women makes easier the assumption that it contains the author's corrections of the text of the Parliament. But the variants themselves do not seem to bear out this theory.

A textual problem fundamentally different from the offered by the Canterbury Tales or the Parliament is presented by the Troilus. In the Conterbury Tales, although there are numerous cases of correction, cancellation, or rearrangement, there is no thorouh-going and sysematic revision. In fact, far from having prepared a second edition, Chaucer never completed a first. But in the Troilus it is agreed that the manuscripts show either two or three distinct stages of composition. Details about the classificaton of the authorities are given below in the Textual Notes and need not be repeated here. The essential facts are that all scholars recognize a first version, a, which stands in many respects closest to the Italian original, and a second (or third) version, γ, which is preserved in the most correct and best authenticated manuscripts. A third form of the text, preserved in manuscripts not wholly distinct from those which contain a and γ, is held by Professors Root, as by his predecessor in the study of the problem, the late Sir William McCormick, to represent a separate version β, which those two scholars have conceived in different ways. More recently professor Root, who continued and completed McCormick's thorough and elaborate study of all the manuscripts, has arrived at the opinion that, β represents Chaucer's final revision—that is, the third stage of his text. While he recognizes the superiority of the best manuscripts, he holds that to arrive at Chaucer's authoritative version an editor would correct the γ text by, β readings wherever these are susceptible of sure determination. The description and classification of manuscripts by McCormick and Root the present edior has found to be thorough and trustworthy. It is, in fact, one of the most substantial achievment of Chaucerian scholarship. But even if two stages are recognized, that represented by the γ manuscripts has, in the opinion of the present editor, the best authority. The β readings have consequently not been accepted in this text, which is based consistently on the γ version. The reconstruction of γ has of course not been in itself always easy, since the γ manuscripts contain errors and omissions. Exclusive γ readings have been examined with special care because of the uncertainty whether they are due to Chaucer or a scribe. But the authority of the γ group, even when it stands alone, seems better to the present editor than it does to Mr. Root. It should be added, however, that the differences between the γ text and Mr. Root's, β version are few and unimportant.

The question of revision arises in relation to several other works of Chaucer besides the Troilus, but it nowehere else presents so serious a practical problem to the editor. In the case of several of the Canterbury Tales, it has been argued that Chaucer made over early poems for use in the collection. There is no question in editing, however, of a choice between versions. Similarly in the case of passages possibly unauthentic or canceled by the author, the editor has simply to decide whether and where to admit them to his text. In the Prologue to the Legend alone is there another instance of thorouh-going revision, resulting in parallel versions and in this case it is clear that both texts should be printed side by side, as has been done in most recent editions.

An editorial problem somewhat different from those far discussed is raised by the Book of the Duchess and, in less degree, by the House of Fame. It may be illustrated by some account of the character of the text in the former of these works. There are only four authorities—the Farfax, Bodley, and Tanner manuscripts, and Thynne's edition. Farfax and Bodley are, as usual, closely related, and in this poem they offer the best text, Thynne furnishes a number of good corrections of their readings. The critical text is easy to construct, and there are very few cases where a choice of readings is difficult. But there are many cases where the authorities agree in readings unsatisifactory in sense or in meter, and it is hard to decide how far an editor should go in mending such passages. It may be freely admitted that the manuscripts are late and none too trustworthy. At the same time it should be remembered that some roughness of workmanship might be expected in so early a work as the book of the Duchess and in a meter of such free traditions as the English octosyllabic couplet. Headless lines were quite as natural there as in the decasyllabic verse, and extra syllables within the line are not hard to accept, though some of them may be due to scribes who supplied works to take the place of finl *-e's* they had wrongfully suppressed. Lines which lack an unaccented syllable in the middle are very unlikely to be right. For verses so constructed, with two abutting streses—a metrical type sometimes called Lydgatian because of its frequent occurence in Lydgate's poems—are almost unknown in those works of Chaucer of which good text is preserved. All these irregularities, which occur commonly in the Book of the Duchess, are easy to remove if an editor feels at liberty to emend his manuscripts at will. The present text is less freely corrected than Skeat's and for that reason less smooth in many places, as the editor is well aware. But one kind of emendation, the restoration of full grammatical forms apocopated in the manuscript to the detriment of the meter, is certainly justifiable and has been freely employed.

The editor of Chaucer, after he has settled the matter of authorities and readings and made his critical texts, still has to consider the question of grammatical rectification. For the best manuscripts contain many forms that are demonstrably incorrect—nouns and adjectives with meaningless final *-e's*, or strong preterites with the same ending incorrectly added in the singular number. These errors cannot be removed by a critical comparison of the manuscripts; they must be treated, if regulated at all, in the light of Middle English grammar. Fortunately the materials are abundant for constructing a grammar of Chaucer's dialect, and the inflections he employed are very fully and precisely known. It is therefore posible to correct with confidence most of the grammatical errors of the scribes. But the practice of editors in making such corrections has varied considerably. Skeat's general policy was to normalize both the spelling and the grammar of his texts, though he was not quite thorough or consistent in removing erroneous forms. The Globe editors differed one from another in their practice, but many incorrect endings were allowed to stand in their text. Professor Root, in his edition of the Troilus, though recognizing that numerous final *-e's* in his text did not represent a syllable, thought it most consistent with his purpose to follow the actual usage of his scribes. His method and that of the Globe edition is of course defensible, and it has its advantage, especially for an investigator of the history of English orthography. For many of the forms under discussion are not, strictly speaking, incorrect, but are rather specimens of a system of spelling divergent from the ordinary practice in Middle English. According to that system final *-e* may denote not only a pronounced final syllable but also, as in modern English, the long quantity of a preceding vowel (as in "hate," over against "hat"). This principle is doubtless to be recognized in some of the spellings of he Chaucerian scribes. In a small number of nouns and adjectives it is not certain whether Chaucer's nominative form had a final *-e'*, and in others he clearly used two forms, one with *-e'* and one without. Words of the latter sort are entered in the Glossary of this edition with a bracketed -e'(*e.g., bliss*(e), *cler*(e), and in the text the form which occurs in manuscript is usually preserved. But the editor's practice has probably not been perfectly consistent in this matter, and the final *-e'* may sometimes have been struck off when unpronounced in the verse. In the case of nouns in the dative construction it is sometimes difficult to decide whether to allow the inflectional *-e*' outside of the stereotyped or "petrified" phrases to which it is mainly restricted. Its use undoubtedly spread somewhat, even to cases other than the dative, but Chaucer's dative was usually without ending, nad the dative *e's* have been struck off in this text unless there was special reason for supposing them to have been preserved. Perhaps the influectional form that makes most trouble with regard to this matter of final *-È* is the second person singular of the imperative of strong verbs and of long-stemmed weak verbs of the first Anglo-Saxon conjugation. Strictly speaking these forms should have no ending (sing, send, heer, etc.). But they are commonly spelled with a final -e', and the ending is occasionally demanded by the rime or verse-rhythm. It can be accounted for as a subjunctive from used in a jussive sense, or as an ending which was developed in the imperative of the verbs mentioned above because of the analogy of the subjunctive and the other weak classes in the imperative. It would be defensible to keep such forms in the text when they occur in the manuscript. In this edition the practice is again not wholly consistent, but in most cases the -e's have been struck off and the correct historical forms restored. One other form, of frequent occurence, may be cited to illustrate this editorial problem. The possessive pronoune his, when used with a plural noun, frequenty takes a final -e (hise) in the best manuscripts. This is very common, almost regular, with the Ellesmere scribe. But the -e is not justified by the Anglo-Saxon form (his) and appears never, or almost never, to be pronounced in Chaucer's verse. It has been struct-off in the present edition. But since the form with -e clearly occurs in Middle English, an editor might with equal propriety allow it to stand where his manuscript has it.

In matters of spelling, apart from questions of inflection or dialect, the procedure of the editor has been conservative. The lack of any autograph manuscripts leaves us without an authoritative Chaucerian standard, and any attempt to construct such a standard (like that Professor Koch in his early edition of the Minor Poems) is sure to encounter many uncertainties. The ordinary critical method fails entirely at this point, since the scribes modified spelling rather freely in copying. A variety of practices is consequently open to the editor, ranging from the "diplomatic" reproduction of a given manuscript to the introduction of a new phonetic spelling of his own. For the purpose of teaching pronunciation and meter this last method would have its advantages, and it has been adopted with selected specimens of the verse (as, for example, with the whole Manciple's Tale in Dr. Plessow's edition). The present text, therefore, in the case of those works that are preserved in the best manuscripts, follows the spelling of the scribe where it is not absolutely or probably incorrect. Final -e's omitted in the manuscripts have not been supplied if they were elided or apocopated in the verse, but they have been restored when necessary to the meter. Grammatical errors, as already explained, and dialectal spellings, where not appropriate and presumably intentional, have been mended with care. But no effort has been made to introduce uniformity in less important matter's, such as the use of *o* and *e* or of i and y, or the doubling of long *o* and long *e*. Such slight modernization as has been adopted in printing will be explained below.

In the case of nearly all Chaucer's works it has been possible to follow this method of close adherence to the spelling of the manuscripts. Indeed such is the excellence and general agreement in these matters, of the Ellesmere copy of the *Canterbury Tales* and the Corpus and Campsall copies of the Triolus, that those manuscripts may be reasonably supposed to represent practices closely similar to Chaucer's own. But there are a few poems in which the masnucript of best verbal authority presents a dialectical or otherwise vagarious orthography. This is notably of the *Legend of Good Women*, where the Cambridge Gg manuscript is the only source of the revised text for the Prologue; and the case is similar with the parliament of Fowls and some of the short poems. Under such circumstances an editor to choose between printing a text of strange and un-Chaucerian appearance and making the spelling conform to Ellesmere and Corpus standards. The latter method seems decidedly preferable, and the orthography of the legend and of a number of the minor poems has accordingly been freely normalized.

Capitals have been used at the beginning of lines of verse. Capital F has been substituted for *ff*, which often takes the place of a majuscular sign in the manuscripts: *th* for the archaic "thorn" (*þ*); and *j* for the capital *I* which sometimes represents it. The letters *u* and *v* have been adjusted to modern practice (use, virtue, love, for the manuscript spellings *vse, uertu, loue*). The apostrophe has been employed with *n*', *t*', and *th*', when the vowel of ne, to, and the (or *thee*) is elided before a following initial. Contractions, like the stroke which designates a final nasal, have been silently expanded unles there was real doubt about their meaning. In the case of words in on, oun (nacioun, condicioun, etc.) which are spelled very inconsistently and may be pronounced with the sound of either *o* or *ou*, it has been necessary to adopt an arbitrary practice. The ending is commonly abbreviated in the manuscript, sometimes with *m* (*n* with with an upper return stroke), sometimes with *n* or *u*. These signs are used inconsistently by the scribes. In the present text, when words of this class have their pronunciation determined by rime (as by such unambiguous rime-words as toun or oon), they are spelled accordingly. When two words of the *nacioun* (*nacion*) type rime with such other, *n* with the return stroke is expanded as *n*, and *n* or *u* wth the makron as *un*. When the scribes use both abbrevations in a single pair of rimewords (nacion: condiciou), as occasinally happens, both are normalized with the spelling *oun*.

In spacing (which varies greatly in the manuscripts) modern usage has been followed except Middle English appears to have had a different sense of unity. Thus upon, into therto, theron, withoute, also whose, nowher, and the participle compound with *y*-and *for* are regularly printed without spacing or hyphen. But combinations which were less clearly recognized as units (such as for sothe, but if, by cause, over al, in the sense of the German überall) are either hyphenated or separated entirely. In this second class of words consistency of practice has been hard to attain, just as in modern spelling there is considerable variation in the use of the hyphen.

To the foregoing explanation of editorial method may be added a word about the Textual Notes in the present edition. They contain accounts of the manuscripts and other authorities for the text of each work, with information about their relations, and lists of the more important variant readings. It was the editor's original plan to register much more fully than he has finally done in print. But various considerations—lack of space, the appearance of Professor Root's edition of the Troilus with full textual apparatus, and the announcement of Professor Manly's projected work on the Canterbury Tales—led him to reduce his citations to about one quarter of those originally collected. The selected list now printed is not intended to exhibit the characteristics of manuscripts or to supply adequate materials for textual investigation. Scholars having these interests in mind will naturally resort directly to the manuscripts or to complete reprints and repoductions. But it is hoped that the variants here given will be found to include such alternative readings as have any literary interest. The different versions of the Troilus have been recorded with some fulness; also rejected passages (including some that are spurious) from the Cannfferbury Tales. Some variants in phraselogy have been registered because they have a bearing on the poet's vocabulary. Finally, in a good many cases where the readings are doubtful the editor has supplied his readers with the material for testing his decisions.

THEORIES OF LANGUAGE

Language like other activities of man is subject to various kinds of pressure arising from changing circumstances. Migration changes in the cultural system of a people, contact with people, contact with peoples speaking different languages, changing needs are some of the causes that brings about changes in language. It is interesting to turn to the problems of the origin and early history of human language. We at once realise that we are deeply ignorant about the origins of language and that we have to be content with some amusing guesses and plausible speculation. We are not certain when language arose, but it seems likely that it goes back to the earliest history of mankind, perhaps over millions of years. We are not so certain how the language was born in the beginning. Various theories have been built up around this problem, based upon certain indirect pieces of evidence. If we question ourselves what language is the answer would be that means what we have in our mind. In other words language helps us to convey to others what we are thinking of or feeling or desiring. But while considering this definition of language, we have to admit that language or speech is not the only means of conveying our ideas to others. To some extent gestures and signs can also do this. For instance we can nod head instead of saying 'yes' and 'no'. Language in the sense in which we are in term is different from signs and gestures as a means of conveying our ideas because it employs sound, have a meaning. These sounds of speech are produced by the deliberate movements of the vocal organs inducing the lips, the jaws, the tongue and vocal cords. This brings us to the definition of speech as the expressions of our thoughts and feelings through sounds produced by the activities of the vocal organ. In speaking a language we are making use of certain sets of sounds called the words of the language to serve as outward symbols of the ideas in our minds. As a symbol stands for something else, only those who are familiar with the symbol and the particular way of using it can recognise or understand it.

The kind of diversification of a language occurred many times in human history and this is why there are today about three thousand languages in the world. An examination of these languages reveals that many of them are closely related in that they share certain common characteristics in phonology, morphology. Languages thus interrelated are metaphorically called a family of languages. Each family has several branches and each branches has several sub-branches:

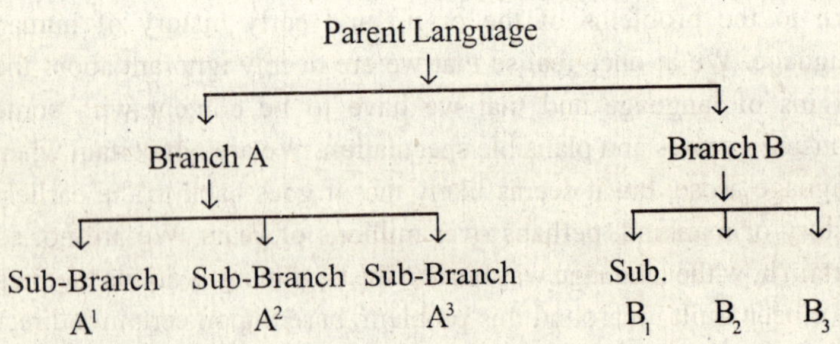

Various theories which have been built up around the language problems are:

1. Bow-wow theory
2. The pooh-pooh theory
3. The ding-dong theory
4. The yo-he-ho theory
5. The gesture theory
6. The musical theory
7. The contact theory

Each of these theories are capable of accounting for a certain aspect and explain a certain probability of the origin of language. According to Edward Sapir, "*A purely human and non-instructive method of communicating ideas, emotions and desires by means of a system of voluntarily produced symbols is language.*"

The use of word system in the definition emphasizes the distinction between speech and language. Speech is an expression of thought or feeling by means or meaningful sounds produced by the vocal organs. These sounds are made deliberately and intentionally for the purpose of being heard and understood properly by the hearer. A collocation of meaningless noises cannot be called a speech because it has nothing to communicate. Sounds are said to be meaningful only when they call up same thing in wind. Communication through spoken word is possible only when there is that correspondence between what the speaker means what the hearer understands. Communication fails when the link is broken. If we wish to understand the real nature of language, it is of highest importance to realize that words which make a language consist of sounds, which are uttered and heard before they are understood. Sounds are the basic realities of language and therefore to study a language means to study a particular set of sounds, and to learn also the ideas for thoughts symbolised by those sounds. Learning of the sounds of a foreign language is made easy by the production of those sounds. Such a study of the sounds of speech is called phonetics.

Detailed study of theories mentioned earlier is are follows:

1. **Bow-Wow Theory.** According to this theory the earliest form of language arose as a result of man's attempt to imitate natural sounds such as the one's of animals, the rustling leaves, the lashing of the wind and so on. This theory tells us that certain words in every language sound as if they were imitative of natural sounds. Words like quack, cuckoo, splash, buzz, hiss, bang, sneeze show a kind of relation with the things or sounds they stand for. Imitation of natural sounds may explain a part of the primitive vocabulary and it is plausible that the imitative noises of primitive man have developed into words and meanings and so on. When once a group of words like the above exists in the language new sets can be cared and new meanings may develop an analogy with other words. But the theory does not explain the origin of many words and words which strike us very appropriate in sound do not give the same impression in a different context. For example initial fl seems to be particularly suitable to words connected with fire (*e.g.* flame, flash, flare) and with flying as in flap, flaunt, flutter and so on. But the same initial group of sound appears in words like flask, flat, flesh, flush and so on which have no direct or indirect relation with fire or flying. The theory fails and have its limitations.

2. **The Pooh-Pooh Theory**–According to this theory, language had its origin in instinctive cries of primitive man, expressive of emotions like pain, joy or fear. This theory holds further that earliest linguistic utterances, interjections or exclamations are expressive of some emotional state of the mind of primitive man. But how did articulation develop

from mere expressive cries? About this the theory is silent. It is easy to imagine how a cry of fear could become a signal of dangers in primitive community as among higher animals. But the theory does not explain how the gulf is bridged between an emotional cry and its articulate symbol.

3. **The Yo-he-ho Theory**–Some of the nineteenth century scholars put forward this theory, according to which, language arose from the noise made by a group of men engaged in joint physical labour like moving a tree trunk or lifting a rock or felling a tree. In any joint effort of this kind we produce involuntary vocal noises. Such vocal noises were produced by tightening the glottis to trap the breath in the lungs and then in sudden violent bursts of physical effort, releasing the air-stream, suddenly making various types of noises, vocal noises produced in such contexts might develop into words with meanings such as 'heave', 'lift' and so on. The two remarkable features of this theory are: *(a)* it gives a plausiable explanation for production of earliest consonants and vowels and *(b)* it envisages the origin of language in a situation involving human co-operation which would not have been possible in primitive community without the prior existence of language. It has been argued against the theory that language must have existed long before primitive man was brought into a situation involving communal co-operation.

4. **The Ding-Dong Theory**–This is a nickname to what is usually known as nativistic theory. The theory is based on the supposed harmony between sound and sense in language. It depends on the uncertain instinctive faculty which primitive man is supposed to have and by which every impression he received was immediately given a vocal expression. Every external impression he received was like the sound of a bell (ding-dong) and produced corresponding utterances. The theory is convincing chiefly because it relies too much on hypothetical instinctive faculty

of primitive man, rather than on more solid ground of evidence.

5. **The Gesture Theory.** According to this theory speech was preceded by gestures. Supporters of this theory point to the extensive use of gestures by certain animals and by some primitive tribes. While it is credible that gesture and speech are closely related, the theory does not take us beyond that. It cannot establish that gesture preceded speech. It appears more probable that speech and gestures grew up together indeed, even in modern times we use gestures to supplement our vocal expressions. An extreme version of the gesture theory holds the view that language came into existence as recently as about 3500 B.C. But this argument can be exploded because it is incredible to believe how man could have developed the elaborate civilization of the old and New Stone Ages without the assistance of speech. A variant of this theory is the mouth gesture theory. Supporters of this theory argue that primitive men used gestures in communication and as his intelligence and technique developed, he needed more precise gestures. As his hands and legs were occupied by his acts and crafts, the mouth, especially the lips are made to copy the gestures of hands. As he continued to use the mouth parts in eating was taken, while we move the jaws and other parts of the mouth to produce the gesture of eating, if we also produce the sounds muyum, muryum, muya, muya, the sense is understood. Supporters of this theory analyse various words in terms of mouth gestures of this kind. Though some of the aspects of this theory are amusing and fanciful it has the virtue of accounting for the articulated nature of speech.

6. **The Contact Theory.** This theory sees the origin of language in man's instinctive need for contact with his fellows. According to this theory, language grew in several stages. At first, contact sound was made which was not

communicative but merely expressive of one's need for contact with his fellows. Examples are the noises made by the gregarious animals. In the second stage came the cry which was directed to the environment in general; such are the mating calls and cries of young nestlings in danger. In the third stage came the call directed to an individual, demanding for satisfaction of some urge: examples are domestic animals, begging for food and infant crying for his mother. In the last stage came the word with its symbolic function. It appears this theory suffers because it places undue emphasis on the instinctive need for contact as the motive for the invention of language. Further, the theory does not explain anything how language acquired articulation.

7. **The Musical Theory.** This theory sees the origin of language in music. It was Otto Jesperson who put forward this theory. By tracing the history of language backward, he arrived at the view that primitive language consisted of long words and jaw-breaking and burdensome sounds and frequent use of tone and pitch and musical intervals. He believes that it was musical, passionate and very irregular and that it dealt with the concrete rather than the abstract. Its earliest form was a song which was a song merely expressive but not communicative. Jesperson's views seem to be romantic. He writes language was born in the courting days of mankind. The first utterances of speech of fancy to myself are like something between the nightly love-lyrics of Puss upon the tiles and the melodious love-songs of nightingale. Like any other theory, this theory is untenable in the absence of historical knowledge of a large number of world's languages.

❐

2

Types of Changes in Present Day Situation

The spelling of English, even in printed books was not finally standardized until the eighteenth century. With such freedom from restraint, especially before the eighteenth century, we must expect the history of spoken English to give evidence of drastic change; but the changes which took place were not all of the same kind.

(1) The most important kind of change tends to affect the realization of a phoneme in all its occurrences. Such changes, not usually being set in motion by any immediate, outside influence, are in this sense independent; they are often known as isolative internal changes. Thus, the ME realization of the phoneme in a word such as house had the sound [u:], which has generally become [*a*ʊ] in modern English; similarly, the ME vowel phoneme having a value of the [a:] type, as in a word such as name, is in most cases realized as a kind of [eɪ] in PressE. Changes of this type apply particularly to the English vowel system, which underwent a remarkable evolution of values, known as the *Great Vowel Shift*, during the centuries preceding the modern period.

(2) Another kind of change which affects the realization of a phoneme is that which is brought about by the occurrence of phonemes in particualr contexts—a dependent change, often called *internal combinative*. Thus, the phonome in mice, having now the sound [aɪ], results from an earlier [i:] by means of an isolative change; but this [i:] sound in

[mi:s] arose as a result of a combinative process of vowel harmony, or i-mutation, through the stages [mu:si], [my:si], >[mi:s] where the change [u:] > [y:] can be explained by the fronting of [u:] under the influence of the [i:] of the following syllable. Such a combinative change belongs to OE, but a more recent change of this type is exemplifed by words such as swan. This word was probably pronounced [swan] in about 1600, but the [w] sound has rounded and retracted the vowel to give the modern form [swɐn]. The large majority of earlier [w] + [a] sequences have now given [w] + [ɐ], or [ɔ:], by reason of this combinative change affecting this particular sound sequence, *e.g.* want, quality, war, water, etc.

(3) Some changes are neither independent nor dependent upon the phonetic context; they may be said to be external to the main line of evolution. Thus, it was fashionable in Elizbethan times to pronounce such words as servant and heard with [ær] or [ar], perhaps originally a dialect form, rather than with [ɛr], the regular form of development; these words, with some exceptions such as clerk have reverted to the normal development of ME [ɛr],—[a:] rather than [a:]. It was also fashionable to pronounce the termination -ing as [ɪn], only now retained as a special form of affectation or of vulgar speech. Such changes, involving a change of distribution of phonemes among word and morpheme classes, do not affect the phonemic system of the language. The introduction of foreign words may, however, at least temporarily and in the speech of a restricted number of individuals, disturb the number of phonemes or their distribution as regards position in the word.

(4) In addition to changes of quality, there have also to be taken into account changes involving quantity and accentual pattern (stress). Thus, the vowel in such words as path, half, pass, still short three hundred years ago, is now long in the South of England. Or again, the vowels in good,

book and breath, death, once long, are now relatively short. Changes of accent are particularly striking in the case of words which have come into the language from French.

RATE AND ROUTE OF VOWEL CHANGE

The English vowels have been subject to more striking changes than have the consonants. This is not surprising, for a consonantal articulation usually involves an approximation of organs which can be felt; such an articulation tends to be more stable in that it is more easily identified and transmitted more exactly from one generation to another. Changes in the consonantal system comparatively rarely involve a modification of sound. Far more common is the type of distributional change involving the conferment of phonemic status on an existing sound (*e.g.* [v, ð, z], allophones of /f, θ, s/ in OE, later obtain contrastive, phonemic, significance), or the disappearance of an allophone (*e.g.* postvocalic [x] and [ç] in such words as brought and right were largely lost in the South of England by the seventeenth century) or the insertion of an existing phoneme in a particular class of words (*e.g.* the initial /h/ in words of French origin such as herb, homage). Whether it is a question of consonantal change, loss, or addition, it is usually possible to explain the type of modification which has taken place and the approximate period during which it occurred.

A modification of vowel quality will, however, result from very slight changes of tongue or lip position and there may be a series of imperceptible gradations before an appreciable quality change in evident (or is capable of being expressed by means of the Latin vowel letters). It is particularly difficult to assess rate and phonetic route of change in the case of those internal independent vowel changes which affect the realization of a phoneme throughout the language. It is known, for instance, that the modern homophones meet and meat had in ME different vowel forms, approximately of the value [e:] and [ɛ:]. The [e:] vowel of meet became [i:] by about 1500 and it might be postulated that by a process of gradual change the [ɛ:] of meat first closed to [e:] and then, by the eighteenth century, coalesced with the [i:] in meet. The available evidence, however, suggests that the change [ɛ: > i:] may not have been either simple or gradual, but that two pronunciations existed side by side for a long period (the conservative [ɛ:] beside another form [i:] which had resulted from an early coalescence with the meet vowel) and that it is the [i:] form which has in most cases survived. In other vowel changes, it may be agreed that the change was gradual, but it is difficult to date precisely the stages of development. thus, the modern /aɪ/ of time results from a ME [i:] value; it is clear that the change has been one of progressive, widening, diphthongization, but there may have been a period of incipient diphtongization when there was hesitation between the pure vowel [i:] and some such diphthong as [ɪi] or [əi]. It is well to remember, therefore, that at any particular time in history there are likely to be a number of different, coexistent, realizations of vowel phonemes, not only as between regions but also between generations and social groups. An example of such variety in modern English is provided by the diphthong in the word home, which in the South of England may be rendered as [əu] by yonger generation and something more like [ou] by the older people. The speech of any community may, therefore, be said to reflect the pronunciation of the previous century and to anticipate that of the next.

SOUND CHANGE AND THE LINGUISTIC SYSTEM

It is convenient to study sound change in terms of the development of particular phonemes or sounds, but it is misleading to ignore the relationship of the sound units to the system within which they function and which may, in fact, not be changing. In other words, although there may be considerable qualitative changes, the number and pattern of the terms within the system may show relative stability. The ME /i:/ phoneme, for instance, is now realized as [aɪ], but there is still a phonemic opposition which contrasts such words as time, team, tame, term, tomb, etc., and, in any case, a new phoneme /i:/ has emerged in words of the team type. On the other hand, the system may change because a sound, without itself changing, may receive a new, phonemic, value, *e.g.* the sound [ŋ] has always existed in English as a realization of /n/ followed by the velars /k/ or /g/, but when the final /g/ in a word like sing was no longer pronounced, /ŋ/ contrasted significantly with /n/ and /m/.

Since the system of our language consists of a framework of significant oppositions by means of which we communicate, it may be assumed that there is a tendency for the system to remain stable, the loss of an opposition involving a possibility of confusion. In fact, of course, the redundancy of English is such that some degree of neutralization of phonemes is easily tolerated: thus, to-day, few speakers in the South of England distinguish saw and sore by means of an opposition /ɔ:/ - /ə ɔ/, yet the loss of the /ə ɔ/ diphthong is no impediment to communication. An example of an earlier coalescence of vowel phonemes in that illustrated by the homophony of meet and meat. On the other hand, new oppositions may emerge in the language, *e.g.* the phonemes /v, ð, z, ŋ/, as we have seen. Nevertheless, despite the adjustments in the number of phonemes which have taken place, the history of the English sound system display, over the last 1,000 years, a considerable degree of stability.

Though the relationships within the system may tend to remain stable, a change of phonetic realization of any phoneme is likely to have qualitative repercussions throughout the system. Such a disturbance may be observed in modern English. The phonetic relationship of the vowel phonemes in set and sat, in one type of pronunciation, is of a front vowel between half-close and half-open to a front vowel between half-open and open. If, however, the vowel of sat has a closer articulation than that described, that of set must be raised, too. Alternatively, if the vowel phoneme of sat is realized as a front open vowel, as in many English regional dialects, the vocalic area in which the phoneme of set can be realized becomes more extensive; in fact, in those kinds of English where this occurs, the vowel in set tends to be a half-open variety. Such considerations of the phonetic relationship of ponemes have a relevance in the historical, diachronic, study of English.

Although, therefore, it is often convenient in diachronic studies to investigate the development of individual phonemes in terms of the quality of their realization, it is clear that many sound changes can be explained only by reference to a readjustment of the phonetic relationships of the phonemes of the system as a whole, Moreover, any particualr point in the development of a language's sound system is not simply to be considered as a stage in the process of change of a number of sound units but rather as the presentation of the functioning of a system at a certain historical moment. The primary significance of the sounds of modern English is their function in the system of to-day; in the same way, the English sound of 1600 are to be viewed in terms not only of their past and future forms but also of their contemporary, synchronic, relationships and functions.

Some sound changes are, indeed, the result of an influence which applies to the system as a whole. A prosodic, or supra-segmental, feature such as the stress-accent provides an example of this kind. English has always possessed a strong stress-accent, certain syllables of a word or utterance being made more prominent than their neighbours because of, amongst other things, the greater force with which they are said. Those drastic changes of vowel quality known as the Great Vowel Shift mainly affect vowels in accented syllables. But vowels in most unaccented syllables (especially those in word final positions) have undergone, in the last thousand years, an equally striking, though different, type of change. Henry Sweet has called OE the period of full endings, stanas being realized as ['sta:nas]; ME, the period of levelled endings, when stones was pronounced ['stɔ:nəs]; and eModE and later English, the period of lost endings, when stones is [sto:nz]; [stəunz]. There is, therefore, a general tendency for all unaccented vowels to shorten (if long) and to gravitate towards the weak centralized vowels [ɪ] or [ə], or sometimes [u], if not to disappear altogether. This fact accounts for the high frequency of occurrence of [ɪ] and [ə] in PresE and for the complete elision of many vowels in unaccented syllables in rapid colloquial speech, *e.g.* suppose [s'pəuz], probably ['prɐbblɪ].

Our conclusions will, therefore, be based on information mostly of an indirect kind; yet such is the agreement generally amongst the various types of evidence that the broad lines of sound change can be conjectured with reasonable certainty:

(1) Theoretical Paths of Development. If in dealing with the changing realization of a particular phoneme we can be reasonably sure of its sound value at two points in hisotry, we can, from our knowledge of phonetic possibilities and probabilites, infer theoretically the intervening stages of development. We can, of course, be sure of the pronunciation of PresE. If, then, the evidence suggested unequivocally that, of instance, the vowel in home was pronounced as [a:] in OE, the development to be described and accounted for would be [a:] > [aʊ]. It is likely that the articulation has always involved the back, rather than the front, of the tongue; the change has clearly meant a closing of the tongue position, to which at some stage there has been added a gliding (diphthonga) movement. We might, therefore, postulate such developments as [a: > aʊ > ɔʊ > oʊ > əʊ] or [a: >ɔ: > o: > oʊ > əʊ]. The available evidence will then confirm or refute the hypothesis—in this case the second solution being more in keeping with the information. Such recognition of phonetic probabilities will always be implicit in the tracing of change. It must be considered unlikely they [a:] on its way to [oʊ] or [əʊ] would have passed through a stage of front articulation, without any combinative influence.

(2) Old English. It is most important in an investigation of the development of English sounds over the last thousand years that the pronunciation of OE should be established with some certainty. If this can be done, we shall have a 'starting point' for the phonetic route of change to PresE. The term old English, however, spans a period of some four hundred years from about A.D. 700 to A.D. 1100. Morevoer, the invasion of the Angles, Saxons, and Jutes in the fifth and sixth centuries introduced four separate varieties of English: the Angles, in the Midlands, north-east England,

and the south of Scotland, using types of English known as Mercian and Northumbrian (or, in general terms, Anglian); the Saxons, in the south and south-west, using the West-Saxon dialect; and the Jutes, settling mainly in the region of Kent and using a dialect called Kentish. Of the four dialects, West-Saxon, which was to become a kind of standard language, is the one about which most is known from the extant texts. In its later form—that in use between about A.D. 900 and A.D. 1100—it is referred to as Classical OE.

The broad lines of the pronunciation of this language can be conjectured from a comparison of the development of the other members of the West Germanic group of languages to which it is related. But by far the most explicit evidence concerning its sounds is to be inferred from the alphabet in which it is written. The earlier Runic spelling was replaced by a form of the Latin alphabet. This alphabet was probably introduced into the country in the seventh century by Irish missionaries. It can be assumed, therefore, that the sounds of OE were represented as far as possible by the Latin letters with their Latin values, with some modifications of an Irish kind. A great deal is known about the pronunciation of Vulgar Latin, whose sound system had much in common with that of modern Italian. If an Italian, knowing no English, were to-day asked to write down with his own spelling the PresE pronunciation of the world milk, [mɪlk], he would have no difficulty in representing the first sound, which he could spell as m; the vowel [ɪ] might, however, seem to him to resemble the sound he would write in Italian as e rather than as i; and 'dark' [l] would appear to have a back vowel glide accompanying it, requiring a spelling such as ol; and, since he has no k letter, he would spell the final [k] as c. His transcription of the word might, therefore, be meolc, which is, in fact, a West-Saxon spelling of the word now written milk. This is a fortuitous example and must not be taken to suggest that OE was pronounced in the same way as PresE. But it does demonstrate the OE spellings, which may appear to be very different, are often less surprising when we keep in mind the Latin values originally attached to the letters.

Sometimes the simple forms of the Latin alphabet were evidently inadequate for representing the English sound; thus, the joined form æ was used to symbolize a sound between C[a] and C[ɛ]; the sounds [θ] and [ð] were writing in the earlier manuscripts as th initially and d medially and finally in a word, and later as ð or the rune þ, regardless of the sound's position in the word or its voiced or voiceless quality; the rune þ frequently replaced the earlier u or uu. The vowel values of the OE system were particualrly difficult to represent with the five Latin vowel letters. Sometimes the spelling used will hesitate between two letters: thus, the vowel of mann, probably of a C[a] or [ɐ] quality, is written either with a or o, indicating a vowel between the open central unrounded value of the Lain letter a and the back half-open to half-close rounded value of o. Unaccented vowels, too, already beginning to be obscured and levelled, presented a problem to the scribes, the Latin alphabet offering no way of showing a central vowel of the [ə] type. Unaccented æ, e and i soon begin to the written as e and unaccented a, u, o later tend to be used indifferently, indicating that the vowel distinction was being lost. A diphthong such as the one written as ea must probably be interpreted as a glide to a central [ə] quality.

Quantity is often shown in the case of vowels by doubling the letter or by the use of an accent and in the case of consonants by doubling the letter. The stress-accent in a word is also sometimes shown by the use of a mark; but, in any case, it is agreed, from a comparison of the West Germanic languages, that the word accent in OE fell generally on the first syllable of words, with the exception of certain compounds.

The written form of OE provides us, therefore, with considerable information concerning the language's pronunciation; we have a working hypothesis from which to begin our investigations. The study of later forms of English will often, in fact, confirm that the OE pronunciation postulated from the spelling and the comparison of Germanic languages in the only one from which later forms can be expected to have developed.

(3) **Middle English.** Spelling forms can also help us to deduce the pronunciation of the ME period, roughly A.D. 1100-1450. Generally speaking, it may be said that the letters still had their Latin values and that those letters which were written were meant to be sounded. Thus, the initial k is a word such as knokke was still pronounced and the vowel in time would have an [i] quality. This persistence of Latin values in spelling was no doubt due to the influence of the Church, which was still the centre of teaching and writing, and the absence of a thoroughly standardized spelling accounts for its predominatly phonetic character. However, English spelling was modified by French influences. Notably, the French ch spelling was introduced to represent the [tʃ] sound in a word such as chin (formerly spelt cinn), where the new spelling form indicates no change of pronunciation; in addition ou, or ow, represents the sound [u], formerly written u, *e.g.* hous, in OE hus. The simple u spelling was retained to express both the French sound [y] in words like duke and fortune and the OE short [u] sound, though this latter sound is often written as o, especially when juxtaposed to letters of the w, m, n type, *e.g.* wonne rather than wunne, to avoid confusion between the letter shapes.

Rhymes, too, have their value, especially as, in this period, they are likely to have been satisfactory to the ear as well as to the eye—in the whole of Chaucer's work, for instance, there are very few rhymes which appear to involve the pairing of different vowel sounds. Nevertheless, evidence from rhymes is valueless unless it is possible to be certain, from other sources of evidence, of the pronunciation of one member of the pair. Thus, the Chaucerian rhyme par cas: : was, because we can be sure that the French word cas had a vowel of the [a] quality, is evidence to confirm the view that the [w] of was had not yet retracted and rounded the vowel to [ɐ] and, the final s in the two words being still likely to represent [s], that the word was probably pronounced [was].

Again, words imported from French can give us information concerning the timing of sound changes. Thus, French words such as age and couch, which we know from French sources had [a:] and [u:] at the time of their introduction into English, fell in with the English vowel development [a:] > [eɪ] and [u:] > [aʊ] in words like name and house; we can conclude, therefore, that at the time the French words came into the language the [a:] and [u:] vowels had not begun their change.

Moreover after the ME period, as we shall see, a great deal of direct evidence is available to us, so that our conjectures from about 1500 onwards can be made with considerable certainty. We my often, therefore, be able to deduce from our knowledge of pronunciation in the sixteenth century the stage probably reached in the ME period in the development of a sound from OE. The OE [i:] sound in time, for example, was beginning to be diphthongized generally very early in the sixteenth century. It is reasonable to suppose (even if other evidence to support the theory did not exist) that time still had a relatively pure [i:] for much of the ME period.

Finally, the metre of verse reveals the stress accent of words. It is for this reason that we know that French words, in Chaucer's verse, generally retained their original accentual pattern, *e.g.* courage [ku'ra:dʒə], and that the accent shift in these cases is a phenomenon of at least late ME.

(4) Early Modern English. The same sources of evidence which we have already considered remain available for the eModE period, roughly A.D. 1450-1600. The introduction of printing brought standardization of spelling and already the spoken and written forms of the language were beginning to diverge. But individuals, especially in their private correspondence, often used spellings of a largely phonetic kind, in the same unsophisticated and logical way that children still do. If a modern child writes He must have gone as He must of gone, he is only representing the phonetic identity of the weak forms of have and of ([əv]), an identity which he will learn to ignore when he adopts the conventional spelling distinction. In the same way, if fifteenth- and sixteenth-century spellings show the word sweet occasionally written as swit, it may be assumed that this original ME [e:] was by now so close that it could be represented by i with its Latin value. Or again, the spelling form sarvant instead of servant reflects an open type of vowel in the first syllable which was current throughout the eModE period in such words. Moreover, the conventional adoption of an unphonetic spelling can sometimes provides us with positive evidence as to its value: thus, when words like delight (formerly delite) began to be spelt with gh, this spelling form gh clearly no longer had the consonantal fricative value which it had formerly represented in light, since there never was a consonantal sound between the vowel and final [t] is delight. We may conclude, therefore, that gh no longer had its former phonetic significance in words such as light.

Care must, of course, be taken to identify the increasing number of learned or technical spellings adopted by printers. The initial letter group gh in ghost (OE gast) indicates no change in pronunciation—goose was also sometimes spelt ghoose in this period. Again, spellings which aim at revealing the etymology (true or false) of a word must usually be discarded as phonetically valueless, *e.g.* debt, island. It is above all from the writings of individuals that some general indications concerning sound changes may be gathered and used to supplement evidence derived from other sources.

Rhymes, too, continue to be useful as complementary evidence. A rhyme such as night: : white confirms the view that postvocalic gh no longer had a consonantal value; or again, can: : swan suggests that the rounding of [a] after [w] had not yet taken place. Yet, just as in the case of ME, rhymes must be treated with caution, more particularly as eye-rhymes were doubtless beginning to become more prevalent. There is, however, in Elizabethan literature, additional evidence afforded by the frequent use of puns, which usually rely for their effect upon similarities, if not identities, of phonetic value. Shakespeare, for instance, plays on the phonetic identity of such pairs as suitor, shooter (both capable of being pronounced [ʃu:tər] and known, none (both [no:n}); such puns suggest that the pronunciation of the two words was commonly sufficiently close to make an immediate impression upon an audience.

The most important and fruitful evidence for this period, is, however, of a direct kind. It is provided by the published works of the contemporary grammarians, orthoepists, and schoolmasters. They are of unequal value and their statements have often to be interpreted in the light of other evidence; yet they provide us with the first direct descriptive accounts of the pronunciation of English. From the sixteenth century ownards, ours conclusions rely more and more on their descriptive statements and less on clues of an indirect kind.Sometimes there appears to be a conflict between the phonetic probabilities, the statements of grammarians, and evidence from other sources. Frequently the solution must be that there existed at any time a variety of current pronunciations, resulting from differences of dialect, generation, fashion, and place in society, in the same way that a description of PresE (even that of a restricted area such as the south of England) would have to take into account a large number of variants.

MODIFICATIONS IN THE ENGLISH SYSTEM

1. **Distribution of Phonemes.** The similarities of the systems given abve may obscure the fact that the same sound, especially as far as the vowels are concerned, may occur in different categories of words according to the period. Thus [u:], now in food, occurred in OE in words such as town; [i:], now in team, occurred in OE in time. The following summary shows some of the most striking changes affecting the vowel quality used in particular word categories

		OE	ME	eModE	PresE
time	.	i:	i:	əi	aɪ
sweet	.	e:	e:	i:	i:
clean	.	æ:	ɛ:	e: (or [i:])	i:
stone	.	a:	ɔ:	o:	əʊ
name	.	a	a:	ɛ:	eɪ
moon	.	o:	o:	u:	u:
house	.	u:	u:	əu	aʊ
love	.	ʊ	ʊ	ɤ	ʌ(or[ä])

2. **Vowel Changes.** Several trends become apparent from a study of quality changes:

   (a) OE long vowels have closed or diphthongized; on the other hand, PresE [əʊ] and [eɪ] show signs of monophthongization.

   (b) Certain phonemic qualitative oppositions have coalesced, *e.g.* OE /e:/ and /æ:/; the orginally separate diphthongs of day and way; the diphthong of know with the originally pure vowel of no; the diphthongs of day, way with the former pure vowel of name; OE /y:, y/ with /i:, ɪ/ (or /ɛ/).

   (c) Short vowels, with the notable exceptions of the OE / a, æ/ (and the short diphthong /ɛə/) in open syllables and ME /ʊ/, have remained relatively stable.

   (d) Rounded front vowels have been lost, *e.g.* OE /y:, y/ and earlier /ϕ:, ϕ/.

   (e) The loss of post-vocalic [r] in the eighteenth century gave rise to the PresE centring diphthongs /ɪə, ɛə, ʊə/, the pure vowel /a:/ and introduced /a:, ɔ:/ into new categories of words (cart, port).

   (f) Vowles under weak accent are increasingly obscured to [ə] or [ɪ], or are elided.

   (g) Changes of quantity affected certain phonemes in particular contexts or sets of words, *e.g.* lengthening of OE /a, æ, ɛə/ in open syllables and of ME /a/ + /f, θ, s/; and shortening of ME /o:/ in words like good, book, blood, and to ME /ɛ:/ in such words as breath, death, head.

3. **Consonant Changes.** Changes in the consonantal system are less striking, but the following may be noted:

(a) Double (or long) consonants within words were lost by late ME; certain other consonant clusters cease to be tolerated, *e.g.* /hl, hr, hn/ by ME and /kn, gn, wr/ in the eModE period; post-vocalic /r/ was lost in the south-east of England in the eighteenth century.

(b) Allophones of certain phonemes have been lost, *e.g.* the [ɣ] allophone of /g/ in late OE and the [x, ç] allophones of /h/ in eModE.

(c) New phonemes have emerged, *e.g.* /tʃ, dʒ/ in OE, /v, ð, z/ in ME, and /ŋ, ʒ/ in eModE; in addition, /h/ is used initially in words of French origin where, originally, no [h] sound was pronounced (habit, herb, humble, etc).

THE PRESENT-DAY SITUATION

The English are today particularly sensitive to variations in the pronunication of their language. The 'wrong accent' may still be an impediemnt to social intercourse or to advancement of entry in certain professions. Such extreme sensitivity is apparently not paralleled in any other country or even in other parts of the English-speaking world. There are those who claim, from an elocution standpoint, that modern speech is becoming increasingly slovenly, full of 'mumbling and mangled vowels and missing consonants'. Alexander Gil and others made the same kind of complaint in the seventeenth century. There is, in fact, no evidence to suggest that the degree of obscuration and elision, often characteristic of a dynamic stress language such as English, is markedly greater now than it has been for four centuries. Of more significance—social as well as linguistic—is the attitude which regards a certain set of sound values as more acceptable, even more 'beautiful' than another. Judgments of this kind suggest that there is a standard for comparison; and it is clear that such a standard pronunciation does exist, although it has never been explicity imposed by any official body. A consideration of the origins and present nature of this unofficial standard goes some way towards explaining the controversies and emotions which it arouses at the present day.

(1) Great prestige is still attached to this implicitly accepted social standard of pronunciation. Often called Received Pronunciation (RP), the term suggesting that it is the result of a social judgment rather than of an official decision as to what is 'correct' or 'wrong', it has become more widely known and accepted through the advent of radio. The BBC formerly recommended this form of pronunciation for its announcers mainly because it was the type which was most widely understood and which excited least prejudice of a regional kind. Indeed, attempts to use announcers who had a mild regional accent provoked protests even from the region whose accent was used. Thus, RP often became identified in the public mind with 'BBC English'. This special position occupied by RP, basically educated Southern British English, has led to its being the form of pronunciation most commonly described in books on the phonetics of British English and traditionally taught to foreigners.

(2) Nevertheless, it cannot be said that RP is any longer the exclusive property of a particular social stratum. This change is due partly to the influence of radio in constantly bringing the accent to the ears of the whole nation, but also, in considerable measure, to the modifications which are taking place in the structure of English society. Just as the sharp divisions between classes are beginning to disappear, so the more marked characteristics of regional speech and, in the London region, the popular forms of pronunciation, are tending to be modified in the direction of RP, which is equated with the 'correct' pronunciation of English. This tendency does not, as yet, mean that regional forms of pronunciation show signs of disappearing, but it has to be recognized that those who wish, for any reason, to modify their speech have models of RP always readily available to their ears while, at the same time, the social inhibitions concerning movement between classes,

which were formerly so strongly operative, no longer, in the face of the standardization of society as a whole, exert the same pressure.

Moreover, it must be remarked that some members of the present younger generation reject RP because of its association with the 'Establishment' in the same way that they question the validity of other forms of traditional authority. For them a real or assumed regional or popular accent has a greater (and less committed) prestige. It is too early to predict whether such attitudes will have any lasting effect upon the future development of the pronunciation of English. But, if this tendency were to become more widespread and permanent, the result could be that, within the next century, RP might be so diluted that it could lose its historic identity and that a new standard with a wider popular and regional base would emerge. Such a change is made more likely through the recent more permissive attitude of the BBC (and of the commerical television companies) in their choice of announcers, several of whom now have markedly non-RP or non-British accents.

(3) Certain types of regional pronunciation are, indeed, firmly established. Some, especially Scottish English speech, are universally accepted; others, particularly the popular forms of pronunciation used in large towns such as London, Liverpool, or Birmingham, are generally characterized as ugly by those (especially of the older generations) who do not use them. This rejection of certain sounds used in speech is not, of course, a matter of the sounds themselves: thus, [paınt] may be acceptable if it means pint, but 'ugly' if it means paint. It rather a reflection of the social cannotations of speech which, though they have lost some of their force, have by no means disappeared. Indeed, RP itself can be a handicap if used in inappropriate social situation, since it may be taken as a mark of affectation or a desire to emphasize social superiority. It may be said,

too, that if improved communications and radio have spread the availability of RP, these same influences have rendered other forms of pronunciation less remote and strange. An American pronunciation of English, for instance, is now completely accepted in Britain; this was not the case at the time when the first sound films were shown in this country, an American pronunciation then being considered strange and even difficult to understand. Speakers of RP are becoming increasingly aware of the fact that their type of pronunciation is one which is used by only a very small part of the English-speaking world.

(4) A comparison to two regional or social types of pronunciation will reveal differences of several kinds:

(a) The system, *i.e.* the number of distinctive (phonemic) terms operating, may be the same, but the phonetic realizations of the phonemes may be different: *e.g.* the RP opposition between the vowels of bet and bat may be maintained, but the realization of both vowels is much more open than in RP so that the sound of /æ/ may come near to that of one type of RP /ʌ/ or when, as in Cockney, an allophone [?] in unaccented positions represents /t/ and often /k/ or /p/ or when the final allophone of /l/ is [l] rather than [ł].

(b) The system may be different, *i.e.* the number of oppositions may be smaller or greater: *e.g.* the RP /æ/ - /a:/ opposition may not be present in those Ulster or Scottish forms which do not distinguish Sam and psalm; or when RP /aɪ/ homophones, as in side and sighed may be differentiated qualitatively or quantitatively, as in some types of Scottish English; or when, as in some forms of RP, /a:/ levels with /aɪ/ and /aʊ/ before /ə/ or when the presence of /g/ after /ŋ/ in such world as sing deprives [ŋ] of its phonemic status.

(c) The system may be the same, but the incidence of phonemes in words is different: *e.g.*, in those Northern forms which have the RP opposition /u:/ - /ʊ/, but nevertheless us /u:/ in book, took, etc., or when /ɐ/ is used instead of /ʌ/ is one, among, etc., though the opposition /ɐ/ - /ʌ/ exists; or when the choice of phoneme is associated with the habits of different generations, *e.g.* /ɔ:/ for /ɐ/ in off, cloth, cross, etc., or /eɪ/ for /ɪ/ in Monday, holiday, etc.

(5) It is possible to make some classification of the various kinds of British English pronunciation in the light of the regional and social criteria mentioned. Features of regional pronunciation, without any contamination from RP, will be fo8und in highly educated and less educated speech (to be distinguished briefly as educated regional and popular regional); lack of conventional education will often, in addition, reveal itself by the use of non-standard grammatical and lexical forms. On the other hand, a regional pronunciation may be termed modified when it has adopted certain characteristics of RP, *e.g.* the adoption of the RP [a:] in words such as ask, after, path rather than [a]. In the case of the speech of the Greater London pupulation, there are a great number of gradations to be noted amongst the popular regional forms, through educated regional to RP; such varying mixtures of regional and RP are typical of the suburban districts.

Within RP itself it is convenient to distinguish three main types: the conservative RP forms used by the other generation and, traditionally, by certain professions or social groups; the general RP forms most commonly in use and typified by the pronunciation adopted by the BBC; and the advanced RP forms mainly used by young people of exclusive social groups—mostly of the upper classes, but also, for prestige value, in certain professional circles. In its most exaggerated variety, this last type would usually by judged 'affected' by other RP speakers, in the same way that all RP types are liable to be considered affected by those who use unmodified regional speech. Advanced pronunciations, however, whenever they are not the result of temporary fashion, may well indicate the way in which the RP system is developing and be adopted in the future as general RP, *e.g.* the originally advanced ('affected') diphthong in home, involving increased centralization and a tendency towards monophthongization, seems likely to become general in a very short time.

These various types of British English pronunciation may be summarized as follows:

Regional	(Reg)	Received	(RP)
educated	(educ)	conservative	(cons)
popular	(pop)	general	(gen)
modified	(mod)	advanced	(adv)

(6) Finally, it has to be recognized that the role of British RP in the English-speaking world has changed very considerably in the last century. Over 300 million people now speak English as a first language, and of this number native RP speakers form only a minute proportion; the majority of English speakers use some form of American pronunciation. However, despite the discrepancy in numbers, RP continues for historical reasons to serve a model in many parts of the world, and, if a model is used at all, the choice is still effectively between RP and American pronunciation.

OLD ENGLISH PERIOD

After the Teutonic tribes had made themselves masters of the greater part of south Britain the English language came into existence as a separate idiom. The settlers spoke dialects which were very much allied, and from the fusion of their dialect resulted the English language. The earliest inhabitants of Britain during the time of the

Roman occupation from 55 B.C. to 410 A.D. spoke a language known as Celtic. The Celtic language must have received Latin element into its fold from the speech of the Roman soldiery. The history of the English language begins with the settlement of the three Germanic tribes, Angles, Saxons and Jutes in the sixth century. The coming of these tribes to Britain brought the Celts into contact with them and the contact influenced the languages of the Germanic tribes. In the area extending north-word from the Thames the Angles settled themselves. The Jutes settled in Kent and the Saxons settled in the rest of England south of the Thames. But the South-West of England was still occupied by the Celtic tribes. The Celts called their Germanic conquerors Saxons indiscriminately and the areas occupied by them was called Saxonia. But soon the Angle came into use and was applied to all the three Germanic tribes in general. The word English is derived from the name of Angles and was applied without distinction to the languages of all the Germanic tribes. Much later, England came into use from name of Angles. Old English was the language which emerged from the fusion of the dialects spoken by the invading Germanic tribes.

The Old English period extends from 450 to 1100. This period is known as the period of full inflexions. This period is described as the period of levelled or weakened inflexions since the inflexions which had began to weaken or become blurred towards the end of the Old English Period, became very much reduced during this period.

The Dialects of Old English

The three Teutonic tribes who settled in Britain spoke dialects which were more or less diverse. These tribes could no doubt understand each other, but there was no common tongue, and no common written language. Old English had four principal dialects Northmbrian, Mercian, West Saxon and Kentish. Northumbrian and Mercian were the dialects of the Angles and are often classed together and called Anglian. West Saxon represents the language of the Saxons and Kentish that of the Jutes.

Northumbrian was the first dialect to produce a literature. A rich body of old English poetry was produced in this dialect towards the end of the seventh century and in the beginning of the eighth century. But Northumbrian could not long retain its pre-eminence. During the reign of Alfred the Great in the West Saxon kingdom, West Saxon became the standard literary language of England. Even the older Northumbrian poetry was recopied into standard West Saxon Speech. Nearly all of Old English literature is preserved in manuscripts transcribed in this dialect. It is for this reason that West Saxon has been made the basis of the study of Old English.

Characteristics of Old English

No language is spoken or written in the same form through centuries. Language is a natural growth, partly mental and partly physical. It follows, therefore, that a language is undergoing constant change. The history of English language since its inception has been one of the continuous development. Hence, although Modern English has been derived from Old English by a regular process of change, Old English has quite respect of a foreign language. The language of Alfred seems to be quite different from Modern English, Old English has evolved into Modern English through gradual changes in pronunciation, spelling, grammar and vocabulary.

A page of Old English presents a look of strangeness to the modern reader because of its employment of certain symbols which are no longer in use today. Old English made use of two symbols xo and p to represent the sound of 'th'. These two symbols are no more used in Modern English. Old English represented the vowel sound as in words man, hat and so on, by the symbol ae. Much of the strange appearance of Old English is due to the frequent appearance of this symbol. Similarly 'sh' sound is represented by 'Sc' in old English as for example Sceap (Sheep), biscop (bishop), Likewise 'K' sound is always represented by c, as for example in words like cynn (Kin), nacod (Naked). In general it may be said that in pronunciation Old English has no silent syllable and its spelling is more or less phonetic, that is to say, its letters represents its sounds quite closely.

In Old English script there are seven vowel symbols- a, e, i, o, u, y and the digraph ae which is called 'ash'.

All the seven vowels represent either long or short sounds. Long vowels are marked by the sign, placed over vowels *e.g.*, a, e etc. The short vowels are pronounced almost as they are pronounced in Modern English. The pronunciation of some of the Old English vowels are indicated below:

OE a Pronounced like the 'a' of father.

" oe Pronounced like the 'a' of hat.

" oe Pronounced like the 'ai' of air.

" i Pronounced like the 'i' of machine.

" u Pronounced like the 'u' of put.

" u Pronounced like the 'oo' of food.

The Old English consonants have mostly the same sounds as in Modern English, but some call for comment. The letter 'h' is more strongly pronounced than it is in Modern English. The letter C has mostly a K-sound, SC the sound of modern 'Sh' and the combination 'Cg' the sounds of 'j' of judge. The letter r is trilled in all positions as in Modern Scotch. Old English script does not have the letter V, f serves for the sounds of both f and V. Old English alphabets contains two symbols P, called thorn and called 'eth' to represent the sound of th; P represents the sound of th in thin an δ the sounds of th in this, when we read Old English we must remember that each symbol is pronounced. In this sense, Old English is phonetic in character.

Therefore we can summarize by saying that Old English is essentially phonetic in character. There are no silent sounds and no superflous symbols, nor are the existing symbols made to overstram too much. In the course of time, Old English test its phonetic nature, especially from the middle English period. Two important characteristics of Old English are the phonetic changes known as graduation and mutation. Modern English have a bearing of these phonetic and sound changes. Gradation is a change in vowel sounds of principal parts of verbs according to whether they occur in a stressed or unstressed syllable. The vowel changes that we find in these old English verbs were due to shifting of stress long ago in the history of the Indo-European group if languages. But the changes in vowel sound in the root syllable of the verb is gradation. The verbs in which this gradation takes place are called strong verbs and the verbs which cannot make past tense by such a change in vowel but of adding suffix 'ed' are called weak verbs. This gradation is also called ablant. A similar change took place in the root syllable of the verb when a suffix was added to it in order to make a or a participle. As examples we may take the following verbs:

Present	*Past*	*Past Participle*
drifan (drive)	draf (drove)	drifen (driven)
radan (ride)	rad (rode)	riden (ridden)
writan (to write)	wrat (wrote)	writan (written)

The more important phonetic change in Old English was mutation, sometimes called amlaut. It should be more strictly called as i-mutation. It is a process in which, in early Old English vowels in accented syllables were modified through the influence of an i or j in the next syllable. The i or j that caused the change totally disappeared at the later stage. This is a very complicated sound change which had a good deal of living interest for modern student. It explains certain anomalies in Modern English. The following are the vowels changes that took place:

Short back vowels	*Short back disphthongs*
a > e	ea > ie
oe > e	eo > ie
o > e	io > ie,
u > y	

It will be noticed that what happened was that the back-vowels were changed to front vowels.

Grammar is the most striking characteristic that distinguishes Old English from the Modern English. It is an inflected language though not so highly inflected as the classical languages like Sanskrit, Latin and Greek. It stands a little more than half way along the linguistic road leading Indo-European synthesis to Modern English analysis. Modern English had dropped almost all the inflexions and has devised other means of expressing grammatical relations. In short Modern English is an analytic language, while Old English is a synthetic one.

A language is said to be in the synthetical stage when it expresses the grammatical relations of words by adding some suffixes to the stems of nouns, adjectives, pronouns and verbs. A language is free from such inflexional endings as far as possible and in their place makes free use of other devices like prepositions and other auxiliary words is said to be in the analytic stage. From this point of view Modern English is analytical. In its Grammar, Old English resembles Modern English. The nature of Old English grammar can be gathered by looking at the inflexions of its nouns, adjectives, pronouns, verbs, and so on.

Old English nouns have two numbers-Singular and Plural, three genders–masculine, feminine and neuter. The system of genders is irrational, because it is not dependent upon the consideration of sex. Where as what we call gender in Modern English is based on sex. Therefore, in Modern English all males are said to be Masculine, Females Feminine and things without life are called Neuter. But in Old English, as in Latin, it is not on sex or absence of sex but on the forms that a noun assumes in the course of its declension. Thus in Old English here (army) is Masculine, Wynn (joy) is faminine, wif (woman) is Neuter and wifman (woman) is Masculine perhaps the second element in the compound is Masculine Strangely mona (moon) is Masculine and sunne (sun) is Feminine.

Another peculiarity of Old English is the adjective like nouns have gender. The adjective takes the gender of the noun with which it is associated.

There are four cases-nominative, genetive, dative, accusative. The system of declension is very intricate.

The Old English noun is inflected according to its number and case. It has chiefly four cases and the endings of these vary with different nouns. There are two chief declensions and a consonant declension. Vowel declension is called strong declension and consonant declension is called weak declension. Whether a noun takes one or the other of the two declension depends upon whether the stem of the noun ended in Germanic in a vowel on in a consonant. The following examples will suffice to understand the nature of the declension of the nouns:

(1) Masculine-a Stem (Stan Stone)

	Singular	*Plural*
Nominative	Stan	Stan-as
Genetive	Stanes	Stan-a
Dative	Stan-e	Stan-um
Accusative	Stan	Stan-as

(2) Feminine O Stem:– giefu (gift)

	Singular	*Plural*
Nominative	gief-u	gief-a
Genetive	gief-e	gief-a
Dative	gief-e	gief-um
Accusative	gief-e	gief-a

(3) Masculine Consonant Stem:– flunta (hunter)

	Singular	*Plural*
Nominative	hunt-a	hunt-um
Genetive	hunt-on	hunt-ena
Dative	hunt-an	hunt-um
Accusative	hunt-an	hunt-an

It is a evident by thus how complicated the inflexions of the Old English noun is. Modern English has discarded most of the case endings except the Genetive case ending.

In Old English adjective, there is a two-fold declension one of them is the strong declension used with nouns when they are not accompanied by a definite article or a demonstrative pronoun. For instance 'god mann' (good man) is strong declension. The other is the weak declension used with nouns accompanied by a definite article. Thus, god a mann (the good man) is a weak declension. Further complication of the adjective in Old English adjective is that it is declined according to number, gender and case. In Modern English the adjectival remains undeclined whatever number, gender and case it is associated with. Such elimination of the complex adjectival inflexion gives a great advantage to the English language, over many other Indo-European languages.

A definite article is inflected according to gender, number and case. Like modern German, Old English had a fully inflected definite article. The little word 'the' assumed twelve different forms according to the gender, number and case of the noun.

Old English had two classes of verbs strong and weak which have passed even in Modern English and are known as regular and irregular verbs. There were only two tenses by inflexion past and present. The present generally served also a future (We go there next month) but million and scullan (will and shall) were occasionally used and their use foreshadowed future developments. In the strong verbs the change of tense is indicated by a modification in their root-vowel as in 'sing, sang, sung'. In the weak verbs such a change in tense is indicated by the addition of suffix. It is estimated that Old English has a few over three hundred strong verbs. Based on the gradation of the vowel they assume, they are classified into six classes and to those six is added a seventh class of verbs called reduplicating verbs. They may be illustrated by the following verbs :–

	Present		*Preterite*	*Preterite*	*Past*
			Singular	*Plural*	*Participle*
1.	drifon	(drive)	draf	difon	drifen.
2.	cheooan	(choose)	ceas	curon	coren
3.	helpan	(help)	healp	hulpon	holpen
4.	beran	(bear)	boer	boeron	boren
5.	sprecan	(speak)	spoec	sproecon	sprecan

In Modern English many of the characteristics of the verb are preserved with some modifications. Old English has distinct forms of the personal pronouns practically for all genders, persons and cases. Instead of two numbers, singular and plural, it has an intermediate number called the dual number, which represents two things. The existence of the dual form in addition to the plural is an unnecessary complication in language and so it has disappeared in Modern English.

After gaining the knowledge of Old English grammar, pronunciations, dialects we must learn about the language of Old English in prose and poetry. The presentation of a good prose style is always with the efforts made by the generations of writers. Old English prose lacks lucidity, simplicity and easy flow, it is often clumsy and unwieldy. But in some of the passages we find an impassioned prose of real merit. Of course the poetic style of the Old English, on the contrary has a great claim. It is marked by a leisurely movement, repetition of ideas and words, alliteration, an abundant use of compounds and synonyms. In Old English poetry there are twenty four synonyms for sea and including compound words and figurative expressions, the number of terms for sea must be at least a hundred.

LEXICAL BORROWING FOLLOWING THE RENAISSANCE

By superimposing the grammatical patterns of one language upon those of another we can determine some of the main grammatical difficulties involved in learning the second language. We find for example that there is agreement in number and gender between noun and adjective in French, but not so in English that the modifier comes before the noun in English, whereas it usually comes after it in French, United Nation giving *Nations Unies, some fresh air/de l'air frais*.

This gives us only the feature which each grammar lacks or possesses in relation to the other. Differential grammar is not, as some practitioners of it would have us believe, simply a matter of superimposing an outline of the grammar of one language on that of another. What is required is a special type of description which accounts for all types of differences and equivalences.

To begin with, we must distinguish between what may be said and what must be said. When a French learner speaks English he is forced into making certain distinctions that he has always ignored in the grammar of his own language. The grammar of English forces him to decide on whether he is referring to a state or an action, whether the action is incomplete and continuous or simply habitual. In his own language, he does not, for example, have to make the distinction between a person who plays the piano regularly as a hobby or profession and one who happens to be playing on the piano at any given moment: the utterance *II joue du piano* covers all such situations. In English, however, the distinction is compulsory, and the French learner must get into the habit of making it, for in one case he will have to say *He plays the piano*, and in the other, He is playing the piano. It is not that he is unable to make this distinction in his own language for he can distinguish *Il joue du piano from Il est en train de jouer due piano*; it is that he is not forced to make the distinction.

Secondly, in what must be said, we must distinguish unique forms from alternate ones. The grammar of our native language may provide a number of different ways of saying the same thing. Only one of these may be possible in the second language. Conversely, a single form in the native language may be equivalent to a number of different forms in the second language. For example, the adverb well in He spoke well of you may be equivalent to an adverb in French (Il a tre's bien parle' de vous) or it may be equivalent to a noun (*Il a dit du bien de vous*).

Although the examples we shall use are of the obligatory type, a complete differential grammar would also show what choices exist in each of the four grammatical categories—(1) the systems of the grammar, (2) the structures of the grammar, (3) the grammatical classes, and (4) the grammatical units.

Differences in System

Not all languages have the same grammatical systems. Some languages have no cases, for example. A French learner of German has to get used to the whole idea of case inflection in nouns—nominative, genitive, dative and accusative—in addition to the use of the right case in the right place.

Languages with the same systems, however, do not use them in the same way. An English learner of French knows that both English and French have a passive voice; but he must learn to avoid equating one with the other, for an English passive may be equivalent to the French "pronominal voice". (E. *It's not done* / F. *Ça ne se fait pas.*)

Not only do different languages have different inflectional categories, but the same category may function differently in one language from the way it does in the other, so that the function of number, case, person and tense is different in each language.

Of the differences with the systems of the verb, let us take as an example the use of tense in English and French. The fact that English and French have many tenses in common does not mean that these are equivalent. Both English and French have a simple present tense, but the English present may often be equivalent to the French perfect, future, or future perfect:

I hear he's coming = E. PRESENT/F.PERFECT

= J' *ai appris qu'il viendra.*

I hope he comes. = E. PRESENT/F. FUTURE

= J' *espere qu'il viendra.*

After we finish. = E. PRESENT/F. FUTURE

= *Apres que nous aurons fini.*

PERFECT

Both English and French have simple past tenses, but the English simple past is often the equivalent of the French imperfect, subjunctive, or present perfect:

He said he knew. = E. PAST/F. IMPERFECT

= II a dit qu'il le savait.

It's time he shut up = E. PAST/F. SUBJECTIVE

= II est temps qu'il *se taise.*

I saw him yesterday. = E. PAST/F. PRES. PERF.

= Je l' *ai vu hier.*

Conversely, if we were to take the French tenses as a starting-point, we would find a similar lack of equivalence with those of English. For example:

F. PRESENT	E. PERFECT
Nous le connaisions depuis des anness.	We've known him for years.

Differences in Structure

Languages differ in the way they put words and phrases together. They differ in the order and interdependence of their items. A description of the structural differences between two languages will show such things as diffferences in word-order. For example, although adverbs are used in both French and English they do not always occupy the same relative position in the sentence.

F. II repond *toujours en francais.* /E. He always answers in French.

F. J' aime beaucoup le the. */E. I like ead very much.*

A differential description will also show the differences in the type of interdependence of words in the sentence. In French, the tag-question is completely independent; in English, it depends on the main verb and must agree with it. A French learner of English must get used to making this agreement.

In the following example, note how the French *n'estce pas* always remains the same, being independent from the main clause with which it is used. On the other hand, the English equivalent is a dependent group which always has to agree with the main clause.

II est prêt, n'est-ce pas?	He's ready, isn't he?
II etait prêt, n'est-ce pas?	He was ready, wasn't he?
II sera prêt, n'est-ce pas?	He will be ready, won't he?
II semble prêt, n'est-ce pas?	He seems ready, doesn't he?
II semblait prêt, n' est-ce pas?	He seemed ready, didn't he?
II n'est pas prêt, n'est-ce pas?	He isn't ready, is he?
II n'etait pas prêt, n'est-ce pas?	He wasn't ready, was he?
II ne sera pas prêt, n' est-ce pas?	He won't be ready, will be?
II ne semble pas prêt, n'est-ce pas?	He doesn't seem ready he?
II ne semblait pas prêt, n'est-ce pas?	He didn't seem ready, did he?

Different Classes

Although most languages have such word-classes or parts of speech as nouns, verbs and adjectives, the number of classes is not necessarily the same for all languages.

In languages with the same number of word-classes, each class does not necessarily do the same work as its counterpart in other languages. And in actual use, a word (*e.g.*a verb) may be equivalent in one language to a word belonging to an entirely different part of speech, in another language. This sort of equivalence is called transposition.

A French verb, for example, may be equivalent to an English adverb, or adjective, or noun:

Il ne tardera pas a rentrer.	F. VERB/E ADVERBE He 'll soon be back.
Des qu'on essaied' êtrearbitraire.	F. VERB/E. NOUN Any attempt to be arbitrary.

A French noun may be equivalent to an English adjective:

Au débuts du 19e siécle. F. NOUN/E. ADJECTIVE In the early 19th century.

And some French nouns are equivalent to English phrasal verbs:

Attention! F. NOUN/E. PHRASAL VERB Look out!

Different Units

Words phrases, sentences, etc., are the units of grammar. Not all languages have the same sort or the same number. Those that exist in both languages do not always correspond. A word in the first language may be equivalent to a phrase in the second, as when the English word agenda is equated to the French *ordre du jour*, or when the German word *druckfertig* has to be rendered into English as ready for printing.

Some of the difference may form a pattern, as may be seen by comparing English phrasal verbs with their french and German equivalents. Examine, for example, the following:

F. VERB	*E. PHRASAL VERB*		*G. PREPOSITION*	
Entrez.	Come in.	Go in.	Herein.	Hinein.
Sortez.	Come out.	Go out.	Heraus.	Hinaus.
Montez.	Come up.	Go up.	Herauf.	Hinauf.
Descendez.	Come down.	Go down.	Herunter.	Hinunter.

Many French verbs are equivalent to an English verb followed by some sort of modifier, giving such combinations as phrasal verbs. The structure of phrasal verbs enables English to make distinctions like the one between come in and go in which the French single verbs like entrer do not reveal.

The most important word units in a language are its structure words—its articles, prepositions etc. Althouth these are limited in number, they are found in almost every utterance. Structure words of the first language, however, are not always equivalent to those of the second. For example, although the English structure word come is equivalent to the French partitive du in a few of its uses, it must very often be equated with other French structure words such as:

en	Give me some	Donnez m'*en*
un	Some fool has...	Un imbecile a...
quelque	For some time	Pendant *quelque* tems
environ	Some forty persons	Environ une quarantaine
certains	*Some say* that....	*Certains* disent que...

Structure words, however, are limited in number, forming part, as they do, of a closed system. If the word is not a structure word, it is part of an unlimited series required a different technique of differential description. This is the function of lexicology.

Differential Lexicology

By far the most numerous items which distinguish one language from another are the items of vocabulary. Some of these may have the same form in both languages, but differ in content; or they may have different forms and the same conent. The vocabulary of both languages may be compared from these two points of view: *(1)* equivalence in their forms of expression, and *(2)* equivalence in meaning, or content.

EXPRESSION EQUIVALENCE

Words with similar expression forms in both languages may be described as to *(1)* what they stand for (their reference), and *(2)* the combinations, or collocations, into which they enter.

Refernece of Cognates

If a word has the same form in both languages, it may *(i)* have the same referent, *(ii)* have different referents, or *(iii)* have some referents in common.

(i) A few words, like jeep in French and English, which look and sound alike in both languages may also refer to the same thing.

(ii) There may be a number of words which look and sound alike in both languages but which refers to different things. The word car in French has not the same referent as it has in English.

(iii) Many of the words which look and sound alike have some referents which are the same and some which are different. The word administration which look in English and French sometimes refers to the same thing. It sometimes, however, refers to something different. In business texts, for example, administration in French is equivalent to management in English. When the reference is not external but internal, reference to feelings or thoughts, the analysis of common and different referents is necessarily more complex.

Collocation of Cognates

Cognates vary greatly in the combintions which each language allows them to enter. The German word Winter may seem like a close cognate of English winter, but in German, winter cannot be "around the corner" it can only be ''at the door" (*vor der Tür*). Even identical geographical place names may have collocations which are quite different. The word Rome may refer to the same city in English and French; but to find the French equivalent of the collocation *When in Rome do as the Romans do*, one would have to consider howling with the wolves.

Yet in the actual use of the language, homophones and homographs can be more a peril than a help. In order to use them safely, one has to go to all the trouble of learning the cases in which they are cognates and the cases in which they are not; and when they are similar, to what extent they are similar. For example, English hound and German hund are similar in form and meaning. But in order to use the English word correctly, the German learner has to forget about the word hound and learn word dog, the usual equivalent of German Hand.

There are many such confusing similarity between genetically related languages like English and German, languages that once have been identical and still are classed in the same family. But each language develops in its own way and undergoes different influences, so that what was once the same has become different in pronunciation, spelling oı meaning.

There is also a great number of confusing similarities between languages which have been in close contact, languages like English and French. Although thousands of English words have been imported from the French language, few are now identical with their French counterparts. The reason is that only part of the meaning may have been imported in the first place, or the meaning may have changed and developed in a different direction from the original. Moreover the imported words has to be fitted into a different phonetic, grammatical and semantic structure.

A third case is where the cognate has been imported from a common language. Words like sugar—sucre—Zucker, coffee—cafe'—Kaffee, tea the'—Tee imported ultimately from the Near and Far East, may differ in spelling and pronunciation but have a number of formal and semantic elements in common.

CONTENT EQUIVALENCE

If two words are different in expression-form in both languages, they may likewise be analysed according to what they refer to and how they combine with other words, that is, according to *(1)* the reference of the counterparts in the other language, and *(2)* the collocations ino which these counterparts enter.

1. **Reference of Counterparts.** If the two words are different in their form of expression, they may be identical in reference. The English word *cod* and the French word morue refer to the same fish. This one-to-one equivalence is popularly supposed to exist between all the words of both languages. And this is what many learners expect to be taught when they study a foreign langauge or when they look up words in a bilingual dictionary.

   What is usually the case, however, is that the content equivalence is only partial, that a word in one language has a number of counterparts in the other. The English word head, for example, has a number of counterparts in French, since it covers an area of content which is only partly equivalent to that covered by the French tέte, as a glance at the following list will reveal:

	tέte	(of a person)
	chevet	(of a bed)
	face	(of a coin)
	pomme	(of a cane)
head =	bout	(of a match)

haut bout	(of a table)
directeur	(of an organization)
mousse	(on beer)
rubrique	(title)

Similarly, the French makes a distinction between rivers which flow into the sea (fleuve) and those which do not (riviére); for English they are all rivers. It is this unexpected and seemingly unreasonable difference in grouping of referents that is responsible for so many of the errors in second language learning. When a German learner of English says "Close the door, please; there's a train." He has no reason to believe that the concepts of train and draught should not have a single label in English as they do in German, where the word Zug covers both.

2. **Collocation of Counterparts.** Even when the counterparts are equivalent, however, the equivalence rarely extends to the complete range of collocations into which each word may enter. The English verb laugh may be the counterpart of the French rire and the German lachen; but when we laugh up our sleeve in English we laugh in our beard in French (dons sa barbe), and in our first in German (*ins Fäustchen*).

   Differences in range of collocations have not been determined for any two languages. There have been studies of deceptive cognates, useful treatments of certain areas of content in two languages, and a large number of isolated instances unearthed in the compilation of some of the more complete bilingual dictionaries.

   All the above differences in vocabulary, grammar and pronunciation do not add up to a complete differential analysis. This is because all levels of language work together as a whole. In the final analysis, what must be known is how each language, working as a system of systems, differs in the production of complete utterances in any given situation. One language may require a long utterance, and in the same situation another language may require not more than a word or simply a gesture. It is a matter of style.

No differential analysis of two languages can be complete unless it includes *(1)* such differences in the contents of the responses to convenional situations. And since responses may themselves be made through diferent levels in each language, vocabulary, grammar, or pronunciation, the description must include *(2)* the differences in the levels of expression.

It is not sufficient to know that words and phrases in two languages may differ in content. These words and phrases appear in different sequences which may relate differently to the same situation. In all sorts of everyday situations involving such things as requests and courtesy, giving and getting, what is normally said in one language does not correspond in either form or conent to what may be said, in the same circumstances, in another. For example, if a German speaker offers a stranger his seat, he will probably begin and end the act with what might be interpreted as please (bitte). No so in English, where he may begin with a slight gesture or remark and end with a Not at all or That's quite all right.

Equivalents lie often in entirely different levels of language. It may be a matter of vocabulary in one language and of grammar in another, of grammar in one language and of phonetics in another. Because each language is absolutely free to represent what it likes with its structure words, inflections, and parts of speech, in any level or combination whatever, the differential analysis of two languages can be a highly complex affair. Such an analysis, however, is necessary if we are to get a picture of the internal problems of foreign-language learning.

NEW LEXICAL ITEMS

The creation of new lexical items is partly because of necessity and partly because of fashion. Necessity arises when a word is lost for linguistic reasons, such as attrition or homonymic clash. Obviously a new one must take its place. Similarly, if the meaning of a word is 'devalued', another one must be put in the gap left by the devalued one. And new inventions such as radar, laser and penicillin require new words. But at other times new words arise purely through fashion.New words spring up alongside older words. At the first, these new alternatives may be regarded as slang, but in course of time many of them become increasingly common. For example, words such as pot, hash, grass are becoming increasingly common.

The continual infiltration of new lexical items is a normal and healthy trend. It testifies to the essential productivity of language–the ability to say new things and deal with new situations.

New lexical items can be assigned to two main classes: items created from resources within the language (internal borrowing) and items created from outside sources (external borrowing).

'When any part of the strucutre of a language is changed by importation of features, whether from some other part of the language or from some external source, the imported features are said to be borrowed'. We distinguish between two types of borrowings: external and internal on the basis of the source of the borrowing.

External Borrowing

Under the heading of external borrowings come those from one dialect to another (dialectical borrowings), those from an earlier stage of the same language (archaisms), and those from the languages (loans). It is very frequent for a language to borrow lexical items from related dialects (regional, social, occupational) for various reason, distinctive meanings, humour, or pleasant or unpleasant connotations of one sort or another.

Borrowing is a very common linguistic phenomenon. In all probabiiity, no language is completely free of borrowed forms.

Languages change through the influence of other languages. Some languages borrow too largely, other only to a limited extent. For example, in English over half of its lexicon is borrowed; in Albaniam, on the other hand, only a few hundred words are thought to have entered the lexicon through borrowing. In periods of mass borrowing, such as Italianism in Elizabethan England or Anglicansim in twentieth century India, entire sectors of vocabulary may become saturated with loan-words. Prestige is the decisive factor in any borrowing.

Borrowing is never a linguistic necessity, since it is always possible to extend and modify the use of existing lexical items to meet new communication needs. A common cause of lexical borrowing is the need to find words for objects, concepts, and places. It is easier to borrow an existing terms from another language than to make one up. The paths of lexical borrowing reflect to a certain extent the paths of cultural influence. For example, Hindi has borrowed from English words as radio, television, telephone, rail, signal, platform, guard, conductor, and so forth. Similarly the influence of Italian music and art can be seen in Italian: opera, tempo. English through these words borrowed from piano, sonata, sonnet, fresco, etc. A large portion of the Arabic words in English pertain to the realm of science: zero, cipher, zenith, alchemy, algebra, nadir, alcohol, etc. Government and other terms that came to English from French include crown power, state, reign, country, peer, court, duke, duchess, prince, sovereign, minister, chancellor, council, authority, parliament, baron; borrowed terms related to military matters are battle, army, war, peace, office, lieutenant, navy, admiral, soldier, sergeant, troops, arms, armour, gallant, company, force.

French borrowings can also be seen in English religious, moral and legal vocabulary. A large number of French borrowing is there in English, because in England for a pretty long time French was the prestige language. and the use of French words in English conversation became a common practice, especially after the Norman Conquest of England in 1066.

Latin and Greek had great prestige in the world of scholarship during the middle Ages. Consequently Latin and Greek have provided

English with the richest resource for borrowing. Most of the words borrowed from Latin and Greek and learned words and the list of such words may run to many thousands. Even the names of many scholarly disciplines are borrowed from the classical language: sociology, psychology, anthropology, philosophy, philology, biology. Many words in English are forms with Latin morpheme ex-'out of form': exact, exaggerate, exalt, exclude, explain, explicit, explode, explore, export, extend, extinct, extort, etc. Similarly ex-husband and ex-wife are the examples of Latin ex prefixed to Germanic forms. Lexical borrowing in English is sometimes of such complexity that a word may be derived simultaneously from two or more different sources. The words typhoon, for example, is derived possibly from as many as three different sources: Urdu toofan (storm) Greek Typhoon, and Cantonese daal fung (big wind).

Semantic borrowing is more elusive, and more difficult to trace, for example, the semantic influence of Judaeo-Christianity on Greek. The lexical form of angel (Fr. ange, Ger. Engel, Rus. angel) is derived from Greek aggelos, but the concept itself is borrowed from Hebrew. Semantic borrowing is a process virtually impossible to forestall. Usually it occurs in one of the two forms: either meaning of an existing word is changed and then new meaning replaces the old one completely, or the old meaning continues to exist along side the new meaning. As an example of the second type, we can take the word red which has become synonymous with socialist and especially communist since the Russian Revolution. As an example of the first type can be cited dialectic which can now-a-days only with difficulty be used in the original sense of 'lexical' disputation'. Traumatic used to refer to physical shock; but this meaning has been superseded by 'a disturbing experience affecting the mind.' In British English snag meant 'a trunk or large branch of a tree embedded in the bottom of a river' until the meaning 'obstacle' was borrowed from American English, which eventually eclipsed the earlier meaning altogether.

Semantic borrowing will be particularly frequent where there is an intimate connection between two languages. This happened, for instance, in the early Christian Church where Hebrew exercised a powerful influence on Greek, and the latter on Latin. It is now happening in the language of sports, which in many countries, is saturated with Anglicanism.

Internal Borrowing

Internal borrowing frequently start out as slang, which later becomes accepted, such as the word snob, squabble, hard up. Bird, now becoming acceptable in meaning of 'girl', is perhaps borrowed from the word 'bribe'. A common type of internal borrowing is the adoption of proper names, as the words sandwich from Lord sandwich, the first person to eat his meat between two slices of bread.

Nevertheless, the following methods of forming new items are important in English:

(a) Affixation—New words can be created by adding prefixes, such as de-, self-, anti- (defence, self-service, antithesis), or suffixes, such as-ise,

(b) Analogy—*e.g.* motorway after railway.

(c) Blends (or Contamination)—Blends occur when two existing words are combined into a new one. They are sometimes called 'portmanteau' words, after the statement of Humpty-Dumpty in Alice Through the Looking Glass: 'You see it's like a portmanteau–there are two meanings packed up into one word.

e.g. smog<smoke and fog

Brunch>brekafast and lunch

(d) Compounds–Two existing words are sometimes juxtaposed to form a new compound lexical item:

e.g. break into

salesman

(e) Shortening–Long words are shortend to form new ones:

e.g. Pram<perambulator

bus<omnibus

❐

3

Family of Languages and Descent of English

Speech is a product of certain muscular movements. Sounds, which are vital elements of speech, are made by the passage of a stream of air from the lungs. Vibration of the vocal cords and movement of the tongue are other important activities that produce any kind of sound. Repeated muscular movements of the organs of speech tend to alter the sounds produced. Thus each individual is constantly and unconsciously contributing to the change of sounds. So, different individuals of a single speech-community differ from one another in their speech habits. The language of a community is the sum total of the individual speech habits of those composing the community. Constant communication in a speech-community merges the individual differences in the speech of the whole community and a sort of conformity prevails. But, for social or political reasons, if a community divides itself into groups and if one group of the community is separated from the other for a considerably long time, differences grow up in speech habits of both communities, resulting in emergence of dialects. But if the length of separation is great, the language of one group becomes unintelligible to the other, and their languages grow separately from one another.

In abysmal depths of the past, when man was nomadic in habit, the primitive tribes which wandered in the lands around the Black Sea, spoke a language which has been variously named by philologists of today, Aryan, Indo-Germanic and Indo-European. The best designation seems to be Indo-European because it not only indicates the geographical extent to which it spread, but, also gives legitimate prominence to Asian and European groups of languages. The nomadic tribes moving in search of food and shelter split up into various groups and moved in different directions across the continent of Euro-Asia. Each of the groups took with it their common language. But long stretch of separation in time and place made their languages grow first into dialects and still later into distinct, independent languages. The multiplicity of languages today is due to repeated differentiation through the ages. Even where the differentiation has gone so for as to create new languages, it is not impossible to recognise certain number of common features among the resulting languages and those common features indicate that at one time all those languages were one.

It is not difficult to perceive kinship between German and English, especially if we notice some English words with their corresponding German Words. A large proportion of words in both the languages are recognisably identical in many respects. German *milch* and English *milk*, *Brot* and *bread*, *Fleisch* and *flesh*, *Wasser* and *water*, *Gras* and *grass*, *Korn* and *Corn*, *Kuh* and *cow*, *Kalb* and *calf*, *Vater* and *Father*, *Mutter* and *Mother*, *Schwester* and *Sister*, *Gehen* and *to go*, *haben* and to *have*. Words like these (there are hundreds of such) indicate the obvious likeness between the two languages. Apart from the common stock of words and their similarity in sound, in their grammar, too, German and English resemble to a certain extent. In the same way English *Father* and Latin *pater*, *brother* and *Frater* indicate the connection between Latin and English. We further notice that English *father* corresponds to Dutch *Vader* Gothic fadar, old Norse fadir, Germam Vater, Greek pater and Sanskrit *Pitar*; English *brother* corresponds to Dutch *broeder*, German *Bruder*, Greek *Phrater*, Sanskrit *Bhrater*. This amazing similarity leads us to a hypothesis that the languages of a large part of Europe and part of Asia were at one time identical and that they have grown into distinct languages, with gradual divergent changes, from a common pre-historic language which Scholars call Indo-European Language.

The Indo-European language was a synthetic language with complex inflexional endings. Simplicity and directness of expression are products of the later stages of the evolution of language. It was centuries later that Indo-European language developed analytical tendencies. The vocabulary of Indo-European language was probably limited, only large enough to Serve the needs of the primitive, aboriginal tribes who spoke it. Some traces of it are still to be found hanging over its descendents. It is noticeable that in most of the modern European languages and their ancestral tongues from which they were derived, the singular, personal pronouns bear a very close resemblance. The Indo-European languages have common words for the primary family relationships like *father, mother, brother*.

Evidently the early tribes did not recognise any relationship outside the family. While there are no anciently common Indo-European words for elephant, Rhinoceros, camel, tiger, lion, etc., there are common words for snow, cold, beech, bear, wolf, deer, rabit, mouse, ox, sheep, pig, dog, etc., the cumulative evidence of this list is that the original community was an inland one. More interesting is the resemblance in the ancient languages and their modern descendents, of the cardinal numbers up to ten. Apparently, early man counted on fingers and could not go beyond ten. More complicated counting was done with the help of pebbles for counters. The Latin word for pebble is *calculus* from which *calculate* was derived.

The Indo-European family split into nine chief branches. These branches seem to fall into two well-defined groups according to the modification which certain consonants of the parent language underwent in each. Those two groups are called *Satem* group and *Centum* (pronounced Kentum) group from the words for hundred in Avestan and Latin respectively. The *Satem* group includes the Indian, Iranian, Armenian, Balto-slavic and Albanian branches. The *Centum* group includes the Hellenic, Italic, Celtic and Teatonik branches. Now, let us have a brief glance at each of these branches.

SATEM GROUP

Indian. The Indian branch of the Indo-European family has preserved for us the oldest literary texts, the Vedas, written in what is called Vedic Sanskrit. A later form of the language was fixed and given a literary form by Indian Grammarians of whom PANINI is chiefly celebrated. This form is known as Classical Sanskrit, which is the medium of rich variety of literature including the two national epics, the *Ramayana* and the *Mahabharata*, and a wealth of dramatic literature and lyric poetry. Though, formerly, Sanskrit was the language of religion, as Latin was in medieval Europe, it is proudly cultivated today as a learned literary language. But, it has long ceased to be a spoken language. A large number of colloquial dialects known as *Prakrits* existed alongside of Sanskrit. One of them, *Pali* was given literary status and was made the language of Buddhism in the 6th century B.C. *Prakrits* gave rise to *Apabhramsas* which in turn gave rise to the present languages of North India and Pakistan. The most important of these are Hindi, Bengali, Marathi and Punjabi, Romany, the language of Gypsies, "those spoilt children of man-kind" represents a dialect of North-Western India from which the nomads carried to many parts of the world, in the course of their long history of wandering.

Iranian. The earliest recorded language of this group is Avestan. It is the language of Avesta, the sacred writings of the Zoroastrians. Some of these writings go as for back as 1,000 B.C. Avestan has left no direct descendents, but it is related to old Persian. Another language belonging to this group is Old Persian which is preserved in inscriptions recording the achievements of Daring and Xerxes. A later form of this language is called Middle Iranian or Pehlavi, from which Modern Persian is descended'. Persian is spoken throughout a large part of Iran and it is also an important secondary speech among Muslims in Pakistan and India. Related to Persian are Kurdish; the language spoken in the mountain regions of Eastern Turkey, Iraq and Western Iran, Balochi, the language of Balochistan and Pashto, the chief language in Afghanistan.

Armenian. The earliest records of Armenian are preserved in a Bible translation of the fifth century A.D. It stands alone as a separate branch of the Indo-European family, although, for sometime, it was thought to belong to the Iranian group. Throughout their long troubled history, the Armenians have preserved their individuality and have not allowed themselves to be dominated by the imperial rulers of Persia, Rome and Byzantium. The modern form of this language is, spoken by about four million people in the southern Caucasus and Eastern Turkey.

Albanian. This is by far the smallest of the eight surviving branches of the Indo-European family. It is spoken by only one and half million people. It constitutes a branch by itself, though some scholars associate it with forgotten Illysian. The evidence is insufficient for certainty. Albanian contains a very large proportion of loan words from neighbouring languages, chiefly from the languages of Turkey. It is wrapped in history and we do not have intimate knowledge of it because, apart from some legal documents, no literature has survived earlier than the seventeenth century.

Balto-Slavic. This consists of two groups, the Baltic and Slavic which have some common features and may be said to have descended from the same branch. The Baltic group includes Lithuanian and Lellish. Of these Lithuanian is important to the student of Indo-European because its conservative nature has preserved some old features that have disappeared in all other members of the Indo-European family. Russian, Polish, Czech, Serbocroation are the chief languages of the Slavic group.

CENTUM GROUP

Hellenic. This consists of the Greek dialects which were spoken in Ancient Greece and in the Islands of the Aegean and in Asia Minor. Until recently its antiquity was dated back to the 9th Century B.C. But recent discoveries have antedated the beginnings of Greek, carrying it back to a time long before the sack of Troy (1183 B.C.). We are fortunate in possessing abundant literature and large mass of inscriptions and documents in the dialect of Attic, the dialect of the city of Athens, which owed its supremacy to the dominant political and cultural position of Athens in the Fifth Century B.C. After the death of Alexander the Great (323 B.C.), it became the general language of Mediterranean countries. The dialects of modern Greece arc descended from this language. Modern Greek has only eight million speakers. Its forms and many of the common expressions have remained unchanged in three millennia. Although by a capricious turn of fortune's wheel the Greek language has shrunk to narrow confines in Greece, it has richly expanded as the inexhaustible source of supply for the ever-growing scientific and technological vocabulary.

Italic. The languages of this group present a larger collection of recorded evidence than any other branch of Indo-European. We have evidences that as early as the Sixth Century B.C., a number of languages were spoken in Italy. Of all the languages spoken in those times, Latin became supremely important because of the political supremacy of Rome where it was a chief language. The minor languages were expelled from the country and they are known today only from inscriptions and place-names. The expansion of the Roman Empire spread Latin into many parts of Europe. The literary form of Latin is called classical Latin. From the spoken form of Latin, called Vulgar Latin, are descended the Romance languages like French, Italian, Spanish, Portuguese and Rumanian. These languages have been carried into different parts of the world. French especially expanded and found home in many regions of the world.

Celtic. This group was extensive in Europe in the beginnings of the Christian era. But, in modern times only four have survived, Breton, Welsh, Irish and Scots Gaelic. These are spoken today by a comparatively small minorities in France and British Isles.

The Germanic Languages. The Branch of Indo-European to which English belongs is called Germanic, and it includes German, Dutch, Frisian. Swedish, Norwegian and Icelandic. The parent language of all these languages was a dialect of Indo-European and it is often called Proto-Germanic. Round about the beginning of Christian Era, the speakers of Proto-Germanic still formed a homogeneous cultural and linguistic group, living in the north of Europe. We have no evidence of the language of this period, but we know something of the people who spoke it from the works of Tacitus.

Tacitus calls them Germans and describes them as a tribal society living in scattered settlements in the woody and marshy country of Northern Europe. It is essentially an agricultural community, keeping flocks and growing grain crops. But their agriculture is not of an advanced type. The family is the basic unity of social organisation among them. They are monogamous and women are held in high esteem in their society. They love war because it is often a means to renown and booty. Such was, in brief, the account of the people who spoke Proto-Germanic. Perhaps because of over-population and the poverty of their natural resources, in the course of time, they spread in different directions. As a result of this expansion of the Germanic peoples, dialect-differences within Proto-Germanic became more marked Three main branches of Proto-Germanic are distinguished. They are, West Germanic, North Germanic and East Germanic. Modern, Scandinavian languages like Norwegian, Swedish, and Danish: belong to the North Germanic branch. Gothic was descended from the East Germanic dialect of Proto-Germanic.

The West Germanic dialect is the most important one, because English, Dutch, Frisian and German are descended from this branch. A family tree for the West Germanic languages is given below:

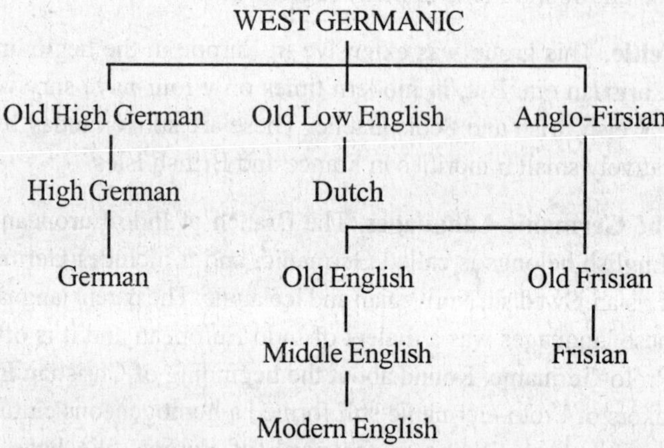

All of these languages and their dialects bear the common Germanic characteristics which distinguish this group of languages from other Indo-European groups. Let us glance for a moment at these characteristic features of all these languages.

As has already been mentioned, we have no records of the earliest form of the Proto-Germanic language. However, by comparing its various descendent languages, we can reconstruct it to quite a considerable extent. The reconstructed Proto-Germanic language shows some structural and phonological affinities with the other Indo-European languages.

Grammar. The one quality that stands out as a marked characteristic of the Proto-Germanic language and many of its descendents, is their inflexional system. Many of the languages in this group make great use of variations in the endings of words. Modem English, however, has lost the inflexional system and has developed other grammatical devices. We can still find some traces of inflexion in Modern English, which may supply us with examples to show what an inflexion is. For example, when we add—s to form the plural in nouns, or to mark the third person singular in the verb, we are using an inflexion. Similarly, when we add—ed to form past tense to the verb, we are using an inflexion. The suffixes—er and—est in degrees of comparison are other inflexional endings.

The role of inflexions in Modern English is not very great. To get a clearer idea of what an inflected language is like, we need to look at classical Latin or Modern German. Take for example, an English sentence, *The master beat the servant*. Here no word is inflected to indicate who is the beater and who is the beaten. The word-order denotes the subject and object and this word-order is fixed unless one changes it for stylistic purposes. But in Latin the subject is inflected by adding the suffix—us and the object is inflected by adding the suffix—um. The English sentence given above can be rendered in Latin, word for word as *Dominus verberavit servum*. You can also write the sentence changing the word-order and *say Dominus servum verberavit* or *Servum verberavit dominus*. So long as the suffixes—us and—um cling to the subject .and the object respectively there is no change in meaning, in whatever position you place them. But in English, there is a world of difference between *The master beat the servant* and *The servant beat the master*. That is not the whole story of inflexions. In many inflected languages nouns have other inflexions based on case, number and gender. We need not enlarge on other inflexions, at this stage. In the parent-Indo-European, in Proto-Germanic and in Modern German, adjectives are inflected according to the case, gender and number of the nouns they are called upon to qualify.

Another outstanding feature of Germanic group is that its verb has properly only two tenses, a present and a past. This extreme simplification of the verb in Germanic group of languages has resulted in a multiplying of compound tenses, a great increase of flexibility and in greater subtlety of those languages.

A third characteristic of Germanic is its development of the two main classes of verbs, strong and weak. Strong verbs are those which show the changes of tense by changing the vowel of their stem, like Modern English, *sing, sang; bind, bound; drive, drove*. Such series of vowel variations to indicate the change of tense are called Ablant series or vowel-gradation. While this is a less frequent device in other languages, a large number of such verbs are found in Proto-Germanic. Besides strong verbs, Proto-Germanic had developed a new class of verbs called weak verbs. Weak verbs are those in which the change of tense is indicated not by change of vowel but by adding a suffix to the verbs as in *walk walked*; *love loved* and so on. The weak verbs, too, have become very important in Germanic languages. In Old English the weak verbs were already in the majority and since then, many strong verbs have crossed the floor and changed over to weak. In Modern English, the strong verbs are a small minority and adding insult to injury, they are frequently called 'irregular verbs'.

Vocabulary. A good number of words are peculiar to Germanic and they have no certain correspondences in other Indo-European languages. Such are *ship, sail, boat, sheet, stay, keel, float,* and *sea*. Since other Indo-European languages have no words corresponding to these, it is held that the Indo-Europeans originally lived inland, and since the Germanic peoples reached the coast and took: to the sea, they developed nautical words. The Proto-Germans borrowed a good number of words from the Celts and the Romans. The Celts were skilled in metallurgy, and the Germanic' words *iron* and *lead* were borrowed from them. The Romans contributed to the Germanic languages words relating to war, trade, building and food. Thus, words like *wall, tile, chalk, mill, pound, cheap, monger, pepper, peas, apple, plum* and so on seem to show that the Germanic tribes were much impressed by-concrete manifestations of Roman civilisation like road, building, food, trade—rather than by Roman law.

Phonology. In pronunciation, Proto-Germanic, at the time of its separation from the parent Indo-European language, had, developed certain changes. One important change was in the matter of accent. Accent is generally of two kinds: musical accent based on pitch or intonation and stress accent based on the-force or weight of utterance. The parent Indo-European language had, perhaps, musical accent, But in its descending languages the stress accent became predominant. But the stress accent used in: many groups of the descendents, of Indo-European was free, that it could be used on different parts of the same word according to context and meaning. The 'free accent' as it is often called can be seen in classical Greek and in some conservative languages such as Russian. But it is characteristic of Germanic languages; to fix the stress on the first syllable of the word. It is this fixing of the stress on the first syllable in Germanic group of languages, that is the primary cause of withering of inflexions, which has been a marked characteristic of English. When the first syllable of the word is stressed, inevitably, the syllables at the end of the word will tend to be first blurred in utterance and finally lost completely. For example, the Proto-Indo-European form of the infinitive of the verb was perhaps something like *bheranom*, which in Proto-Germanic became *beranan*. In pre-historic Old English the final—*an* was lost and so the recorded Old English had the form beron. As a result of the stress falling on the first syllable, the last syllable—an was weakened to—en, giving Early Middle English *beren*. During the Middle English Period the final—n was lost leaving the *bere*. Finally, by the fifteenth century the final—e was lost and the modern form *bear* came into existence. This serves us as an example to show how similar process of attrition might have taken place in the other Germanic languages.

CHARACTERISTIC FEATURES OF ENGLISH

It is difficult to characterize a language in general terms. Languages are not always amenable to such description. Nevertheless, t can be said that the English language is the most receptive and heterogeneous tongue. From almost every language of the world it has taken to itself, the vocabulary, grammatical forms and habits of spelling and pronunciation. The historical study of the language shows that in the fifth and sixth centuries when the Angles, Saxons and Jutes conquered England, it was a 'pure' unmixed language with an extraordinary flexibility to make compound words from its own elements, to express new ideas. But throughout its history it has received foreign words with readiness and ease and has assimilated the alien elements to its own character. Hence the copiousness and rich variety of its vocabulary.

The second important characteristic feature of English is its extraordinary simplicity of inflexions. Old English was a highly inflected language, but modem English has evolved through progressive simplification of inflexions. As a result of dropping out inflexional endings, the relationship of words in a sentence is indicated, unlike in some European languages, by fixed word-order. Otto Jesperson illustrates this by taking a German sentence, *alle diejenigen wilden tiere, die dort laben*. Here almost every word carries the plural impression. But the English version "all the, wild animals live there" the adjective, the articles and the relative pronoun do not carry any plural mark. Reduction in such superfluous inflexions is hardly considered any thing but an advantage.

The third important feature of English is its fixed word-order. In inflected languages like Latin, German, the inflexions indicate the relationship of words in the sentence and the word-order can be fairly free. But in English, word-order is fixed in relation to meaning in the sentence. We cannot reverse, the word order of a sentence like "the dog bit the man" without making it a startling news.

The fourth quality which gives English an exceptional advantage is natural gender in place of grammatical gender of other European languages. In learning English, the student does not have to labour under the burden of memorizing, along with the meaning of every noun, its gender. In Romance languages, as in Hindi, there are only two genders. Everything on the earth is either masculine or feminine. Though in Germanic languages there are three genders, the way the gender is attributed to the noun is arbitrary to the point of being irrational. Thus in German, *Sun* is feminine, *moon* is masculine while *child, maiden* and *woman* are neuter. In English, Gender is determined by the sex of living creatures, while inanimate nouns are called neuter. This is undoubtedly a great advantage in facilitating the acquisition of English by foreigners.

The fifth quality is that in its phonetic structure, English presents an impression of precision and neatness. The two groups of consonants, the voiced and the voiceless are well defined and present a picture of symmetry. They are so precisely pronounced that there is no scope for ambiguity in sound. Fortunately English is free from indistinct or half slurred consonants; excepting that *r* when not followed by a vowel sound is indistinct. But then, *r* has been gradually giving up its claims to the rank of a consonant. In English, modification of consonant by the surrounding vowels .is less frequent than in some other European languages. The vowel sounds, too, are clear, precise and relatively independent of their surroundings.

The next important quality of the English language is that, in great many ways, it is particularly suited to terse and vigorous ways of expression. Notice the condensed force of monosyllables, in expressions like, '*first come, first served*'; '*no cure no pay*'; '*live and learn*'; '*haste makes waste and waste makes want*'. The absence of connecting words like articles and prepositions delivers the language from prolixity in style.

English sentences are amenable to abbreviations which render the language business-like and convenient. For instance, 'while fighting in Germany he was taken prisoner', he would not answer when spoken to', 'once at' home, he forgot his fears'. Shortening of sentences like this is called Syntactical shortening. English abounds in shortening of words too: *bus for omnibus, cob for cobriolet, photo for photograph* and *phone for telephone*. This, in a way, reflects the temperament of the English, who do not usually—speak more words or more syllables than necessary. By avoiding hyperbolic expressions which do not mean 'what they say, English has acquired a kind of balance and sobriety.

Judged from the standard of logic there is no other language so high as English. It has a tense-system that is superior to any other of European language. While we find the time divided into present, past and future in many languages, further division of each of those tenses into simple perfect, perfect continuous and progressive is nowhere seen so consistently and precisely as in English. The distinction subtle and difficult as it is, is superior to anyone found in other languages.

English grammer, difficult as it is for a foreigner, allows certain, freedom as, for instance, in the use of a number of words like, *family, clergy, committee, club* are of plural number from the logic of facts, and singular from the grammatical point of view. But there are no rigorous rules in the use of them either as singular or plural depending on the meaning to be conveyed. Where the idea of unity is conveyed 'the committee is of the opinion' is accepted and where the idea of division or plurality is essential, it can be said, 'the committee have divided in their opinion". Very few languages offer such freedom. Similar freedom is exercised in expressions like, '1 do not think I have ever spent a more delightful three weeks', 'for quite a twenty minutes', and' 'nine years is a big slice of one's life-time'.

Otto Jesperson sums up the characteristics of English in these words: "The English language is a methodical, energetic-, business-like and sober language, that does not care much for finery and elegance, but does care for logical consistency and is opposed to any attempt to narrow—in life by police regulations and strict rules either of grammar or of lexicon". Thus the language reveals the soul of the nation.

❐

4

Landmarks in the History of English

Language is in a constant state of flux; it changes gradually and is perpetually changing. Language, like the thoughts and feelings of a nation or tribe, is not, at all times, the same, but is capable of enrichment, expansion and modification in a hundred ways with the advance of civilization and fortunes of history. The progress of change is continuous one, and one period passes by insensible gradations into another. There are transitions and overlappings between any two periods, because ,changes in languages do not take place overnight. There are certain great historical events which have profound influence upon men's lives, their thoughts and ideas, their way of life and upon the language they speak. Study of such external events and their impact on language is called the history of the language.

The English language, in common with all other languages existing today, has an eventful history in the past. It was not always as what we know it now. It is our present effort to enumerate briefly those external historical events which have left a definite impress upon the English language.

Historians of the English language distinguish three great periods of its development. The first is the Old English Period (sometimes called the Anglo-Saxon) which lasts from about the year 600 until about 1100. This is followed by the Middle English Period extending from 1100 to 1500. The third is the Modern English Period beginning from 1500 and extending to the present time. It should not, however, be imagined that these three are sharply marked periods, and that between the close of one period and beginning of another there was a complete and sudden change, In fact, the Old English Period passes imperceptibly into the Middle English Period and the latter slowly passes into the Modern English Period. But, for the sake of convenience and clarity, historians of the English language have erected landmarks, choosing these dates for their historical significance in the life of the language and of the nation. Thus, about the year 600 is taken as beginning of the history of English, because Angles and Saxons established their power and implanted their language in Britain, And, by 1100, the Normans consolidated their hold on England and Norman-French began to influence the English Language. And 1500 is taken as another landmark because by that time the full tide of the Renaissance had reached the shores of England. Now, in next few chapters, it will be our effort to trace the history of the English language, the influences it received and the changes it underwent through the ages. The following may serve as a brief introduction to each of the periods of its growth.

The Old English Period. The earliest inhabitants of England were the Britons (or Celts) and their language was Celtic. Probably Celtic language was spoken in England throughout the period of Roman occupation from 55 B.C. to 410 A.D. Soon after the withdrawal of the Romans from England, the 'English' tribe called Angles, Saxons and Jutes descended with their hordes and began to settle and fight their way up the rivers and along the coasts from about the first half of the fifth century. The Superior Celtic civilization, their spiritual and intellectual supremacy came rapidly to an end. The 'English' tribes drove them more and more westwards. The coming of the two races into 'contact brought a number of Celtic words and with them some Latin words into the English language. But many of the Celts fled into the hills of Wales, Cornwall and Scotland and there, their language was perpetuated, and the language of the invading tribes became the language of England and came to be known as Old English or Anglo Saxon.

During the closing years of the sixth century, Pope Gregory sent the mission of St. Augustine to England to gain new converts to the Catholic church. King Ethelbert of Kent and most of his people embraced the new religion and in less than hundred years after the arrival of St. Augustine and his monks, the whole of England was Christian.

Towards the end of the eight century, piratical rovers (including Swedes, Norwegians and Danes) from Scandinavia first attacked and plundered the east coast and finally established a few settlements. From that time onwards there were occasional invasions by the Scandina ians and King Ethelwulf and Wessex and his sons after, were continually fighting the sporadic invaders. This time the invaders did not confine their attacks to the east coast, but they penetrated deep in land and, established more numerous settlements. But King Alfred finally reduced them to submission in 878. By a treaty they were permitted to settle in England and they accepted Christianity. Again, more than a hundred years later, a fresh army of the Danes invaded England and plunged it into bloodshed. The sporadic attacks of the Scandinavians reached a climax when Canute, a Danish King sat on the English throne from 1017 to 1035. These events though political in character are important, because they were destined to have their effects on the development of the English language.

The Middle English Period. Another most important landmark in the history of English was the conquest of England in 1066 by William of Normandy. The Norman Conquest, as the event is often called, had greater, effect on the English language than any other In the course of its history. The immediate results of the Norman Conquest were that Government passed out of the hands of English men into those of the Normans. Norman bishops, Norman knights and Norman barons flooded the country. However, it must be realised that the English language had come into contact with the French even before the Norman Conquest. The contact actually started with Aethelred, who married a French princess in 1002. He had sent his son, who later became Edward the Confessor, to school in France and he came back to England with French habits and French friends. During the reign of Edward the Confessor, between 1042 and 1066, a good amount of Norman French must have been spoken at the English Court. William the Conqueror hastened and completed the contact between the two languages which had already existed. After the Norman Conquest for some years, two languages were spoken, English by the Saxon Nobility and French by the Norman barons and official classes. But the Norman French enjoyed greater prestige and higher social status, because it was the language of the Court, of the nobility, of the law courts and of learned professions. But the Englishmen naturally clung to their own speech and about 90 per cent of the population still spoke English, and some Englishmen even continued to produce literary works in it. There was no evidence of any attempt to put down or discountenance the speaking of English. The natural and inevitable intercourse between the two races and occasional inter-marriages between them caused the mingling of the two languages. The result of such interaction of the two languages was the emergence of what is called Middle English.

The Middle English Period is the one of series of momentous changes in the tife of the nation and in the history of the language. The changes of this period affected both the grammar and the vocabulary of the English language. In grammar, from highly inflected Anglo-Saxon, English set on a new era of levelled inflexions; English started growing analytical. In vocabulary, English lost a good number of words of Old English stock and received words from French and Latin. At the beginning of the Middle English Period, English is a strange language which must be learned like a foreign tongue. But at the end of the period, it is almost like our present day English. Such was the extent of the changes that took place during the Middle English Period.

The Modern English Period. In 1453 Constantinople fell to the Turks and classical scholars fled to Germany and Italy. That was the beginning of the intellectual awakening in Europe which has come to be known as the Renaissance. With the closing years of the fifteenth century the New learning spread to England from Italy. With the introduction of Greek into Oxford and Cambridge, a new era began in the cultural life of England. New scholarship and learning produced new forces and added new words to the vocabulary. Greek and Latin filtered into the English language because they were necessary to express the new needs, new ideas and aspirations. While men of action, navigators, fighters and adventurers were making voyages and discovering new worlds beyond the sea, scholars and men of letters were busy enriching the fund of national ideas from rediscovered worlds of thought.

In the wake of the Renaissance, followed a religious movement known as Reformation. Though its significance is chiefly political and religious, it had left its impress on the language. The most important outcome of the Reformation in relation to the language, was the various English translations of the Bible, the most important being the Authorised Version of 1611. This was greatly responsible for fixing the language and for setting a kind of standard to the language.

Another important event in the Modern Period in the history of the English language was the invention of printing. Printing discredited dialect and contributed to the establishment of 'standard' to the language. It tended to fix the English spelling which had been a little less than chaotic before. Printing also made it possible to bring books within the reach of all. Thus, it proved a powerful force for promoting a standard uniform language and to spread it all over the country. Such a widespread influence would not have been possible, were it not for the fact that education was making rapid progress and literacy was becoming much more common among the people. It is probable that in Shakespeare's London, about half of the people could at least read. In the seventeenth and eighteenth centuries many of the people had the means of education and leisure to enjoy the study of books. There was a great increase in the number of schools, and journalism came into existence and the novel was beginning to grow popular.

In recent times, the world is brought together by the growth of science and the consequent invention of rapid means of transport and communication. The expansion of the British Empire enlarged the English vocabulary by borrowing words from almost every known language of the world. Further, it has also spread the language over vast areas of the world. The easy means of travel and communication, the steam-ship, the rail-road and automobiles, the post office, the telegraph, the telephone, the ubiquity of the radio and television, the cinema, have been great forces in modern times, in standardizing the language and giving it the shape, the size and the structure it has attained today. In the chapters that follow, we shall trace in greater detail the growth of the language through its eventful history.

THE OLD ENGLISH PERIOD

The history of the English language begins with the settlement of the three Germanic tribes, Angles, Saxons and Jutes in the sixth century. The coming of these tribes to Britain brought the Celts into contact with them and the contact influenced the languages of the Germanic tribes. The Angles settled in the area extending northward from the Thames. The Jutes settled in Kent and the Saxons settled in the rest of England south of the Thames. But the South-West of England was still occupied by the Celtic tribes. The Celts called their Germanic conquerors Saxons indiscriminately and the area occupied by them was called Saxonia. But soon, the Angle came into use and was applied to all the three Germanic tribes in general. The word *English* is derived from the name of *Angles* and was applied without distinction, to the language of all the Germanic tribes. Much later, *England* came into use, from the name of Angles. Old English was the language which emerged from the fusion of the dialects spoken by the invading Germanic tribes.

CHARACTERISTICS OF OLD ENGLISH

Spelling and Pronunciation of Old English. A page of Old English presents a look of strangeness to the modern reader because of its employment of certain symbols which are no longer in use today. Old English made use of two symbols ð and $\overline{\text{p}}$ to represent the sound of *th*. These two symbols are no longer used in Modern English. Old English represented the vowel sound as in words *man, hat* and so on, by the symbol $\overline{\text{æ}}$. Much of the strange appearance of Old English is due to the frequent appearance of this symbol.

Similarly *sh* sound is represented by *sc* in Old English, as for instance *sceap* (sheep), *biscop* (bishop). Likewise *k* sound is always represented by *c*, as for example in words like *cynn* (kin), *nacod* (naked).

There are certain other genuine differences of pronunciation between Old English and Modern English. Some of them call for comment. The symbol *f* represents in .Old English both sounds f and *v* and therefore *v* symbol was not in use. When *f* occurs in the middle of a word before a voiced sound, and is not doubled, it is generally pronounced *v*. Examples are *giefan* (give), *seafan* (seven), *lifde* (lived). In all other positions *f* symbol is pronounced *f* as in *fxder* (father), hæft (haft, hand).

The symbol *s* is common in Old English, but *z* is unusual, since *s* stands for both sounds *s* and *z*. The rules for their distribution are exactly the same as for *f* and *v*. The symbol *s* represented z sound in the middle of a word before a voiced sound and when it was not doubled. Examples are *nosu* (nose), *bosm* (bosom). But the same symbol represents *s* sound in all other positions. Form example *stanas* (stone), *cyssan* (to kiss), *hus* (house). Likewise, the distribution of p̄ and ð is the same as that of *s* and *z*.

The symbol *g* is difficult to interpret. Sometimes it is a semi-vowel as in the words *gear* (year), *geong* (young). Sometimes it is a stop as in *god* (good), *ges* (geese) and yet sometimes it is a fricative sound produced by narrowing the air-stream, as in words like *fugol* (word) *lagu* (law). The letter *h* represents a stronger and mofle articulate sound than what it is today. When we read Old English we must remember that every symbol is pronounced. In this sense, Old English is phonetic in character. *h* must be pronounced in *niht* (night) and *k* must be pronounced in *cneo* (knee). *r* in Old English is a less troublesome sound. In whatever position it occurs it is pronounced clearly. Examples are wæter (water), (*beam* child). The quality of the vowel is not changed by the presence of *r*, or by being followed by *r* or *1*. Final *e* in any word has phonetic value in Old English. Thus, *e* at the end of *moppe* (moth) and *cwene* (queen) is clearly pronounced.

It can be summed up that Old English is essentially phonetic in character. There are no silent sounds and no superfluous symbols, nor are the existing symbols made to overstrain too much. In the course of time, Old English lost its phonetic nature, especially from the Middle English Period.

Sound Changes in Old English. Two important characteristics of Old English are the phonetic changes known as *gradation* and *Mutation*. These sound changes have a bearing upon modern English. Gradation is a change in vowel sounds of principal parts of verbs according to whether they occur in a stressed or unstressed syllable. This can be illustrated by taking the sentence given below and uttering it thrice with accent on three different places.

(a) Can' you do it?

(b) Can you' do it?

(c) Can you do' it?

In *(a)* the accent is on *can*; in *(b)* the accent falls on *you* and in *(c)* it falls on *do*. The shift of the accent changes the vowel in *can*. In *(a)* it is ǣ (kæn); in (b) it is pronounced *kʌn* and in (c) it is pronounced with a short sound; ə (kə̆n). A similar change took place in the root syllable of the verb when a suffix was added to it in order to make a tense or a participle. As examples we may take the following verbs:

Present	*Past*	*Past Participle*
drifan (drive)	draf (drove)	drifen (driven)
riden (ride)	rad (rode)	riden (ridden)
writan (to write)	wrat (wrote)	writan (written)

The vowel changes that we find in these Old English verbs were due to shifting of stress long ago in the history of the Indo-*Europe* an group of languages. But the changes still persist in Modern English verbs. Such change in vowel sounds in the root syllable of the verb is gradation. The verbs in which this gradation takes place are called strong verbs and the verbs which cannot make past tense by such a change in vowel but by addition of suffix-ed are called weak verbs. Gradation is also known as *ablaut.*

The more important phonetic change in Old English was *mutation*, sometimes called *umlaut.* It should be more strictly called i-mutation. It is a process by which, in early Old English, vowels in accented syllables were modified through the influence of an i or *j* in the next syllable. The *i* or *j* that caused the change disappeared altogether at a later stage. This is a very complicated sound change which has a good deal of living interest for the modern student. It explains certain anomalies in Modern English. For example, irregular plurals like *teeth, mice, geese* can be convincingly explained by i-mutation. Similarly, formation of abstract nouns like *strength* and *length* from *strong* and *long*, derivation of verbs from certain cognate nouns like *doom-deem*, *food-feed* and so on would not look anomalous, if we knew the operation of i-mutation. The following are the vowel changes that took place:

Short back vowels	*Short back diphthongs*
a > e	*ea > ie*
ǣ > e	*eo > ie*
o > e	*io > ie*
u > y	

It will be noticed that what happened was that the back-vowels were changed to front vowels. This is true of also long vowels which were changed to their respective long front vowels. The results of this process, as they are evident in the present day English, are as follows:

(a) Mutated Plurals. In Old English, a number of nouns formed their plural by the addition of the suffix -iz. For example the word *toð* (a tooth) had *toðiz* as its plural. By the influence of i in the plural, *o* became e, thereby giving *teðiz*. Since the stress fell on the first, -iz which forms the last syllable slowly disappeared and hence the modern form teeth. The whole process can be represented by the following formula:

toð	>	*toðiz*	>	*teðiz*	>	*teð*	>	*teeth*
(singular)		(plural)		(due to the influence of *i*)		(disappearance of-*iz*)		(Modem *form*)

In the same way we can explain the mutated plurals mice, feet, geese, men and so on.

(b) Mutated Abstract Nouns Derived from Adjectives. In Old English an abstract noun was formed from an adjective by adding the suffix *ið* to the adjective. Thus, from the adjective *long*, the abstract noun *longið* was formed. By operation of i-mutation *o* in *longið* was changed to *e*, and later *i* was dropped, so we get the modern form length. The following formula makes it clearer:

long	>	*longið*	>	*lengið*	>	*length*
(Old English adjective)		(O. E. Abstract noun)		(due to operation of i-mutation		subsequent disappearance of *i*)

By the same process the abstract nouns like *strength*, *health*, *filth* were formed from their respectives *strong*, *whole* and *ful* (foul) were formed.

(c) Verbs Derived from Nouns. In Old English, a verbal infinitive was formed by adding the suffix-jan to a noun. Thus from the noun dom (judgment) the verbal infinitive *domjan* was formed. This became *dumjan* by operation of j-mutation and subsequently the suffix-jan was dropped, thereby giving the modern form *deem*. Now look at the following formula.

dam	>	*domjan*	>	*demjan*	>	*dem*	>	*deem*
(O.E. noun)		(O.E. Verbal infinitive)		(change of *o* to *e* due to operation of j-mutattion)		(dropping of the suffix)		(Modern form)

By the same process we get the modern verbs like *feed, breed, deal, meet* from the Old English forms of *food, brood, dole* and *mot*. The word *mot* is no longer found in Modern English.

(d) Verbs Derived from Adjectives. In Old English, certain verbs were made by adding the suffix-jan to adjectives. Thus from the word *hal* (whole) *haljan* was created. This underwent j-mutation and became heljan, and as in earlier cases, the suffix was dropped and thus we get the modern form *heal*. Similarly, with the word fill from O.E. full. The following formula is easier to remember:

hal	>	*haljan*	>	*heljan*	>	*hel*	>	*heal*
ful	>	*fulljan*	>	*fyljan*	>	*fyl*	>	*fill*
(O.E. adjectives)		(O.E. verbs by adding the Suffix-jan)		(due to operation of j-mutation		(dropping of the Suffix)		(Modern forms)

(e) Mutated Degrees of Comparison. In Old English the comparative degree was formed by adding-ira, and the superlative degree by adding-ist. These two suffixes are in fact ancestors of the modern-er and est. By operation of *i*-mutation, Old English *eald* (meaning old) gave rise to *elder* and *eldest*. In recent times, on the analogy of the positive, alternative degrees of comparison were formed from old. They are *older* and *oldest*. These are more generally used, while *elder* and *eldest* have a limited use. These are generally used to refer to persons and that, too, to the people within the family, as in *eldest brother, elder sister*.

Gradation and Mutation, though they took place in a distant past, have direct bearing on certain forms in Modern English.

Grammar of Old English. The most fundamental feature that distinguishes Old English from Modern English is its grammar. Old English in the main was a Synthetic language, with full of complicated inflexions. A language is said to be in the Synthetical stage when it expresses the grammatical relations of words by adding some suffixes to the stems of nouns, adjectives, pronouns and verbs. A language that is free from such inflexional endings as for as possible and in their place makes free me of other devices like prepositions and other auxiliary words is said to be in the Analytical stage. From this point of view, Modern English is Analytical. In its grammar, Old English resembles Modern German. The nature of Old English grammar can be gathered by looking at the inflexions of its nouns, adjectives, pronouns, verbs and so on.

The Old English Noun. The Old English noun is inflected according to its number and case. It has chiefly four cases and the endings of these vary with different nouns. There are two chief declensions, a vowel declension and a consonant declension. Vowel declension is called strong declension and consonant declension is called weak declension. Whether a noun takes one or the other of the two declensions depends upon whether the stem of the noun ended in Germanic in a vowel or in a consonant. The following examples will suffice to understand the nature of the declensions of the noun.

(1) Masculine-a stem—(stan stone)

	Singular		*Plural*
Nominative	stan	—	Stan-as
Genetive	stanes	—	stan-a
Dative	stan-e	—	stan-um
Accusative	stan	—	stan-as

(2) Feminine 0 stem: giefu (gift)

	Singular	*Plural*
Nominative	gief-u	gief-a
Genetive	gief-e	gief-a
Dative	gief-e	gief-um
Accusative	gief-e	gief-a

(3) Masculine Consonant Stem : Hunta (hunter)

	Singular	*Plural*
Nominative	hunt-a	hunt-an
Genetive	hunt-on	hunt-ena
Dative	hunt-an	hunt-um
Accusative	hunt-an	hunt-an

It is evident by this how complicated the inflexion of the Old English noun is. Modern English has discarded most of the case endings except the Genetive case ending-'s.

Grammatical Gender. The gender of Old English nouns is not dependent upon consideration of sex. What we call gender in Modern English is based on sex. Thus, in Modern English all Males are said to be Masculine, Females Feminine and things without life are said to be Neuter. But in Old English, as in Latin, it is not on the sex or absence of sex, but on the forms that a noun assumes in the course of its declension. Thus, in Old English *here* (army) is Masculine, *wynn* (joy) is feminine, *wif* (woman) is Neuter, and *wifman* (woman) is Masculine perhaps because the second element in the compound is Masculine. Strangely *mona* (moon) is Masculine and *sunne* (sun) is Feminine. These examples illustrate the illogicality of the gender of Old English nouns.

Another peculiarity of Old English is that adjectives, like nouns, have gender. The adjective takes the gender of the noun with which it is associated.

The Adjective. The adjective in Old English has a two-fold declension. One of them is the strong declension, used with nouns when they are not accompanied by a definite article or a demonstrative pronoun. For example *god mann* (good man) is a strong declension. The other is the weak declension, used with nouns accompanied by a definite article. Thus, *se god a mann* (the good man) is a weak declension. Further complication of the adjective in Old English adjective is that it is declined according to number, gender and case. In Modern English the adjective remains undeclined whatever number, gender and case it is associated with. Such elimination of the complex adjectival inflexion gives a great advantage to the English language, over many other Indo-European languages.

The Definite Article. Like modern German, Old English has a fully inflected definite article. It is inflected according to gender, number and case.

The Personal Pronoun. Old English has distinct forms of the personal pronoun practically for all genders, persons and cases. Instead of two numbers, singular and plural, it has an intermediate number called the dual number, which represents two things. The existence of the dual form in addition to the plural is an unnecessary complication in language and so it has disappeared in Modern English.

The Verb in Old English. The Old English has two great classes, the weak and the strong. These two classes are found even in Modern English and are known as regular and irregular verbs. In the strong verbs, the change of tense is indicated by a modification in their root-vowel as in *sing, sang, sung.* In the weak verbs such a change in tense is indicated by the addition of a suffix. It is estimated that Old English has a few over three hundred strong verbs. Based on the gradation of the vowel they assume, they are classified into six classes, and to these six is added a seventh class of verbs called reduplicating verbs. They may be illustrated by the following verbs:

	Present		*Pretirite Singular*	*Preterite Plural*	*Past Participle*
I	drifon	(drive)	draf	drifon	drifen
II	cheosan	(choose)	ceas	curon	coren
III	helpan	(help)	healp	hulpon	holpen
IV	beran	(bear)	bǣr	bǣron	boren

V	sprecan	(speak)	sprǣc	sprǣcon	sprecan
VI	faran	(fare, go)	for	foron	faren
VII	feallan	(fall)	feoll	feollon	feallen

It should be noted that in Modern English many of these characteristics of the verb are preserved, with some modifications. But Preterite Plural is completely lost and thus eliminating a part of the complexity of the verb.

The Vocabulary of Old English. Old English is in the main a pure language, that is, in its vocabulary, it is essentially Teutonic. It contains very few words that were of foreign origin. But Modern English has received and naturalised a number of foreign words almost from every known language in the world. In fact, borrowing from other languages started even in Old English Period. The history of the English language from the Old English Period to present day is but the history of the chain of borrowings from other languages.

When the Angles, Saxons and Jutes first settled in Britain, they came into contact with the Celts. The contact between the two races should have brought larger number of Celtic words into English than we really find. The reason for the fewness of Celtic-words in English is not for to seek. The Celts were the conquered race and it would not be fashionable for the conquering race to show their acquaintance with the language of the inferior natives. Nevertheless, certain amount of foreign elements is seen in Old English. Some Latin words flowed into the language of the Angles, Jutes and Saxons on the continent long before those tribes settled in England. After their establishing their settlements, Celtic words and some Latin words through Celtic found their way into the English language. With the introduction of Christianity, a large number of words forced their way into Old English. Later, the Scandinavian invasiom resulted in yet another wave of foreign element. But unlike Modern English, Old English did not borrow foreign element with great enthusiasm. Only when it was inevitable it allowed a foreign word into its fold. Otherwise it managed to express new concepts, new ideas by coining new words out of its own resources.

The great resourcefulness and the rich possibilities of Old, English in coining new compound words can be best gathered when we look at the principal compounds of some roots. Thus, from the root word *god*, a large number of compounds were made; *godcund* 'divine, religious', *godcundness* 'divinity' *godferht* 'god fearing or pious' *godgield* 'idol', *godhad* 'divine nature' *godcyld* 'impiety' *godspell*, *godspellbodung* 'gospel preaching' and so on. Similarly, from the word *mod* which meant in Old English 'heart, mind,. spirit', a good number of compounds were made, *modig* 'spirited, bold, arrogant', *modiglice* 'boldly, proudly', *modigness* 'pride, magnanimity', *modfull* 'haughty', *modleas* 'spiritless', *modcræft* 'intelligence', *gladmodness* 'kindness', *modlufu* 'affection'. Compounds as these demonstrate the remarkable capacity of Old English for word formation; its flexibility, variety and above all its familiarity even to the ordinary man of those times. It utilises its rich native resources before it went in search of foreign words.

Another interesting feature of the Old English vocabulary is its wealth of self explaining compounds. Self-explaining compounds, sometimes called kennings, are compounds of native words whose meaning is either self-evident or made clear by usage and association. Just as in Modern English, railroad, steamboat, electric-light, one-way traffic are self-explaining, in Old English we have *leoh-foet* literally light-vessel meaning lamp, *dǣg-red* literally day-red meant dawn; *corth-crǣft* 'geometry', *number-crǣft* 'arithmetic" *luch-crǣft* 'medicine' and so on. Of course, Modern English and many other languages, too, have got their capacity to form such self-explaining compounds. But in Old English these were more prevalent and more useful.

A part of the flexibility and richness of Old English was due to its generous utilisation of prefixes and suffixes, to form new compounds or to extend the root idea by expanding the word. Suffixes like-ig,-full,-leas, -lice.-ness,-sum,-dom were prevalent in'

Old English. Prefixes like be-, for-, fore-, mis-, ofer-, underwere frequently brought into service. In general, it can be said that Old English could express difficult and new ideas and things with certain amount of ease and familiarity. It had variety, flexibility and wealth of synonyms more useful in poetry than in daily life. It is not surprising that very few foreign words, filtered into Old English, which had a rich and colourful vocabulary of its own.

We have spoken of the characteristics of Old English, its spelling, its grammar and its vocabulary. To enable the student to become more familiar, here are given some specimens of Old English followed by their translations into Modern English.

THE MIDDLE ENGLISH PERIOD

The Norman Conquest of England in 1066 by William of Normandy had profound influence both upon the history of the country and upon the language. Upto this time English was, by and large, a pure and unmixed language with a few Latin, Celtic and Scandinavian words. But after the Norman Conquest English was destined to become a hybrid language with a large percentage of French words drawn into its fabric. The immediate result of the Norman Conquest was that, for a few centuries, English ceased to be the language of the governing classes. It was left without a standard literary dialect, and was reduced to the position of the language of the conquered. Latin and French usurped the earlier respectable place of English and they became the prestige languages in the country. Latin was the language of the Church, of scholarship and of international communication. French was the language of the rulers, of administration and of the upper classes in England, till in 1362 when an Act was passed making English the official language of the law courts, instead of French. In the same century, English instead of French was made the medium of grammar school education.

The Normans who conquered England in 1066 came from Normandy, the northern parts of France. They had been originally Scandinavian Vikings who occupied Normandy earlier in history. They spoke Norman French, a northern dialect of the language and like Chaucer's Nun, they did not know the French of Paris, which is sometimes called Central-French. In England the Norman French of the invaders sieveloped characteristics of its own and was then called Anglo-Norman. It was in the thirteenth century that the Central French began to exert its influence on the English language. So the influence of French on English has to be looked at two stages, one of Norman French and another of the Central French.

Having said so much we must correct two misconceptions. In the first place we must realise that the contact between the English language and the French had existed even before the Norman conquest. The contact actually had begun in the time of Aethelred, who had married a French princess in 1002. He sent his son, who later became Edward the Confessor, to school in France. At least twenty-five years of his life had been spent in Normandy and he knew as much Norman French as English. All his friends, his courtiers and all his manners were Norman. From this it is clear that a good deal of Norman French was heard at the English Court, even from 1042, when Edward the Confessor came to the throne. The Norman Conquest in 1066 brought a great impetus to hasten and complete the process of contact between the English language and French.

Another frequent misconception is that all the changes that the English language underwent during the Middle English Period, were due to the Norman Conquest. Doubtless, it was a period of momentous changes in the English language. Some of them were the result of the Norman Conquest and conditions that were created in the wake of the Conquest. But there were certain changes which were but continuation of tendencies that had begun to manifest themselves in the Old English Period. These would have taken place independent of the Conquest, but at a slower pace. The Norman Conquest hastened the process of change that had already set in. The changes of this period were extensive and fundamental and they affected the language in all its facets, spelling, pronunciation, grammar and vocabulary. Now we shall take these aspects in turn.

I. Spelling. Changes do not occur in spelling as they do in pronunciation. The Middle English scribes went on writing in their traditional way. But the Norman scribes disregarded the English spelling conventions and simply spelt the language as they heard it, using the conventions of Norman French. Thus, the long u was written as *on* by the French scribes. Old English *hus* and *mus* were spelt *hous* and *mous* in the Middle English Period. It was still pronounced u and not as diphthongal sound. Similarly long o was represented by oo as in words like *hoom*, *coom, foo* and so on.

In consonants, the hard c of Old English as in words like *cyning, cene, cepan* came to be represented by *k* before the front vowels c, i, and y and those words were spelt *king, keen* and *keep.* But c was retained before back-vowels like a, o, and u. Where c was pronounced *tʃ* as in Old English, *ch* was introduced after the Norman fashion and as a result the original Old English *cild* became child. It can be stated that words where ch is pronounced *tʃ* had similar origin.

In Old English g has always been pronounced as the modern y. The French scribes substituted the symbol y wherever g was pronounced as y. Thus, for Old English *giefan* and *gearn* (give and year), Middle English had *veven* and *year*. This change was introduced, perhaps because the soft g (pronounced y) before front vowels caused some confusion. Where g was pronounced as dz the symbol was retained as in *gentle*, *gesture* and so on. The Native symbol *ð* was replaced in Middle English by *th* and the Old English *sc* as *scip* was replaced by the French *sh* (ship) Again under French influence the original *cw* as in *cwen*, *ciwic* was replaced by *qu* and so those words became *queen* and *quick.*

Changes in Pronunciation. Since pronunciation relates solely to the spoken language, it is difficult to get such documentary evidences as we could get on matters of spelling, grammar and vocabulary. Besides, it was probable that there was no uniform pronunciation throughout the Middle English Period. Nevertheless,' there are some facts about pronunciation which can be said with a fair degree of certainty.

One of the important phonetic changes in Middle English was that the long *a* as in words like *ham, stan, hlaf* became long *o* often represented by *oo*, as in *hoom, stoon, hloof* and so on. They later became *home, stone, loaf* in Modern English.

Another most important phonetic development was the lengthening of short vowels when they stood in open syllables, and the shortening of long vowels when they stood in closed syllables. An open syllable is one in which the vowel is not followed by a consonant, as in words like *so, me, he, she*. Where a single consonant occurs between two vowels in English, the consonant normally belongs to the second syllable and therefore, the first syllable is an open one. For example, in words like broken, taken, the consonant k is preceded and followed by vowel and so k belongs to the syllable ken, and the first syllable is, therefore an open one. These words must be divided *bro-ken*, *ta-ken*. A closed syllable is one in which the vowel is closed or stopped by a following consonant, as for example in *man, can,* and so on. If there are two or three consonants between two vowels as in *grammar, bolster,* one of them belongs to the first syllable and the other one or two belong to the second syllable. So in such words there cannot be any open syllable. Examples are *gram-mar, bol-ster*. Now, the point is that in open syllables short vowels were lengthened in the Middle English Period; as *intiling, filing, lady, caning*. But in closed syllables long vowels Were shortened as in *tilling, filling, laddy, canning* and so on. But, if it be asked why words like *find, blind, climb, old* and *field*, which have closed syllables are pronounced with long vowels are diphthongs, the answer is that there are some exceptions. The vowels before consonant combinations *md, mb, Id* in most cases remained long. Even the word *friend* was pronounced with long vowel in Middle English.

The third important change was about the long vowels, whatever might be their origin, and their change to different vowels or diphthongs. The results of the change can be briefly mentioned as follows:

(a) long e became long i. For example *feet* was pronounced In Early Middle English more or less like the Modern *fate*. But in later Middle English it came to be pronounced with long i.

(b) long o became long u in later Middle English. For example, *food, doom, boon, shoe,* were originally pronounced with long o to rhyme with the modern *mode, dome, bone, show*. But in the fourteenth century the change came about and they began to be pronounced with long u as they are still pronounced today.

(c) Certain long vowels like a, i and u became their corresponding diphthongs. Thus, long a became *ei* as in words like, *game, name, fame*. The long i became *ai*, as in *find, fire* and so on. In the same manner, the long u became *au* as in *house, cow* and so on.

The fourth change that took place in the Middle English Period was, what is called to day Metathesis. Metathesis is the name given to change of position that took place for certain consonants like and s. By this process, the Old English words *beornan, bryd, ðurh* became *brennan* (burn), *bird, thruh*. It should be noticed that r in each of these words changed its position. From the word *brennan* words *brand* and *brunt* are derived. Similar changes of *lipse, wops*, became by metathesis *lisped* and *wasp*.

Grammatical Changes in Middle English. Languages do not usually borrow grammar. The grammatical changes that took place in the Middle English Period were not very much due to French influence. The tendency had already begun in the Old English Period and the Norman conquest only hastened the process.

We have seen that Old English was a highly inflected language. In grammar, Middle English witnessed a great reduction in inflexions inherited from Old English. So the Middle English Period is often referred to as a period of levelled inflexions. The levelling of inflexions was partly due to phonetic changes partly to the operation of analogy and partly due to English, coming in contact with Norman French, and Scandinavian languages. As the decay of the inflexional system progressed, more and more new grammatical devices came into use. It is difficult to say for certain whether the decay of inflexions was the cause or effect of the use of new grammatical devices.

Among the nouns, two main declensions became generalised in the course of the Middle English Period. In Old English, noun was declined in nominative plural by adding as (stanas, 'stones'), and in genetive singular by adding es (stanes, 'stones'). But in Middle English both these were levelled to-es. Só in nominative plural and genetive singular the noun had the same form *stones*.

Again, in Old English, in certain nouns, nominative plural and genetive singular were formed by adding -an. Thus eage (eye) became eagan (eyes' and of an eye') in Old English. In Middle English -an was changed to -en. In most dialects of Middle English -en became a stock plural termination. But the Midland dialects showed a predeliction for -es, and since the East Midland dialect attained supremacy and literary importance;-es became the common plural ending. Perhaps the French plural termination was also responsible for this change.

Another most important feature of Middle English was the elimination of troublesome grammatical gender and substitution of natural gender in its place. As we have seen in earlier chapter, in Old English, there was no relation between gender and the sex or absence of sex of the object. But, by the middle of twelfth century, gender had begun to be determined by meaning. The possible reasons for this shift from grammatical gender to natural gender are three. First, the ordinary people who spoke the language must have found it difficult and burdensome to master the intricacies of the irrational gender system. Secondly, certain nouns imported in English from French might be having a gender different from English. Thirdly, as the adjective lost their inflexions, gender has lost its importance. So the natural drift was towards simplification, making every thing of the male sex masculine, of the female sex feminine and all other things neuter.

As in nouns, in adjectives and in the articles, case distinctions were lost in Middle English. In adjectives only two forms were used; the normal form *fair* as in Chaucer's "the weder is fair" and "she hadde a fair forheed"; and a form with the ending -e faire, as in Chaucer's "fairewyves" (plural form) and "this faire Pertelote" (weak form after the demonstrative pronoun). The final -e was lost by the end of the Middle English Period and adjective became undeclinable, as it is today.

In Old English, the definite article had three forms for three different genders, *se* masculine, *seo* feminine and p̄æt neuter. Each of them was declined to indicate all four cases and singular and plural. In late Old English p̄e appeared and from this, the modern *the* is derived. In the course of Middle English, other forms gradually disappeared and *the* had been used for all of them. In Modern Period, *the* became the only definite article.

The verb in the Middle English Period had undergone a number of changes. Here it serves one purpose to speak of the infinitives of verbs. In Old-English -an was the regular ending for the infinitives of verbs. From -an was derived the ending -en, in the early Middle English Period. Later *to* was used, before the verb as a sign of the infinitive and therefore the ending -en was felt to be redundant and was finally dropped in Modern English. In Chaucer we find all forms of the infinitives. The more usual was -en infinitive as in *to ryden out, to seeken straunge landes, to tellen you*. But the form with to before the verb was frequently used by Chaucer, are in *to take our wey, the holy blisful martir for to seeke, to drawe folk to heven*.

The decay of inflexions and the consequent simplification of the grammatical structure of English were only indirectly due to the use of French in England. The Norman Conquest had not created the changes but brought about conditions favourable to such changes. By reducing the English language to the level of a spoken language of uneducated people, the Norman Conquest made.

The Vocabulary of Middle English. The influence of the Norman Conquest is much more direct and extensive upon the vocabulary. As has been mentioned in the introductory paragraphs to this chapter, French died out in England in 1362, after enjoying a position of supreme respect for a period of three-hundred years. But it left its marks on English vocabulary. A flood of French words reached the English shores, in different waves and in intervals of different sizes. In spite of the quantum of French influence on all facets of English, English remained still English. Its grammar was simplified; thousands of French words flooded the English language; it lost some of its vitality to create new compounds out of native roots, which was the proud characteristic of Old English, but the basic element of its grammar and vocabulary were still English. Though it witnessed a number of profound changes, its predominant features were those inherited from the Germanic tribes that settled in England in the fifth century. The Englishman of the Middle English Period, as A. C. Baugh remarks, "*ate, drank* and *slept* so to speak in English, *worked* and *played, spoke* and *sang, walked, ran, rode, leaped* and *swam* in the same language. The house he lived in, with its *hall, bower, rooms, windows, doors, floor steps* and *gate* remind us that his language was basically Tutonic. His *meat* and *drink, bread, butter, fish, milk, cheese, salt, pepper, wine* were inherited from pre-Conquest days, while he could not refer to his *head, arms, legs, feet, hands, eyes, ears, nose, mouth* or any common part of his body without using English words for the purpose".

Dialects of Old and Middle English. The Anglo-Saxon tribes conquered England in a piece-meal way and that led to profusion .of small kingdoms and dialect differentiation. There were probably dialect differences from the beginning, because Angles, Saxons and Jutes were not one tribe. Jutes, who came first, settled in Kent. Then the Saxons came later and occupied the rest of England south of the Thames, and then Angles came and settled in regions North of the Thames. These tripartite division of England was naturally reflected in language and dialect.

There were four dialects of Old English, Northumbrian, spoken in regions North of the Humber, Southumbrian or Mercian spoken in South of the Humber, Kentish and West Saxon. In the seventh century, in literature, culture Northumbrian was powerful. In the eighth century this leadership passed to Mercia, for a short period. In the ninth century the West Saxon led, because Wessex kings finally succeeded in unifying the country. In later half of the ninth century King Alfred saved the South and West of England from Danish invasions. During this period Winchester, the capital of West Saxon remained the centre of culture and learning in England. The unification of England under the West Saxon kings brought recognition of the West Saxon dialect as a literary standard. But strangely, it is not the direct ancestor of Modern Standard English.

With the Norman Conquest, all the dialects were put once more on the mettle. One of the striking characteristics of Middle English is great dialectal variety. The chief dialects in the Middle English Period were, Northern, West Midland, East Midland, Southern and Kentish. Just as in Old English, the West Saxon dialect attained the position of a kind of standard, in Middle English the East Midland dialect came to occupy that enviable position. There are some important reasons for this. First, it was the dialect spoken in and around the city of London which was the centre of English life and affairs. Secondly, it was the dialect favoured by the Court and thirdly, it was the dialect used in both universities, Oxford and Cambridge, and so became the language of scholarship. Later Chaucer and other important writers used it, thus establishing it as a literary dialect. Still later Caxton printed his earliest books in it. So by 1450, 'English' became synonymous with "East Midland".

THE RENAISSANCE

The beginning of the Modern English Period is conveniently placed at 1500. Certain new conditions and events of far-reaching: influence came into play from the beginning of the sixteenth century. They were the revival of learning usually known as the Renaissance the Reformation which followed in the wake of it, the invention of the

Printing Press, the rapid spread of popular education, the increased means of communication, the rapid growth of science and technology and the growth of what is called social consciousness. All these factors have left their impact as much on language, as on the life of the nation.

In 1453 Constantinople was captured by the Ottoman Turks. The scholars fled from that seat of learning to Western Europe. They first settled in Germany and Italy and started that intellectual awakening of Europe which has since been known as the Renaissance. The full tide of the Renaissance reached the shores of England about the year 1500. The new scholarship and learning and all that it implied created new forces which had a remarkable influence on the English language. The impact fell more on the vocabulary of English. Hitherto English borrowed words from French. But henceforth, words from Latin, Greek and Italian started pouring into the English language.

The Revival of learning had revealed the wealth of knowledge and experience preserved in the civilizations of Greece and Rome. There was much to learn for the sixteenth century from the writings of the ancients, their ethical and spiritual views, their ideas of Government, their political precepts, theories of education and their knowledge of many other things. The Revival of learning would have had a limited impact if these ideas had remained the property of a few academic men. There was popular demand from men of all classes to share the fruits of the Renaissance. The demand was soon fulfilled by translations.

The Protestant Reformation, which was a phase of the Renaissance, though it was chiefly a religious and political affair, left its abiding marks on the English language. It gave rise to bitter religious controversies. These religious disputes contributed a good number of words like *Puritan, saintly reprobate, selfish, self-denial conscientious* and so on. One important outcome of the Reformation was various English translations of the Bible, the Chief being Tyndale's and the Authorised version of 1611. The Bible fixed the language in a way and set some kind of standard. It has been a strong formative influence on the style of many eminent writers. It has contributed in a rich measure to English vocabulary, especially in metaphoric expressions and house hold phrases.

The invention of Printing was destined to have a profound influence on the language. It made so rapid a progress since its invention that by the year, as many as 35,000 books were printed in Europe. By 1640, about 20,000 titles appeared in English. Thus printing was a powerful force in bringing knowledge within the reach of all. It tended to establish a sort of standard form of language, by discrediting dialects. It popularised and gave currency to new words and phrases, and finally it tended to fix spelling by bringing uniformity into it.

But even the invention of printing would not have produced such widespread effects, had not education and literacy made rapid progress. In the later Middle ages quite a good number of people could read and write. It is probable that in Shakespeare's London, a little less than half of the people could, at least read. In the centuries that followed education had taken "giant leap forward" so that it has now become universal. So, as a result of rapid spread er education the printing press has been able to exert its great influence both on the language and on thought.

All this is only one side of the picture. The account given above seems to promise uninterrupted growth of the English language. But the fact remains that English had to struggle against great odds, before it attained an established position as a language of popular literature in the sixteenth century. It had to face three important problems, *(1)* the problem of recognition, *(2)* the establishment of uniform spelling and *(3)* enrichment of the vocabulary.

(1) The Problem of Recognition. Till 1362, English had fought the battle with French, and came out victorious. But in the Renaissance, English had to fight a more formidable rival, Latin. A strong tradition sanctioned the use of Latin in all fields of knowledge. Besides, the tradition was strengthened by the Revival of Learning. Moreover,

Latin was a kind of universal language in those times, because every educated man in Europe could communicate in it. Now, when English began to claim recognition, classical scholars zealously guarded the tradition of Latin. They contended that if the use of English language were carried too for classical learning would suffer. Nevertheless, English found some strong defenders in men like Elyot, Ascham, Wilson, Puttenham and Mulcaster. These champions of English were tired of being told that the English language was immature, unpolished and limited in resources and that it could not express abstract ideas and shades of thought. In an eloquent mood, Mulcaster declares "I love Rome, but London better, I favour Italic, but England more, I honour Latin, but worship English." Influential utterances such as these, backed by popular demand, played an important role in establishing English as the sole literary medium in England.

Religious disputs played no less part in contributing to the victory of English. Ever since Wycliff refused to carry on his quarrel with the Church in Latin and took his case directly to the people, in their own tongue, Latin had lost one of its strongholds. Since many of the people who were attracted to Protestantism lacked classical education, most of the controversial books and pamphlets were written in English. Thomas More himself, the author of *Utopia* in Latin, wrote his arguments against the Reformers in English. We should not forget that the rivalry between Latin and English had a commercial side.

Another factor which worked for the victory of English was the rise of social and occupational groups which had little Latin and less Greek. Explorers, Navigators craftsmen and other classes had something to say and they said it in English.

Another factor which worked in favour of English was the dawn of national feeling and fervent patriotism. This national feeling and patriotic fervour led to a greater interest and pride in the national language. While scholars and religious leaders were busy disputing over the relative merits of Latin and English, translators worked for the growth and enrichment of the English language. Thus, slowly Latin fell into the background. While English was slowly gaining its supremacy, it was at the same time under greater influence of Latin than it was in any other phase of its history.

(2) The Problem of Spelling. Though spelling is a Pedestrian subject in present times, it was a matter of great importance to the English in the Renaissance. English spelling is bad today. But it was worse in the sixteenth century, because there was no generally accepted system to which everyone could conform. English spelling is said to be unphonetic today, but in the sixteenth century it was neither phonetic nor fixed and uniform. The trouble goes back to the Middle Ages; when Norman scribes tampered with spelling in the Middle English Period and introduced confusion by writing English after the manner of French habits. Later the confusion was increased because, while spelling remained static, pronunciation went on changing from, time to time. The confusion was multiplied later, when, in the Renaissance, certain symbols were inserted in words where they were not pronounced. Thus *b* was inserted in *debt, doubt* after the fashion in Latin *debitum, dubitare* and similarly, *gh* was inserted in *delight, tight* on analogy with words like *light* and *night*. So variability and inconsistency were the characteristics of English spelling in the sixteenth century. Scholars like Sir John Cheks, Richard Stany hurst had evolved their own systems of spelling. Mulcaster, who was a teacher of Spenser, brought a kind of spelling reform based on custom and usage. He felt that it was futile to make English spelling phonetic. He steered a midway of compromise between the ideal and the practical. While others, trying to remove an existing difficulty, were substituting a new and a greater difficulty, Mulcaster used common sense and convenience to remove defects in the existing system. He got rid of superfluous letters in words in *putt, ledd, grubb* and made them *put, led, grub*. He allowed double consonants when they had a syllabic value as in *witting* (wit-ting). Except in words like *tall* and *generall*, he did use double consonants at the end of a word.

(3) **The Problem of Enrichment of English.** We have observed that the Renaissance was a period of widened horizons and increased activity. The spirit of enquiry, adventure and experiment led to amazing discoveries, and influential theories that revolutionised thought in many fields of life. Language was not left untouched. The same spirit of the Renaissance prompted the English improve their language. Moreover, when Latin lost the battle, the deficiencies of English came to surface. It was universally agreed that English was inadequate to accommodate the rapidly expanding civilization. Translators realised the limitations of their medium. There was a remarkable need for new words in various fields. So, many words from Latin and Greek were carried over into English. The import of words from other languages was made with a conviction that English would be better for having it and it was patriotic duty to use one's knowledge to the cause of enriching the national speech. Every writer, small or great, felt it was his duty to redeem the English language of the charge of inadequacy and inelegance.

But, the borrowing was not greeted with cheer. Many people objected to borrowing strange and unfamiliar words. The use of such words was considered pedantry and the words were ridiculed with the name "inkhorn terms", that is, words that existed in the ink-bottle of pedants and not in the living speech of men and women.

While the prevailing attitude was one of opposition to strange and obscene words, there were some who did not hesitate to approve of judicious borrowings. They often pointed out that English had already borrowed from French and Latin in the past. In fact, classical languages themselves were enriched in this manner. They argued the strangeness of new words would disappear as they grew acquainted with them. The defence of borrowing was as powerful as the opposition to inkhorn terms. The controversy soon spent its force and both parties arrived at a sort of compromise. Now, the attack was not so much against the borrowing itself as against the abuse of the borrowing. The safest course, it was agreed, was a middle one, to borrow within certain limits, and "without too manifest insolence and too wanton affectation". Dryden's opinion expressed somewhat later was typical of the spirit of compromise; "I trade both with the living and the dead, for the enrichment of our native tongue. We have enough in England to supply our necessity, but if we will have things of magnificence and splendour, we must get them by commerce".

Sound Changes in the Sixteenth Century. By the year 1500, English consonants were more or less fixed, that is, no significant changes took place in consonantal sounds. When we come to the vowel changes in Modern English, we find that all Middle English long vowels underwent extensive changes, while short vowels remained relatively stable. So for as the short vowels are concerned a person today would have no difficulty in understanding the English of the sixteenth or even the fifteenth century. We note only two important changes in short vowels in passing from Middle English into Modern English. Chaucer's a became *a* in the sixteenth century as in words like *cat, thank, apple, back.* In Chaucer's time u was a rounded vowel as in modern *full*. But it was unrounded in

Shakespeare's time, as in words like *but, cut, sum* and so on. In all these words *u* is retained in spelling.

The Great Vowel Shift. In the fifteenth century a great change in long vowels is seen to be under way. In Chaucer's time, long vowels had 'continental' value, that is, *a* was pronounced long as in *father* and not as in *fate*; *e* was pronounced as *a* in *mate*, but not like *i*: as in *meet, feet*. By the sixteenth century all long vowels were raised to the maximum and those that could not be raised further were diphthongised.

The following examples taken from Chaucer and Shakespeare will explain the process better :

Middle English

Vowel.	*Chaucer*		*Shakespeare.*
(1) a :	na:me	*name*	neim
(2) e :	klg :n	*clean*	kle:n (now kli:n)
(3) e :	me:d	*meed*	mi:d
(4) i	fi:f	*five*	faiv
(1) o :	go:t	*goat*	go:t
(2) o :	ro:t	*root*	ru:t
(3) u :	du:n	*down*	daun

It is evident from the illustrations above how for removed Chaucer's English was from today's and how close Shakespeare's English was to Modern English. The change illustrated above is called the Great Vowel Shift. As we proceed from *a:* to *i:* and again from *o:* to *u:* we are gradually elevating the tongue and closing the mouth. *i:* and *u:* are called raised vowels. Further raising of them was not possible and so they became diphthongs.

Grammatical Features of the Sixteenth Century English. We have seen in the last chapter that the inflexions of Old English were levelled in Middle English. By the end of the Middle English Period, the process of reduction of inflections was completed and they were reduced to Modern Proportions. In Grammar, as in sound changes, there was not much left for the Modern English Period to complete. "The Great mutations of the world were acted."

The Noun. The noun inflexions in early Modern English were almost the same as they are today. The plural and possessive singular of nouns ended in-s, as in *theives, ringes, poynts,* and *uncles lamby*. But in possessive case apostrophe was not in use. In the sixteenth century, however, 'certain -in plurals survived. Most of them became plurals in Modern English; Examples are *fon* (foes), kneen (knees), shoon (shoes), eyen (eyes).

An interesting feature of this period is the frequent use of his - genetive. In Middle English and Old English, the genetive ending was es. But since it is usually unstressed it was frequently written -is. This ending was similar to the pronoun *his* which was also written *is* omitting *h*, when unstressed; so people were led to believe that genetive case-ending was only a contracted form of *his*. We find in Shakespeare and many other writers of the sixteenth and seventeenth centuries, expressions like *Count his galleys* (Count's galleys), *Mars his heart* (Mars' heart). The use of this form was given up in the eighteenth century when people realised the illogicality of such usage in expressions like *maiden his beauty, virgin his delicacy, woman his husband.*

The Adjective. The adjective lost all its inflexional endings even in the Middle English Period. It was no longer declined according to number, gender and case in the sixteenth century. But in degrees of comparison the adjective of the sixteenth century differs from that of the Modern Period. There was variation in the use of *-er* and *more*, *-est* and most as signs of the comparative and superlative degrees. Double comparatives and double superlatives are abundantly seen in Shakespeare and his contemporaries; *more larger, most boldest, most unkindest* and so on.

The Pronoum. The history of English pronoun is interesting. In Old English *thou* was the singular form and *ye* was plural. In Middle English *thou, thy, thee* were used in addressing familiars, children and inferiors and *ye, your, you* were used as a mark of respect. By the beginning of Modern period, *thou, thee, thy* totally disappeared from polite speech.

Another important feature of the pronoun is the history of *ye* and *you*. Originally *ye* was the nominative and *you* objective. In the fourteenth and fifteenth centuries they exchanged their roles; you was used as a nominative and *ye* as an objective. But the Bible preserved the old usage of the two words, as in "No doubt *ye* are the people, and wisdom shall die with *you*." In many writers the distinction was either lost or they used them confusingly. In the seventeenth century *ye* was banished and *you* became the regular form for both cases.

The most interesting aspect of the pronoun was the emergence of a new possessive neuter *its*. In Old English the neuter pronoun had had four forms, *hit* (nominative), *his* (accusative), *him* (Genetive) *hit* (dative). In Middle English *him* as the genetive Was lost and a new possessive needed and *his* was frequently used, though it was identical with the possessive pronoun of *he*. In Shakespeare, we have *How for that little candle throws his beams* and in the Bible, we "*if the salt have lost his savor, wherewith shall if be salted.*" In both examples *his* is used where we use *its*. The emergence of *its* was from *it* which was the weakened form of *hit*.

The Verb. By the sixteenth century the verb had lost all its burdensome inflexions and acquired the modern form. But there are certain differences in usage between the sixteenth century and the present day. The expressions like "*Goes the King hence to-day*" interrogative form was made without the present day auxiliary (*do* or *does*). Another important feature of the verb is scarcity of progressive forms of the verb; Example "*what do you read my Lord*?" for "*what are you reading*".

THE EIGHTEENTH CENTURY

From the second half of the seventeenth century, the adventurous individualism and spirit of independence, so characteristic of the sixteenth century, declined and gave way to a desire for system and regularity. The sublime indifference to rules with which Shakespeare used the language, verbing nouns and adjectives, gave way to hesitation and uncertainty. The ambition of the eighteenth century was correctness in everything written or spoken. They brought logic and reason from philosophy into the domains of language. The results of these tendencies were the efforts of this period to standardize, refine and fix the language. People became acutely conscious of the absence of a standard, and so the century tried to reduce the language to a set of rules and set-up a standard of correct usage. The efforts of the period to standardize the language was summed up in Swift's proposal for "correcting, improving and Ascertaining the English tongue".

The Problem of 'Refining' the Language. The absence of standard led to corruptions creeping into the language, at least scholars so believed. The so-called corruptions which Swift resented were shortening of words like *hyp* from *hypochondriac, rep* from *reputation, extra* from *extraordinary, mob* from *mobile vlugus*. Swift thought that there was dignity in polysyllabic form of words. He would have objected to shortened words of the modern period, like *taxi, phone, bus* and so on.

A succession of writers felt that a few generations after them, their works would not be understood, because the language was not permanently fixed. It was one of the ambitions of the century to stabilize the language. In Italy and France this problem of their languages was taken care of by academies. From the example of France and Italy, it was suggested that England should have an academy. The Royal Society with its Committee for improving the English language was entrusted with the task of refining and stablilizing the language. Dryden was the moving spirit and pioneer in this field. But the Committee failed in its mission perhaps because its terms of reference were vague, or because the Royal Society was more absorbed in matters of scientific research.

When the idea of an academy was in the air, Addison published a paper (no. 135) in "The 'Spectator" pleading for a kind of universal grammar, which can serve as the final court of appeal in disputed points of grammar, and settle all controversies about correctness, idiom and usage. A few months later Swift published his proporsal "for Correcting, Improving and Ascertaining the English Tongue". He said that the daily improvements in the English language were by no means in proportion to its daily corruptions and "that the pretenders to polish and refine it have chiefly multiplied abuses and absurdities; and that in many instances it offends against every part of grammar."

However, the idea of establishing an academy soon died out. At least some people realised that language had a way of taking care of itself and that, after all, features which Were objectionable to one period were either eliminated by time or accepted by another period. Dr. Johnson himself said in an authoritarian voice, "Those who have been persuaded to think well of my design, require that it should fix our language, and put a stop to these alterations which time and chance have hitherto been suffered to make in it without opposition. With this consequence I will confess that I flattered myself for a while; but now begin to fear that I have indulged expectation which neither reason nor experience could justify. ...Sounds are too volatile and subtle for legal restraints."

Now, some individuals thought that what could not be imposed by legislation in matters of grammar might be adopted through reason and persuasion. They tried to bring about linguistic reforms which, they believed, where necessary, to set up a standard. Dr. Johnson, through his dictionary conferred certain amount of stability and uniformity on the English language, especially in matters of Orthography and vocabulary. The grammarians of the eighteenth century tried to do for the syntax, what Johnson had done for the vocabulary and spelling. There was a striking outburst of interest in English grammar from 1760. Joseph Priestly, Robert Lowth, James

Buchanan, John Ash and Noah Webster in America, were some of the distinguished grammarians of this century. All these grammarians aimed at chiefly three things: *(a)* to codify the principles of the language and to reduce it to a set of rules; *(b)* to settle disputed points and decide, perhaps, with a voice of authority cases of divided usage; and *(c)* to point out what were supposed to be common errors and thereby to improve and correct the language.

Authority and Usage. From what has been said above, it is evident that the eighteenth century grammarians had two ambitious functions; to record facts and pronounce judgements and to legislate. To the eighteenth century, which tried to see order and regularity in everything, of any two alternate forms of expression, one must be wrong. Which was wrong, which correct, was to be decided by the grammarians. When once the question was decided and choice made, all other forms were condemned. The grammarian set up a prescriber. He decided not only what people should not speak or write, but also what people should. He was busy discussing the propriety of using *whose* as the the possessive *which*, of expressions like had rather, had better, which have been since accepted as normal conventions of expression. Some of the opinions stated by the eighteenth century grammarians are, however, accepted by later generations.

But, tile later half of the eighteenth century witnessed a signal revolt against Prescriptive and Proscriptive grammar and their abuses. The modern doctrine that usage should be the criterion of correctness, began to be advanced. It was recognized that the peculiarities and deviation from grammatical norms in any language were established by usage and they must be complied with. As Horace put it earlier "usage is the sole arbiter and norm of spee:h". Language is what people speak and not what grammarians think they ought, or ought not to speak. Joseph Priestly and George Campbell advocated this doctrine in later decades of the eighteenth century. In his Philosophy of Rhetoric, Campbell says, "Language is purely a species of fashion. ...It is not the business of grammar, as some critics seem preposteriously to imagine, to give law to the fashion which regulate our speech. On the contrary, from its conformity to these and from that alone, it derives all its authority and value.

The Old Prescriptive grammarians set up the standard themselves and then arrogantly proceeded to label every divergence from it an 'error'. But the new grammarians have not done anything better. They have taken the whole story back where we started. The doctrine of usage amounts to letting each native speaker and each foreign learner speak and write whatever he pleases. If this be allowed, confusion gets compounded as well as confounded. So, the new grammarians set up two separate 'standard' and substandard' English which were not materially very much different from the Old Grammarians' 'correct' and 'incorrect' labels. The new grammarians have rebuilt grammar but not totally discarded it. Descriptive grammar, with linguistics as the basis evolved by the American School of linguistics is nothing but the Old grammar in the new robes of brand-new complicated terminology. The path of moderations seems to be to choose the best from both the old and new schools of grammar.

Now, let us take our eyes from these controversies about the language and about various schools of grammar. Let us look instead, at some characteristic developments in English grammar, in the eighteenth century. One of the developments was the extensive use of progressive forms of the English verb, to indicate an action as in progress at the time implied by the auxiliary. Examples, He is *laughing, she is singing*. The origin of such forms is interesting. The chief factor in their growth is the use of the Present Participle (laughing, singing, dancing) as a noun governed by the preposition *on*. Thus, the progressive form began originally as "*he burst out on laughing*." This was weakened in rapid speech *to he brurst out a-laughing* and further weakened to *he burst out laughing*. Similarly, *he was on laughing* became *he was a-laughing* and finally *he was laughing*.

Another important development is the growth of the progressive passive out of progressive forms of the verb. Thus, a form like "*the house is on building*" suggested that the house was under construction.

But the phrase *on building* was weakened in course of time to a-building and further weakened to *building*. So the original sentence came to be "*the house is building*", active form, with progressive passive meaning. Based on this, at least in Colloquial English, the following expressions are heard : *there is nothing doing at the mill this week, the dinner is cooking* and *the tea is drawing* and so on. But in some cases this has to be used very carefully, because it can be either active or passive sometimes. For example, when we say the *waggon is making*, the meaning is passive, but in the *waggon is making noise*; both construction and meaning are in active.

These changes in grammar, a few as they are, indicate that English is a living and growing thing. Its grarnmar is not fixed and the flux of change continues even if at a slower pace, in spite of grammarians of all schools.

THE NINETEENTH CENTURY AND AFTER

First, let us enumerate some of the chief events of the two centuries under review. The most important political event of great magnitude was the beginning of the expansion of the British empire in the eighteenth century which had laid the foundations for the wide diffusion of English in the world as a result of which English has been used throughout more than a quarter of the earth's surface. With Nelson's famous victory at Trafalgar in 1805, England emerged as the supreme naval power in the world. The growth in importance of some of England's larger colonies, their steady march towards autonomy and the rapid growth of the United States have given significance to the varieties of English spoken in different parts of the world. But this has been counteracted by the establishment of the first cheap newspaper (1816) and of penny Postage (1840) and vastly improved means of travel and communication, which have the influence of spreading the standard form of speech. Naturally, this brings us to the rapid development in science and technology. All these factors havo contributed to immense growth of the vocabulary. The great reform measures like the revision of Penal Code and the Poor Laws, and restrictions placed on child labour established English society on democratic basis. The gulf between the rich and the poor was bridged by increased opportunities and even the humblest worker has been enabled to share the economic and cultural advantages of the period. The progress that the nation has made in all aspects is reflected in the language of the period, and in no period language mirrored the progress of the nation better.

Science and the English Language. Science enriches the language, in the same fashion and to the same extent as it enriches the daily life of each one of us. The relation between science and language is close, very close. Language is the medium of spreading the results of scientific research and at the same time science contributes to the growth of language. It has been estimated that fully one half of the vocabulary of all civilized languages of the world, consists of scientific and technical words. There is yet a third relation. Science in recent times has cast a new light on the mechanics of language, namely, the production, transmission and reception of sound. The telephone, the radio, and such others, are artificial devices to convey the human voice. In return, language furthers the advances of science by placing its semantic resources at the disposal of science, for the dissemination of knowledge among scientists as well as among lay-men. All languages, especially Greek and Latin unlocked the treasure-chests of their vocabularies to science. Words like *gastrogue*, and *plasmagene* in nutrition, and names of diseases like *acidosis, anaemia, appendicitis, bronchitis, diphtheria,* have come into English either from Latin or from Greek. Words like *psychosomatic, mania phobia, cybernetics,* in medical psychology, have come into English straight from Greek. We speak familiarly of *penicillin, streptomycin, hormones, endocrine glands, stethoscope, bronchoscope, metabolism, proteins, carbo-hydrates, enzymes and allergy*. All these words have come into use during the last one hundred years.

Every other field of science has contributed to the bulk of the vocabulary. Physics has given the language, terms like *dynamo comutator, alternating current, calorie, ultraviolet rays, electron, protons, quantum theory* and *relativity* and so on. From Chemistry have come terms like *alkali, benzine, cyanids, firmaldehyde, glycerine, radium, ozono, stratosphere* and so on. Psychologist brings to the language words like *egocentric, extrovert, introvert, inferiority complex* and such others, The familiarity of many of these technical and specialists' words is due to the common man's conscious interest in ever growing science and technology. Scientific cnventions like the radio, the moving picture, the automobile have contributed to the expansion of the vocabulary. The word autombile is an addition to the vocabulary. Other words which have come in the wake of the invention of the automobile are *motor car, sedan, coach, runabout, packing, spart, plug, choke, clutch, gear shift, steering wheel, self-starter, shock absorber,* besides many others. The moving picture has given terms like *screen, reel, film, scenario, projector, close-up, fade-out,* and so on. From the invention of the radio, the English language added to the stock of its vocabulary terms like *radio-frequency, kilocycle, loudspeaker, transformer, aerial, listener, announcer, broadcast, reception, tone-control,* and *radio-gram* and others. The radio has been helping the English language yet in another way.

Scientists need technical terms for an enormous number of things, new inventions, new discoveries :md concepts of all kinds. To meet this need scientists have drawn on various sources. One of the devices to build up scientific vocabulary is to take an already existing word and put it in a special context and, thus, give it a scientific meaning. This is what has happened to words like *salt* in the hands of Chemistry, *pollen* and *fruit, parasite* in the hands of botanists and biologists. Metallurgists have done the same thing to *fatigue*, as physicists have done to words like *work, force, current, power* and *resistance*. The second important device is to borrow words straight from classical languages, or to invent new words out of classical material. Thus, words like *corrolla, focus, genus, saliva* have been taken from Latin. From Greek have come words like *larynx, thorax, iris, pyrites* and so on. But *chlorophyl* is an English word made of Greek elements *chloros* (light green) and *phyllan* (leaf). Similarly, from Latin *vita* (life), has been coined the word *vitamin*. Certain words have been coined by combining Greek and Latin elements. For example, *haemoglobin* is one such word. Sometimes objections were raised ito such words as borrowed or coined from classical tongues, on the ground that they are opaque, that is, their meaning is not immediately evident to an Englishman.

The expansion of the scientific vocabulary is not a recent affair. It has been going on at an ever-increasing pace for over three hundred years. The sixteenth century introduced words relating to human body, *skeleton, abdomen*, and so on and names of diseases like *epilepsy, small-pox, mumps*. The seventeenth century introduced some more medical and biological terms like *vertebra, tonsil, pneumonia* and some mathematical terms like *formula, logarithm* and *series*. In the eighteenth century, biological terminology was enriched enormously. Descriptive terms of zoology and botany, like *albino, anther, fauna, habitat, pistil* belong to this period. Some chemical words like *hydrogen, oxygen, nitrogen molecule* also belong to this century. In the nineteenth century, the expansion became explosive because, the century witnessed the rapid growth of many specialised fields of science. It is practically impossible to list out all new words of the nineteenth and twentieth centuries.

There is yet another way in which science has influenced the English language. The rise of scientific writing in English from the days of Bacon and Harvey, helped to establish a simple referential kind of prose as the central kind in Modern English. Rhetorical style is no longer the norm and scientific writing and cientific attitude in general, played a part in establishing what is called plain prose style.

CHARACTERISTICS OF THE PRESENT DAY ENGLISH

Several historical and social factors have given stability to English grammar. During the period under review, very few changes in grammatical forms and conventions can be observed. We have already seen some of the characteristic features of English, in the early chapters of this section. We may, however, add to them, the following prominent features of modern English.

The most important feature of English is its analytical quality. The story of English from the Old English Period to modern times is the story of its growth from synthetic state to the analytic. Today, there are numerous parts of speech that are not inflected. For example, the definite article has got the same form in all contexts, whether it is placed before the singular, or plural, before, the masculine, feminine or neuter, or before the noun of any case, nominative, objective, genetive, or dative. The indefinite article, of course, has two forms *a* and *an*, but, they alternate euphonically according to the initial sound of the word that follows, and not according to the gender of the noun. In the same manner, modern adjective does not change its form according to number and gender. *Good or bad* remain the same to whatever sex you apply the word. There are two forms of each of the two demonstrative pronouns, *this* and *these*, *that* and *those*. The first pair is applied to the things near and the second pair to the things for away and long ago. The distinctions between *this* and *these*, and between *that* and *those* apply to number. But, while many of the parts of speech have cast their inflexions, in pronouns of all kinds, personal, possessive, relative and interrogative, certain complexities, of number and case have survived in modern English; *I, me, we, us, my, mine, who, whom*. The noun in Modern English has discarded all its case-endings save for a genetive as in *boy's, man's*. The plural of the noun is generally made with -s or -es, with a few exceptions like *men, oxen, ,children, mice, feet* and so on where the mutated plurals have survived.

The Modern English verb, unlike its Middle English and Old English counterparts, has an extremely simple mechanism. The forms of weak verbs have been reduced to four, *love, loves, loving* and *loved*, and those of strong verbs to five, as for example *write, 'writes, wrote, writing, written*. Excepting the forms like *loves* and *writes*, all others are applied to all kinds of subjects, irrespective of person, gender and number. This is a definite improvement over the synthetic forms of Latin, Greek and some modern languages. The forms like *loves, writes, goes* are reserved for third person singular, when the verb is in simple present. But while the main verb does not distinguish between sex, person, and number, auxiliaries differ according to number and person of the subject. Thus, auxiliaries like *is, are, was, were, has, had, shall, will* are chosen to be used in a sentence according to the person and number of the subject. But they do not distinguish between sexes.

But the structure of modern English is not one of unmixed blessing. While many of the grammatical features of modem English make the language easy for a foreign learner, it can be seen that some other grammatical features are inconsistent; for example, the past of strong verbs is not always the same. It is unpredictable; it can be as varied as *sing sang, cling, clung; bring, brought; buy, bought*; and so is the unpredictability of the form of the past participle: *seek-sought*, but *speak-spoken*. The use of *do* as an auxiliary, as an interrogative and in negative is a recent development. Where Shaksespeare had written "goes the king hence?", we say *does the king go* and again Shakšepeare would say, "no, the king goes not", but we say, "no, the king does not go." But, the use of *do* and its inflected forms *did* and *does* is not universal; it is not applied to the verb *to be*. Nobody would say "*does he be here*", just as nobody would answer in the affirmative yes, *he bes here adding-s* to the verb, as is usual with other verbs in this context. Again *do* as an auxiliary mayor may not apply to the verb *to have*.

While it is true, in general, that the grammatical features of modern English are simple, we cannot forget the fact that its spelling is the greatest stumbling block. It is often said to be a monument of traditionalism. It is anachronistic; that is, the spelling system is of Stuart period while its pronunciation is modern. It is inconsistent and the relation between spelling and pronunciation is capricious. Bernard Shaw ridicules the spelling, sound relation in English by inventing a new spelling *ghoti* for fish, where *gh* represents *f* as in *enough, o* represents *i* as in *women* and *ti* stands for *f* as in *nation*. This, however, is an extreme form of ridicule. But the difficulties of the spelling-sound are at once felt by taking a few random examples. For example, the so-called -s plurals are sometimes pronounced with -s at the end, but only sometimes, as in *books, lips, cots*. Sometimes the same plural ending -s is pronounced with-z sound, as for example, in *girls, boys, nibs* and so on. Same is the story of the genetive-s ending, *cat's (s) paw,* but *God's mercy.* The same difficulty appears in the present tense verb forms with -s ending, when the subject is in third person singular; *she writes, she speaks, she weeps* (all with s sound), but she *reads, she kisses, she sings* (all with z sound). There are numerous other difficulties (For details please see the chapter on Spelling and Pronunciation).

In spite of the disadvantages (and not because of its merits), English manages to hold the ground it has gained and make further progress. The progressive expansion of the English-speaking world has been chiefly due to the colonizing habits of English speakers who have transplanted their language in different corners of the world.

The tremendous sweep of territory and population over which English has gained control has created several diverging forms of English speech. Now, this brings us to the problem of English dialects.

English Dialects. There are several varieties of English speech and each of the varieties can be sub-divided into local sub-varieties. The chief varieties are the British variety, with its numerous and widely diverging dialects, the American variety with its three sub-divisions, like Eastern, Western and Central American; the Canadian variety which tends to approach the American; the Australian and New Zealand, which have many things in common; and the South African. In addition to them there are other varieties of English spoken in India, China and other parts of Asia.

The most important of the varieties of English speech is the dialect of Scotland. In its origin it is a variety of Northern English which had an important position upto the sixteenth century. But the Renaissance and Reformation brought the influence of Southern English on the northern variety. The influence of Southern English is also due to the growing importance of London as the political and cultural centre of the English speaking world.

Northern dialect or Scots as it is often called, has certain characteristic differences in pronunciation and vocabulary. The 'Words *who, whose, so, well, neighbour, good* are spelt and pronounced in Scottish as *wha, whase, sae, weel, neebour, geed.* Some of the 'old words which are no longer in standard English, have survived in this dialect. Examples are *ain* for *modern own, bairn for child, auld* for *old, muckle* for *great, bonnir* for *beautiful* and so on.

English in the Empire. The migration of English speakers and the consequent transplantation of the language in vast territories have caused certain divergencies to grow up which distinguish English of one nation from that of the other. The peculiarities are partly due to separation of immigrants, in time and space, from the British community. They are also partly due to the influence of a new environment, differences in material civilization, differences in the flora and fauna of the new territories which received English.

The differences between the English of Britain and that of America is so great that an American writer says that interpreters are for more needed between American and the English than between either and the French or German. It is said that continental Europeans hang out such signboards as "English spoken here—American understood" and as "English taught in three months and American in two months." In England also, such signs are seen. Sometimes, theatres in London write on signboards "New, sensational American Western film—English subtitles." Things like these are often advanced as a form of humour and often they exaggerate the differences between American and British English. Nevertheless, they point out to certain divergencies in pronunciation, vocabulary, spelling and grammar.

Among differences in pronunciation the following are worthy of note. Speakers of King's English pronounce words like *bath*" *dance, half, past,* with long a (a:). But in American English they are pronounced with æ sound, as in *cat, man* and so on. It is estimated that about twenty-five per cent of English words show differences in pronunciation between the American and King's. English varieties. In matters of stress, we can take the following examples. The British stress *necessary* and *primarily* on the first syllable, while in America they stress the second syllable.

In spelling and usage, the following differences may be noted. In Britain words like *honour, labour, flavour, colour* are spelt with—*our* and in America their spelling is simplified to *honor, labor, fiavor, color*. Americans use *ct* where in some cases the British use *x* as in connexion, and inflexion. Nouns like *defence, licence* are spelt in Britain with *-ence* and in America they are spelt with *-ense defense, license* and so on. Many individual words show drastic differences in spelling. The British *jail, tyre, programme, cheque, jewellery* have become in America *gaol, tire program check, jewelry*. Besides, there are many semantic and grammatical differences.

Australian English has distinctive features in vocabulary, because a certain number of words were borrowed from the native Australian tongues. The settlers in Australia, found themselves in the midst of new flora and fauna which needed many new words. So they had either to borrow words from native languages or had to put old words to new use. Thus, the word *robin* is applied in Australia to various birds unknown in Europe. *Jackass* is a new bird whose noise is like *donkey's* bray. *Cockatoo*, originally the name of a bird, is applied to a small farmer in Australia. Australian *Kangaroo* and *boomrang* have been accepted in British English. The Australian calls a street loafer a *larrikan*. The striking differences in pronunciation between Australian and British English can be summed up in the following sentence.

New Zealand English has borrowed words from the Polynesian Maori of the original inhabitants. The word *Kiwi* for instance is one such borrowed word, applied for a wingless bird native to New Zealand. Similarly *kapai* is a word borrowed from the natives and is used as a slang for "Attaboy" .

Before the English took control, South Africa had been successively occupied by the Bushmen, Hottentots, Bantus, the Portuguese and the Dutch. English which reached rather late, had to borrow words freely from all these languages, especially from Dutch. Some of the Dutch words which are indispensable to South African English are *baas* (master, counterpart of American boss), *banket* (gold-bearing quartz reef), *biltong* (pieces of dried meat), *brak* (soil with excess soda or salt), *kloof* (ravine), *morgen* (land measure, a unit of two acres), *trek* (journey by waggon), *dorp* (village), *stolp* (verandah). In South Africa *mason* is simply a bricklayer and not the one who dresses stones. *Boy* means grandfather when it is applied to a native. The meaning of the word *land* has been specialised to barren and uncultivable lands. In South African English *canteen* is a low class drinking place. English *cinema* or the moving picture is often called *bioscope*. Certain words in South African English have fortuitous identity in their meanings with American English. As in America, in South Africa *store* means a shop, *storekeeper* is shopkeeper and *store clothes* are ready-made clothes. Some of the syntactical constructions in South African English do not carry much sense in England and America.

Canadian English has many things in common with American English and a few things in common with British English. Many of the earlier settlers in Canada came from the United States. So, the English of Canada can only be described as a variant of American English. Canadianisms which have no counterpart in the United States or in Britain are very rare. In Canada, The *Gridiron* is used, as a form of slang, for 'old glory'; *toadskin* is the word for 'dollar bill', and to *stand sam* is used to mean 'to treat' someone to something.

Pidgin English. The force of expansion of the English language has besides causing divergencies in Syntax, spelling and Pronunciation, also created Pidginized versions of English. Pidgin variety of any language is at once a monument to human ingenuity and to man's erroneous thinking. In various parts of the world, intercourse between the English and others has given rise to various Pidginized versions of English which are sometimes called *Contact* English. The origin of Pidgin English is partly in the contempt of the English for the native and in the erroneous belief that the English can make English easier for the native by speaking in the truncated idiom of mothers or lovers. It springs from the ill-founded notion that by simplifying the language: by stripping it of its existing inflexions and reducing the grammar to the minimum, and making English grammar and syntax agree with the syntax of the native language, it becomes easier for the foreigner to learn English. But the difficulty is that too much simplification leads to grammatical incorrectness.

Pidgin English had its origin in the trade port of China, where English words were first put to hinese syntactical arrangement to make English easier for the natives. But, from the ports of China it spread to different parts of the world, wherever English is learnt and spoken imperfectly. It is not a unified speech; there are several varieties of Pidgin English; Chinese Pidgin, Melanesian Pidgin current in the Solomon and Fiji islands, New Guinea Pidgin, Pidgin of islands of Polynesia, West African Pidgin, 'Hobson-Jobson' English spoken by Anglo-Indians in India, besides many others. Here are some of the samples of Pidgin expressions current in different parts of the world. In Chines Fidgin *girl* is called *cow-child* and boy is a *bull-child*. To 'worship' is to 'chin-chin' and 'chop chop' means 'quickly'. Simple 'Bishop' is called 'top-side-piece-Heaven-Pidging-man'. In Melanesian Pidgin *kinkinan* means to 'steal'; 'kai-kai' means 'to eat' and 'shoot me kai kai' means 'serve me the dinner'. A friendly act of "pouring coffee in the cup" is described by the phrase "capsize im coffee along the cup". 'Frenchman' is called in this Pidgin 'man-a wiwi' (the man who says oui-oui). The Pidigin expression for "I am hungry" is "belly-belong-me plenty-walk-about." If you want to say "I am going to study", you have to say it in as many words as "maken head-belong-me-walk-about longa-too-much pappa-Yabber." To the speaker of normal English this is nothing but idiotic. Many orthodox linguists paid scant attention and held no respect for the variety of speech. But, Frederick Bodmer says, "to the student of language-planning for world co-operation, they have salutary effects.

Basic English. The multiplicity of mutually unintelligible regional languages has been held to be great stumbling block in international communication. So, many of the linguists of earlier generation toyed with the idea of creating an artificial language which would serve the world as a second language—a common medium for people of all speech-communities. The ideal of having single *auxiliary* language for supra-national communication has given rise to artificial languages like Volapiik, Esperanto, Ido, Espelantido, Interlingua, Novial and so on. They are all artificial languages constructed from the vocabulary and grammatical forms of several European languages. But these linguistic test-tube babies have not survived for long. Still there are people who cherish the hope of arriving at all international medium.

Basic English was first constructed by Ogden and Richards, and was later stamped with official approval by Churchill. It is based upon the assumption that any effective communication requires the minimum of vocabulary and the minimum of grammatical forms. While working on *The Meaning of Meaning*, Ogden and Richards were struck by the recurrence of certain common, frequently used words in defining involved and very obstruse terms covering all subjects. They concluded that it was possible to express everything in daily life with as few as 850 words. They addressed themselves to the question "what other words do we need in order to define something when we do not already know the right word for it". For example, if we do not know the plough, we can define it as the machine we make use of to get the ground ready for sowing. The actions expressed by the verbs like *burn, finish, err* can be defined by phrases like "to make fire", "to make an end", and "to make a mistake".

In addition to the basic verb-list given above., Basic English consists of about four hundred 'general', or frequently used nouns such as *control, machine, government*; about two hundred picturable objects like *man, woman, apple, island, monkey*; one hundred and fifty adjectives like *full, important, ready, good* and so on. In addition to the 850 words Basic English permits the formation and use of compounds like *without, undertake, understand, scientists*, economists and such others pursuing specialized fields of knowledge are granted extra sets of words. Measurements, numerals, calendar, currency, such other terms as cannot be translated or defined are additional to the basic-word-list. Now, including all these special classes of words the basic-word list swells upto nearly 8,000 which is a sufficient minimum for everyday expression of normal English. King's English can be spoken with such a large list. Then why give up King's English and use impoverished English? This is one of the objections raised against the use of Basic English. Further objections are, that the elimination of the bulk of English vocabulary is a little less than stupidity. It is like throwing the motor out of the car because that is where all the troubles spring up.

There is yet another aspect of Basic English. From the point of view of the speakers of English as a mother tongue, it is confusing, involved and circumlocutory. To them it involves a process of forgetting a wealth of words which they have mastered, and to learn, in their place, a new set of words which are often inaccurate, sometimes to the point of absurdity.

❐

5

Foreign Influence on Language

During first seven hundred years English was brought into contact with three other languages of the Celts, the Romans, and the Scandinavians. Here is the influence of these languages:

(1) **The Celtic Influence.** Nothing would seem more reasonable than to expect that the conquest of the Celtic population of Britain by the Teutons and the subsequent mixture of the two races should have resulted in a corresponding mixture of their languages; that consequently we should find in the Old English vocabulary numerous instances of words which the Teutons heard in the speech of the native population and adopted. For it is apparent that the Celts were by no means exterminated except in certain areas, and that in most of England large numbers of them were gradually absorbed by the new inhabitants. The Anglo-saxon chronicle reports that at Andredesceaster or Pevensey a deadly struggle occurred between the native population and the newcomers and that not a single Briton was left alive. The evidence of the place-names in this region lends support to the statement. But this was probably an exceptional case. In the east and southeast, where the Teutonic conquest was fully accomplished at a fairly early date, it is probable that there were fewer survivals of a Celtic population than elsewhere. Large numbers of the defeated fled to the west. Here it is apparent that a considerable Celtic-speaking population survived until fairly

late times. Some such situation is suggested by a whole cluster of Celtic place-names in the northeastern corner of Dorsetshire. It is altogether likely that many Celts were held as slaves by the conquerors and that many of the Teutons married Celtic women.

When we come, however, to seek the evidence for this contact in the English language investigation yields very meager results. Such evidence as there is survives chiefly in place-names. The kingdom of Kent, for example, owes its name to the Celtic word Canti or Cantion, the meaning of which is unknown, while the two ancient Northumbrian kingdoms of Deira and Bernicia derive their designations from Celtic tribal names. Other districts, especially in the west and southwest, preserve in their present-day names traces of their earlier Celtic designations. Devonshire contains in the first element the tribal name Dumnonii, Cornwall, means the 'Cornubian Welsh,' and Cumberland is the 'land of the Cymry or Britons'. Moreover, a number of important centers in the Roman period have names in which Celtic elements are embodied. The name London itself, although the origin of the word is somewhat uncertain, most likely goes back to a Celtic designation. The first syllable of Winchester, Salisbury, Exeter, Gloucester, Worcester, Lichfield, and a score of other names of cities is traceable to a Celtic source, while the earlier name of Canterbury (Durovernum) and the name York are originally Celtic. But it is in the names of rivers and hills and places in proximity to these natural features that the greatest number of Celtic names survive. Thus the Thames is a Celtic river name, and various Celtic words for river or water are preserved in the names Avon, Exe, Esk, Usk, Dover, and Wye. Celtic words meaning 'hill' are found in place-names like Barr (ef, Welsh bar,'top, summit'), Bredon (ef. Welsh bre, 'hill'), Bryn Mawr (ef. Welsh bryn 'hill' and mawr 'great'), Creech, Pendle (ef.

Welsh pen 'top'), and others. Certain other Celtic elements occur more or less frequently such as cumb (a deep valley) in names like Duncombe, Holcombe, Winchcombe; torr (high rock, peak) in Torr, Torcross, Torhill; pill (a tidal creek) in Pylle, Huntspill; and brocc (badger) in, Brockholes, Brockhall, etc. Besides these purely Celtic elements a few Latin words such as castra, fantana, fossa, portus, and vicus were used in naming places during the Roman occupation of the island and were passed on by the Celts to the English. It is natural that Celtic place-names should be commoner in the west than in the east and southeast, but the evidence of these names shows that the Celts impressed themselves upon the Teutonic consciousness at least to the extent of causing the newcomers to adopt many of the local names current in Celtic speech and to make them a permanent part of their vocabulary.

It does not appear that many of the Celtic words attained a very permanent place in the English language. Some soon died out and others acquired only local currency. The relation of the two races was not such as to bring about any considerable influence on English life or on English speech. The surviving Celts were a submerged race. Had they, like the Romans, possessed a superior culture, something valuable to give the Teutons, their influence might have been greater. But the Anglo-Saxon found little occasion to adopt Celtic modes of expression and the Celtic influence remains the least of the early influences which affected the English language.

(2) The Latin Influences on Old English. If the influence of Celtic upon Old English was slight, it was doubtless so because the relation of the Celt to the Teuton was that of a submerged race and, as suggested above, because the Celt was not in a position to make any notable contribution to Anglo-Saxon civilization. It was quite otherwise with the

second great influence exerted upon English–that of Latin–and the circumstances under which they met. Latin was not the language of a conquered people. It was the language of a race with a higher civilization, a race from which the Teutons had much to learn. Contact with that civilization-at first commercial and military, later religious and intellectual, extended over many centuries and was constantly renewed. It began long before the Anglo-Saxons came to England and continued throughout the Old English period. For several hundred years, while the Teutons who later became the English were still occupying their continental homes, they had various relations with the Romans through which they acquired a considerable number of Latin words. Later when they came to England they saw the evidences of the long Roman rule in the island and learned from the Celts a few additional Latin words which had been acquired by them. And a century and a half later still, when Roman missionaries reintroduced Christianity into the island, this new cultural influence resulted in a really extensive adoption of Latin elements into the language. There were thus three distinct occasions on which borrowing from Latin occurred before the end of the Old English period, and it will be of interest to consider more in detail the character and extent of these borrowings.

The greatest influence of Latin upon Old English was occasioned by the introduction of Christianity into Britain in 597. The new faith was far from new in the island, but this date marks the beginning of a systematic attempt on the part of Rome to convert the inhabitants and make England a Christian country. According to the well-known story reported by Bede as a tradition current in his day, the mission of St. Augustine was inspired by an experience of a man who later became Pope Gregory the Great.

The religion which the Anglo-Saxons shared with the other Teutonic tribes seems to have had but a slight hold on the people at the close of the sixth century; but their habits of mind, their ideals, and the action to which these gave rise were often in sharp contrast to the teachings of the New Testament. Teutonic philosophy exalted physical courage, independence even to haughtiness, loyalty to one's family or leader that left no wrong unavenged. Christianity preached meekness and humility, patience under suffering, and said that if a man struck you on one cheek you should turn the other. Clearly it was no small task which Augustine and his forty monks faced in trying to alter the age-old mental habits of such a people. They might even have expected difficulty in obtaining a respectful hearing. But they seem to have been men of exemplary lives, appealing personality, and devotion to purpose, and owed their ultimate success as much to what they were as to what they said.

(3) **Effects on English Civilization.** The introduction of Christianity meant the building of churches and the establishment of monasteries. Latin, the language of the services and of ecclesiastical learning, was once more heard in England. Schools were established in most of the monasteries and larger churches. Some of these became famous through the possession of great teachers and from them trained men went out to set up other schools at other centers. The beginning of this movement was in 669 when a Greek bishop, Theodore of Tarsus, was made archbishop of Canterbury. He was accompanied by Hadrian, an African by birth, a man described by Bede as "of the greatest skill in both the Greek and Latin tongues." They devoted considerable time and energy to teaching. A decade or two later Aldhelm carried on a similar work at Malmesbury. He was a remarkable classical scholar. He had an exceptional knowledge of Latin literature, and he wrote Latin verse with ease. In the north the school at York became in time almost as famous as that of Canterbury. The two

monasteries of Wearmouth and Jarrow were founded by Benedict Bishop, who, had been with Theodore and Hadrian at Canterbury, and who on five trips to Rome brought back a rich and valuable collection of books. His most famous pupil was the Venerable Bede, a monk at Jarrow. Bede assimilated all the learning of his time. He wrote on grammar and prosody, science and chronology, and composed numerous commentaries on the books of the Old and New Testament. His most famous work is the Ecclesiastical History of the English People (73), from which we have already had occasion to quote more than once and from which we derive a large part of our knowledge of the early history of England. Bede's spiritual grandchild was Alcuin of York; whose fame as a scholar was so great that in 782 Charlemagne called him to be the head of his Palace School. In the eighth century England held the intellectual leadership of Europe, and it owed this leadership to the church. In like manner vernacular literature and the arts received a new impetus. Workers in stone and glass were brought from the continent for the improvement of church building. Rich embroidery, the illumination of manuscripts, and church music occupied others. Moreover the monasteries cultivated their land by improved methods of agriculture and made numerous contributions to domestic economy. In short, the church as the carrier of roman civilization influenced the course of English life in many directions, and, as is to be expected, numerous traces of this influence are to be seen in the vocabulary of Old English.

(4) Earlier Influence of Christianity on the Vocabulary. From the introduction of Christianity in 597 to the close of the Old English period is a stretch of over five hundred years. During all this time Latin words must have been making their way gradually into the English language. It is likely that the first wave of religious feeling which resulted from the missionary zeal of the seventh century, and which is reflected in intense activity in church building and the establishing of monasteries during this century, was responsible also for the rapid importation of Latin words into the vocabulary. The many new conceptions which followed in the train of the new religion would naturally demand expression and would at times find the resources of the language inadequate. But it would be a mistake to think that the enrichment of the vocabulary which now took place occurred overnight. Some words came in almost immediately, others only at the end of our period. In fact it is fairly easy to divide the Latin borrowings of the Second Period into two groups, more or less equal in size but quite different in character. The one group represents words whose phonetic form shows that they were borrowed early and whose early adoption is attested also by the fact that they had found their way into literature by the time of Alfred. The other contains words of a more learned character first recorded in the tenth and eleventh century and owing their introduction clearly to the religious revival that accompanied the Benediction Reform. It will be well to consider them separately.

It is obvious that the most typical as well as the most numerous class of words introduced by the new religion would have to do with that religion and the details of its external organisation. Words are generally taken over by one language from another in answer to a definite need. They are adopted because they express ideas that are new or because they are so intimately associated with an object or a concept that acceptance of the thing involves acceptance also of the word. A few words relating to Christianity such as church and bishop were borrowed earlier. The Anglo-Saxons had doubtless plundered churches and come in contact with bishops before they came to England. But the great majority of words in Old English having to do with the church and its services, its physical fabric and its ministers, when not of native origin were borrowed at this time.

Since most of these words have survived in only slightly altered form in Modern English, the example may be given in their modern form. The list includes abbot, alms, alter, angel, anthem, ark, arian, candle, canon, chalice, cleric, cowl, deacon, disciple, epistle, hymn, litany, manna, martyr, mass, minister, noon, nun, offer, organ, pall, palm, pope, priest, provost, psalm, psalter, shrine, shrive, shrift, stole, sub-deacon, synod, relic, rule; temple, and tunic. Some of these were reintroduced later. But the church also exercised a profound influence on the domestic life of the people. This is seen in the adoption of many words, such as the names of articles of clothing and household use-cap, sock, silk, purple, chest, mat, sack, words denoting foods, such as beet, caul (cabbage), lentil (O.E. lent), millet (O.E. mil), pear, radish, doe, oyster (O.E. ostre), lobster, mussel, to which we may add the noun cook, names of trees, plants, and herbs (often cultivated for their medicinal properties), such as box, pine, aloes, balsam, fennel, hyssop, lily, mallow, marshmallow, myrrh, rue, savory and the general word plant.

SCANDINAVIAN INFLUENCE ON OLD ENGLISH

Next to Latin and Greek another important language that influenced English was the Scandinavian. The Scandinavians, or Vikings as they are sometimes called consisted of both Danes and Norweigians and they were alike in both blood and speech to the Angles, Saxons and Tutes who earlier had conquered the celts and settled in Britain. The Old English language, as we have seen, was almost a purely Teutonic language, its foreign elements were few and did not modify the essential character of the language. From the close of the Old English Period foreign elements began to enter the language and much have been contributed to the unparalleled richness and variety of the English vocabulary. The main additions to the language were from three sources the Scandinavian, the Latin and the French, Jasperson has aptly said, "that they were three super-structure, as it were, that came to be erected on the Anglo-Saxon foundation, each of them modifying the character of the language, and each preparing the ground for its successor."

The influence of the invaders became clearly visible in Middle English. It was because Northumbria, where they settled, did not produce any literature which has been preserved, and because it was in the middle English period that the areas they occupied produced literature which has come down to us. Only a few Scandinavian words entered English before the twelfth century. A great army of them appeared in English in the thirteenth century. After the middle English period Scandinavian borrowings have been only casual and occassional.

The Scandinavian element has been brought into the language by the Danes, who after several sporadic invasions ultimately settled down by the side of the Anglo-Saxons in the Northern and Midland districts of England. There had been no English literature before the Danish invasion, we should have found it impossible to say whether commonplace nouns like man, wife, father, life, sorrow, house etc. are of Scandinavian or of Anglo Saxon origin. The same things can be said about verbs like will, can, meet, brings, hear, smile, stand, sit, etc. The consequence do this close similarity between the two languages was that the Danes considered the Old English language as one with their own. So the amalgamation of the two races was easily facilitated by, besides the kingship, the effort of the English kings and the natural adaptability of the Scandinavians. It may be recalled here that, speaking of the fusion of the two races, Ottu Jesperson says, "they fought like brothers and afterwards settled down peacefully, like brothers, side by side." Besides English, Scandinavian has inherited a great deal of the common Sentonic vocabulary and a large number of corresponding words in the two languages were identical and therefore, the two languages borrowed from other spontaneously. Recent researches have shown that the contribution of Scandinavian had played a vital part in the growth of English. And some linguists claim that the process of infectional decay that led to the death of Anglo-Saxon and the birth of Middle English was started not by the Normans, but by the Danes.

The English and the Scandinavians were kindered races and the relations between them were cordial and peaceful. The daily social and commercial intercourse between the two races and the consequent interaction of the two languages left their marks on the English language. It may be recalled here that Old English especially Anglorian dialect, resembled the language of the Scandinavian invaders. Many of the commoner words in two languages were identical. This identity though facilitated the fusion of the two races makes it difficult to a modern student of English to decide whether a given word in Modern English is a native word or a borrowed one. To overcome this difficulty certain tests of borrowed words are devised.

The English vocabulary owns a great deal to the Scandinavians. There are about 900 Scandinavian words in English, besides thousands in the English dialects. The simplest of the tests to recognize the borrowed words is to distinguish between words having ks and sh sounds. Except in the combination of scr as in scream in Old English ks, sound became usually sh. Now most of the words with sh sounds as ship, shall, fish, shirt are native words, while the words with sk sound are scandinavian in origin. Example of scandinavian words resisted the change to sh sound. Similarly, where we get k, j and g it is an indication of Scandinavian origin, as for example deke (ditch), kid, give, get, egg, gild. In native word k became j, (g). We have two slightly differing forms for many words, one being many words, one being the original Anglo-Saxon form and the other the corresponding Scandinavian one. This is illustrated by the following pairs of words in each of which the first word is Anglo-Saxons and the second Scandinavian:

(1) Whole-hale (5) Shirt-skirt

(2) no-nay (6) shriek-screach

(3) rear-raise (7) edge-egg

(4) from-fro (8) less-lose.

Inspite of all these there are certain other Scandinavian words which are now confined to the dialects of Scotland as the North of England. The literary language has long given up these forms in favour of the Anglo-Saxons ones. In the following pairs of words the first word is used in the literary language while the second is confined to dialectal usage:

dew-dag	churn-kirn
neat-nowt	mouth-much
church-kirk	yarth-garth

In some instances, after the Anglo-Saxon and Scandinavian forms have continued side by side for a time the native form has succeeded in crowding out the foreign one. In each of the following pairs of words the first one being Anglo-Saxon has survived, while the second which is Scandinavian has been driven out of use:

(1) goat-gate	(4) naked-naken
(2) heathen-heythen	(5) star-sterne
(3) few-fa	(6) bench-bennk

About 1400 places mostly in the north and east of England, bear Scandinavian names. The place name suffixes-back, by thorp, date, toft, thwaite, etc. one Scandinavian. They occur in such place names as Whitby, Althorp, Nortoft, Dorby, Raugloft, Linthwaite. The invadors, who had a highly developed legal sense modified the legal ideas of the anglo-Saxon and the number of Scandinavians law-terms entered the English language. We may mention a few of those which have remained in common use in modern times-law, by-law, out law, thrall, crave etc. A host of Scandinavian law terms disappeared from the language, when the Norman conquerors took into their own hands the court of Justice and legal affairs, generally."It is interesting to note that, if there had been no Norman conquests to wipe out Scandinavian influence our legal vocabulary would probably have consisted largely of Scandinavian words, and not French words, as it does today." The most important of these judicial imports is the word law. It entered the English language in the 10th century in the form 'lagu' which was the exact Scandinavian form. There was an intimate fusion of the English and the Scandinavians and in every sphere of life they lived in close contact and on equal terms. Through the give and take of everyday life a large number of hemdy words of different varieties entered the English language.

Scandinavian gave a fresh base of life to some words which existed in Old English but had gone out of use. The preposition tell, for instance occurs in the hyme of Caedman, a poet of the 7th century but after Caedman it was not used until Middle English times except in Norse writings. Under the Scandinavian influence the word began to be very frequently used in the North from where it spread southward. As in Danish, it was used both in time and space. Some other words which had become obsolate but got a fresh base of life under the Scandinavian influence are dale, barn and bend.

The number of Scandinavian words that appear in Early Old English are very smaller, perhaps because the early relations of the invaders with the English were very hostile. Words connected with sea running and predatory habits belong to this period. They are banda (leaked ship), cnearr (small warship), dreug (warrior), orrest (battle), ran (robbery) and a few others.

Ever since Scandinavian had started setting down in peace and entered into the ordinary relations of life with the English, the Scandinavian words had been flowing into the English language. It should be remembered that the Scandinavian invasions were not like the coming of christianity learning the English into contact with different civilization and introducing them to many things physical as well as spiritual, that they had not known before. The civilization of the invaders was very much like that of the English themselves, if anything somewhat inferior to it. Consequently, the Scandinavian elements that entered the English language are such as would make the way into it through the give and take of every day life. There are sources of such common words of Danish origin in English. Examples one band, bank, birth, brill, crook, dirt, egg, fellow, gap, guen, link, source, scese, sister, snare, want, window. The number can be multiplied. Name of some parts of the body also came from the same origin as calf, leg, skill, skin. Among common and ordinary verbs of everyday use were to bait, bask, batter, call, crawl, drill, droop and soon.

Many Scandinavian words, unknown in standard English are heard everyday in dialects source of them live in proverbial lore inherited from old times. For example, "a bonny bride is soon *Iriskit* (is ready) and a short horse is soon *wispit* (bedecked)", "a toom (empty) purse makes blate (unenterprising and bashful)maerchant." The Scandinavians were possibly superior to the English is then manorial organisations, local government and law. Many legal terms imported into English from Scandinavian bear witness to this.

"Scandinavian words will crop up together with the Anglo-Saxon ones in any conversation on the thousand nothings of daily life or on the five or six things of paramount important to high and low alike."

Some Old English and Scandinavian words were identical in form or had developed from the same Teutonic root, but different in meaning. The word viking is a common Teutonic word which is found in Old English Texts long before the Scandinavians. It is historically significant that a certain number of grammatical terms, which usually are not borrowed by English from Scandinavian. These borrowings indicate how the Scandinavian and English languages were woven very intimately together as a result of the intimate fusion of the two nations speaking two languages. The natural conclusion of the two nations speaking two languages Scandinavian nature, the civilization of the Scandinavian settlers could not have been of a higher order than that of the English.

Generally pronouns, prepositions, adverb and forms of the verb to be are not transferred from one language to another. That some of these parts of speech were borrowed into English shows the intimate relation that existed between the two races and the two languages. In place of Old English hie, hiera, him, Scandinavian pronouns they, their, them were found in English. Similarly 'both' and 'same' are Scandinavian. The preposition 'till' in the sense of to and fro in the sense of from were commonly used at one time. Conjunction 'though' had the same Scandinavian origin. Many of us do not know that the modern word also was at one time Scandinavian as do. The adverbs aloft, aye (ever) and seemly were derived from Scandinavian source.

Not only the English vocabulary but also English grammar and syntax in a fundamental way affected the Scandinavian influence. "Scandinavian influence on English was almost entirely confined to vocabulary, and there is no marked influence on grammar and syntax."—C.L. Barber.

The above statement cannot be justified because most of the English and Scandinavian words were nearly the same but the ending were different. These endings aroused confusion and put obstacles in the way of mutual understanding. Both the English and the Scandinavians who cared more to make themselves understood to each than to observe the niceties of grammar, tended to discard their inflexional endings and relyer for mutual understanding on vocabulary and syntactical devices, such as the order of the word and the use of preposition. Thus the Scandinavian influence started the process of inflexional decay and the simplification of English grammar.

There are many striking resemblances between the syntax of the two language. It seems probably that the intimate fusion of the two language influenced syntactical relations. Relative clauses without any relative pronoun are rarely found in Old English. Owing to the Scandinavian influences such clauses became common from the Middle English period. The rules for the use of shall and will in Middle English correspond with those in Scandinavian.

In Old English if an auxiliary was used to express futurity it was 'sceal', wile was very rarely used. The most normal way to indicate futurity in Old English was to use the present tense. The new future with 'shall' and 'will' came in vogue from the Middle English period under the Scandinavian rule. In Old English the genetive case was often placed after its noun. But under the Scandinavian influence from the Middle English period the genetive acquired its position before its noun.

It can be noticed easily that many of the borrowed words from Scandinavians, except the forms words, could have supplied no real needs in the English vocabulary. The English language of that time had words corresponding to the borrowed words. The Scandinavian and the English words were possibly in use side by side for a long time. It was perhaps the matter of chance that one or the other had survived, where an idea was expressed by different words in the two languages, it was often the English word that survived. In all other cases the Scandinavian word ousted the native word. For example, the Old English word eye (aye) was replaced by the Scandinavian word awe, after the two had remained for long in use side by side. The same thing happened with the two words for egg, ey (Old English word) and egg Scandinavian. Similarly in words like sister, boon, loan, weak the Scandinavian words survived then Old English counterparts and lived on to the present day. Thus, the verb take (Scandinavian) replaced the English word heman. The Scandinavian sky replace the English welk in (only used in poetry now a days) and window replaced the Old English egg thyrl (eye-bole).

Sometimes both the Scandinavian and the English words lived on to today, with some differences in meaning and use. Besides enriching the English vocabulary, Scandinavian influenced the inflexioned endings of English and hastened the withering away of the cumbersome inflexions. To sum up, we can say that the Scandinavian influence was on the whole a salutory one.

In the Scandinavian attacks upon England three well-marked stages can be distinguished. The first is the period of early raids, beginning according to the Anglo-Saxon Chronicle in 787 and continuing with some intermissions until about 850. The raids of this period were simply plundering attacks upon towns and monasteries near the coast. Sacred vessels of gold and silver, jeweled shrines, costly robes, valuables of all kinds, and slaves were carried off. Noteworthy instances are the sacking of Lindisfarne and Jarrow in 793 and 794. But with the plundering of these two famous monasteries the attacks apparently ceased for forty years, until renewed in 834 along the southern coast and in East Anglia. These early raids were apparently the work of small isolated bands.

The second stage is the work of large armies and is marked by widespread plundering in all parts of the country and by extensive settlements. This new development was inaugurated by the arrival in 850 of a Danish fleet of 350 ships. Their pirate crews entered in the isle of Thanet and the following spring captured Canterbury and London and ravaged the surrounding country. Although finally defeated by a West Saxon army they soon renewed their attacks. In 866 a large Danish army plundered East Anglian and in 867 captured York. In 869 the East Anglian king, Edmund, met a cruel death in resisting the invaders. The incident made a deep impression on all England, and the memory of his martyrdom was vividly preserved in English tradition for nearly two centuries. The eastern part of England was now largely in the hands of the Danes, and they began turning their attention to Wessex. The attack upon Wessex began shortly before the accession of King Alfred (871-99). Even the greatness of this greatest of English kings threatened to prove insufficient to withstand the repeated thrusts of the Northmen. After seven years of resistance, in which temporary victories were invariably succeeded by fresh defeats, Alfred was forced to take refuge with a small band of personal followers in the marshes of Somerset. But in this darkest hour for the fortunes of the English Alfred's courage and persistence triumphed. With a fresh levy of men from Somerset, Wiltshire, and Hampshire, he suddenly attacked the Danish army under Guthrum to Ethandun (now Edington, in Wiltshire). The result was an overwhelming victory for the English and a capitulation by the Danes (878).

The Treaty of Wedmore (near Glastonbury), which was signed by Alfred and Guthrum the same year, marks the culmination of the second stage in the Danish invasions. Wessex was saved. The Danes withdrew from Alfred's territory. But they were not compelled to leave England. The treaty merely defined the line, running roughly from Chester to London, to the east of which the foreigners were henceforth to remain. This territory was to be subject to Danish law and is hence known as the Danelaw. In addition the Danes agreed to accept Christianity, and Guthrum was baptized. This last provision was important. It might secure the better observance of the treaty, and, what was more important, it would help to pave the way for the ultimate fusion of the two groups.

The third stage of the Scandinavian incursions covers the period of political adjustment and assimilation from 878 to 1042. The Treaty of Wedmore did not put an end to Alfred's troubles. Guthrum was inclined to break faith and there were fresh invasions from outside. But the situation slowly began to clear. Under Alfred's son Edward the Elder (900-25) and grandson Athelstan (925-39) the English began a series of counterattacks that put the Danes on the defensive. One of the brilliant victories of the English in this period was Athelstan's triumph in 937 in the battle of Brunanburh, in Northumbria, over a combined force of Danes and Scots, a victory celebrated in one of the finest of Old English poems. By the middle of the century a large part of eastern England, though still strongly Danish in blood and custom, was once more under English rule.

Toward the end of the century, however, when England seemed at last on the point of solving its Danish problem, a new and formidable succession of invasions began. In 991 a fleet of ninety-three ships under Olaf Tryggvason and his associates suddenly entered the Thames. They were met by Byrhtnoth, the valiant earl of the East Saxons, in a battle celebrated in another famous Old English war poem, The Battle of Maldon. Here the English, heroic in defeat, lost their leader, and soon the invaders were being bribed by large sums to refrain from plunder. The invasions now began to assume an official character. In 994 Olaf, who shortly became king of Norway, was joined by Svein, king of Denmark, in a new attack on London. The sums necessary to buy off the enemy became greater and greater, rising in 1012 to the amazing figure of £48,000. In each case the truce thus bought was temporary, and Danish forces were soon again marching over England, murdering and pillaging. Finally Svein determined to make himself king of the country. In 1014, supported by his son Cnut, he crowned a series of victories in different parts of England by driving Ethelred, the English king, into exile and seizing the throne. Upon his sudden death the same year his son succeeded him. Three years of fighting established Cnut's claims to the throne, and for the next twenty-five years England was ruled by Danish kings.

Scandinavion Influence Outside the Standard Speech

We should miss the full significance of the Scandinavian influence if we failed to recognize the extent to which it is found outside the standard speech. Our older literature and the modern dialects are full of words which are not now in ordinary use. The ballades offer many examples. But it is sufficiently evident that there is much Scandinavian material in the dialects besides what has found its way into the standard speech.

Effect on Grammar and Syntax

That the Scandinavian influence not only affected the vocabulary but extended to matters of grammar and syntax as well as less capable of exact demonstration but is hardly to be doubted. Inflections are seldom transferred from one language to another. A certain number of inflectional elements peculiar to the Northumbrian dialect have been attributed to Scandinavian influence, among others the –s of the third person singular, present indicative, of verbs and the participal ending –and corresponding to –end and –ind in the Midlands and South, and now replaced by –ing. The words scant, want, athwart preserve in the final t the neuter adjective ending of Old Norse. But this is of no great significance. It is much more important to recognize that in many words the English and Scandinavian languages differed chiefly in their inflectional elements. The body of the word was so nearly the same in the two languages that only the endings would put obstacles in the way of mutual understanding. In the mixed population which existed in the Danelaw these endings must have led to much confusion, tending gradually to become obscured and finally lost. It seems but natural that the tendency toward the loss of inflections, which was characteristic of the English language in the north even in Old English times, was strengthened and accelerated by the conditions that prevailed in the Danelaw, and that some credit must be given the Danes for a development which, spreading to other parts and being carried much further, resulted after the Norman Conquest in so happily simplifying English grammar. Likewise, the way words are put together in phrases and clauses–what we call syntax–is something in which languages less often influence each other than in matters of vocabulary. The probability of such influence naturally varies with the degree of intimacy that exists between the speakers of two languages. In those parts of Pennsylvania–the 'Pennsylvania Dutch' districts–where German and English have mingled in a jargon peculiar to itself, German terms of expression are frequently found in the English spoken there. It is quite likely that the English spoken in the districts where there were large numbers of Danes acquired certain Danish habits of expression. A modern Dane like Jespersen notes that the omission of the relative pronoun in relative clauses (Rare in Old English) and the retention or omission of the conjunction that are in conformity with Danish usage; that the rules for the use of shall and will in Middle English are much the same as in Scandinavian; and that some apparently illogical uses of these auxiliaries in Shakespeare (*e.g.*, 'besides it should appear' in the Merchant of Venice, III. ii. 289) do not seem strange to a Dane, who would employ the same verb. Logeman notes the tendency, common to both languages, to put a strong stress at times on the preposition, and the occurrence of locutions such as 'he has some one to work for', which are not shared by the other Teutonic languages. It is possible, of course, that similarities such as these are merely coincidences, that the Scandinavian languages and English happened to develop in these respects along similar lines. But there is nothing improbable in the assumption that certain Scandinavian turns of phrase and certain particular usages should have found their way into the idiom of people in no small part Danish in descent and living in intimate contact with the speakers of a Scandinavian tongue.

FEATURES OF MIDDLE ENGLISH GRAMMER

The Middle English period (1150-1500) was marked by momentous changes in the English language, changes more extensive and fundamental than those that have taken place at any time before or since. Some of them were the result of the Norman Conquest and the conditions which followed in the wake of that event. Others were a continuation of tendencies that had begun to manifest themselves in Old English. These would have gone on even without the Conquest, but took place more rapidly because the Norman invasion removed from English those conservative influences that are always felt when a language is extensively used in books and is spoken by an influential educated class. The changes of this period affected English in both its grammar and its vocabulary. They were so extensive in each department that it is difficult to say which group is the more significant. Those in the grammar reduced English from a highly inflected language to an extremely analytic one. Those in the vocabulary involved the loss of a large part of the Old English word-stock and the addition of thousands of words from French and Latin. At the beginning of the period English is a language which must be learned like a foreign tongue; at the end it is Modern English.

Decay of Inflectional Endings

The changes in English grammar may be described as a general reduction of inflections. Endings of the noun and adjective marking distinctions of number and case and often of gender were so altered in pronunciation as to lose their distinctive form and hence their usefulness. To some extent the same thing is true of the verb. This leveling of inflectional endings was due partly to phonetic changes, partly to the operation of analogy. The phonetic changes were simple but far-reaching. The earliest seems to have been the change of final-m to-n wherever it occurred, *i.e.*, in the dative plural of nouns and adjectives and in the dative singular (masculine and neuter) of adjectives when inflected according to the strong declension. Thus müðum (to the mouths) > müðum, gödum > gödun. This –n along with the –n of the other inflectional endings was then dropped. At the same time, the vowels a, o, u, e in inflectional endings were obscured to a sound, the so-called 'indeterminate vowel', which came to be written *e* (less often i, y, u, depending on place and date). As a result, a number of originally distinct endings such as –a, –u, –e, –an, –um were reduced generally to a uniform –e, and such grammatical distinctions as they formerly expressed were no longer conveyed. Traces of these changes have been found in Old English manuscripts as early as the tenth century. By the end of the twelfth century they seem to have been generally carried out. The leveling is somewhat obscured in the written language by the tendency of scribes to preserve the traditional spelling, and in some places the final n was retained even in the spoken language, especially as a sign of the plural. The effect of these changes on the inflection of the noun and the adjective, and the further simplification that was brought about by the operation of analogy may be readily shown.

The Noun. A glance at the few examples of common noun declensions in Old English given will show how seriously the inflectional endings were disturbed. For example, in the first declension the forms müð, müðes, müðe, müð in the singular, and müðas, müða, müðum, müðas in the plural were reduced to three: müð, müðes, and müðe. In such words the –e which was organic in the dative singular and the genitive and dative plural (*i.e.*, stood for an ending in the Old English paradigm) was extended by analogy to the nominative and accusative singular, so that forms like stöne, müðe appear, and the only distinctive termination is the –s of the possessive singular and of the nominative and accusative plural. Since these two cases of the plural were those most frequently used, the –s came to be thought of as the sign of the plural and was extended to all plural forms. We get thus an inflection of the noun identical with that which we have today. Other declensions suffered even more, so that in many words (giefu, sunu, etc.) the distinctions of case and even of number were completely obliterated.

In early Middle English only two methods of indicating the plural remained fairly distinctive: the –s or –es from the strong declension and the –en (as in oxen) from the weak. And for a time, at least in southern England, it would have been difficult to predict that the –s would become the almost universal sign of the plural that it has become. Until the thirteenth century in the south the –en plural enjoyed great favour, being often added to nouns which had not belonged to the weak declension in Old English. But in the rest of England the –s plural (and genitive singular) of the old first declension (masculine) was apparently felt to be so distinctive that it spread rapidly. Its extension took place most quickly in the north. Even in Old English many nouns originally of other declensions had gone over to this declension in the Northumbrian dialect. By 1200 –s was the standard plural ending in the north and north Midland areas; other forms were exceptional. Fifty years later it had conquered the rest of the Midlands, and in the course of the fourteenth century it had definitely been accepted all over England as the normal sign of the plural in English nouns. Its spread may have been helped by the early extension of –s throughout the plural in Anglo-Norman, but in general it may be considered as an example of the survival of the fittest in language.

The Adjective. In the adjective the leveling of forms had even greater consequences. Partly as a result of the sound-changes already described, partly through the extensive working of analogy, the form of the nominative singular was early extended to all cases of the singular, and that of the nominative plural to all cases of the plural, both in the strong and the weak declensions. The result was that in the weak declension there was no longer any distinction between the singular and the plural: both ended in –e (blinda > blinde and blindan > blinde). This was also true of those adjectives under the strong declension whose singular ended in –e.

By about 1250 the strong declension had distinctive forms for the singular and plural only in certain monosyllabic adjectives which ended in a consonant in Old English (sing. glad. plur. glade). Under the circumstances the only ending which remained to the adjective was often without distinctive grammatical meaning and its use was not governed by any strong sense of adjectival inflection. When in the fourteenth century final e largely ceased to be pronounced it became a mere feature of spelling. Except for a few archaic survivals, such as Chaucer's *oure aller cok*, the adjective had become an uninflected word by the close of the Middle English period.

The Pronoun. The decay of inflections which brought about such a simplification of the noun and the adjective as has just been described made it necessary to depend less upon formal indications of gender, case, and (in adjectives) number, and to rely more upon juxtaposition, word order, and the use of prepositions to make clear the relation of words in a sentence. This is apparent from the corresponding decay of pronominal inflections, where the simplification of forms was due in only a slight measure to the weakening of final syllables that played so large a part in the reduction of endings in the noun and the adjective. The loss was greatest in the demonstratives. All the other forms indicative of different gender, number, and case disappeared in most dialects early in the Middle English period. The same may be said of the demonstrative *pës, pëos, pis* (this). Everywhere but in the south the neuter form *pis* came to be used early in Middle English for all genders and cases of the singular, while the forms of the nominative plural were similarly extended to all cases of the plural, appearing in Modern English as *those* and *these*.

In the personal pronoun the losses were not so great. Here there was greater need for separate forms for the different genders and cases, and accordingly most of the distinctions that existed in Old English were retained. However the forms of the dative and accusative cases were early combined, generally under that of the dative (him, her, (th)em).In the neuter the form of the accusative (h) it became the general objective case, partly because it was like the nominative, and partly because the dative him would have been subject to confusion with the corresponding case of the masculine. One other general simplification is to be noted: the loss of the dual number. Language can get along without such nice distinctions as are expressed by separate pronouns for two persons and more than two. Accordingly the forms wit, zit, and their oblique cases did not survive beyond the thirteenth century.

It will be observed that the pronoun *she* had the form *hëo* in Old English. The modern form could have developed from the Old English *hëo,* but it is believed by some that it is due in part at least to the influence of the demonstrative *sëo.* A similar influence of the demonstrative is perhaps to be seen in the forms of the third person plural, they, their, them, but here the modern developments were undoubtedly due mainly to Scandinavian influence. The normal development of the Old English pronouns would have been *hi (he), here, hem,* and these are very common. In the districts, however, where Scandinavian influence was strong, the nominative *hi* began early to be replaced by the Scandinavian form *pei* (O.N. *peir*), and somewhat later a similar replacement occurred in the other cases, *their* and them. The new forms were adopted more slowly farther south, and the usual inflection in Chaucer is *thei, here, hem.* But by the end of the Middle English period the forms *they, their, them,* may be regarded as the normal English plurals.

The Verb. Apart from some leveling of inflections and the weakening of endings in accordance with the general tendency, the principal changes in the verb during the Middle English period were the serious losses suffered by the strong conjugation. This conjugation, although including some of the most important verbs in the language, was relatively small as compared with the large and steadily growing body of weak verbs. While an occasional verb developed a strong past tense or past participle by analogy with similar strong verbs, new verbs formed from nouns and adjectives or borrowed from other languages were regularly conjugated as weak. Thus the minority position of the strong conjugation was becoming constantly more appreciable. After the Norman Conquest the loss of native words further depleted the ranks of the strong verbs. Those that survived were exposed to the influence of the majority, and many have changed over in the course of time to the weak inflection.

Losses among the Strong Verbs–Nearly a third of the strong verbs in Old English seem to have died out early in the Middle English period. In any case about ninety of them have left no traces in written records after 1150. Some of them may have been current for a time in the spoken language, but except where an occasional verb survives in a modern dialect they are not recorded. Some were rare in Old English and others were in competition with weak verbs of similar derivation and meaning which superseded them. In addition to verbs that are not found at all after the Old English period there are about a dozen more that appear only in Layamon or in certain twelfth century texts based directly on the homilies of Aelfric and other Old English works. In other words, more than a hundred of the Old English strong verbs were lost at the beginning of the Middle English period.

But this was not all. The loss continued in subsequent periods. Some thirty more became obsolete in the course of Middle English, and an equal number, which were still in use in the sixteenth and seventeenth centuries, finally died out except in the dialects, often after they had passed over to the weak conjugation or had developed weak forms alongside the strong. Today more than half of the Old English strong verbs have disappeared completely from the standard language.

Strong Verbs Which Became Weak. The principle of analogy–the tendency of language to follow certain patterns and adapt a less common form to a more familiar one–is well exemplified in the further history of the strong verbs. The weak conjugation offered a fairly consistent pattern for the past tense and the past participle, whereas there was much variety in the different classes of the strong verb. We say sing–sang–sung, but drive–drove– driven, fall–fell–fallen, etc. At a time when English was the language chiefly of the lower classes and largely removed from the restraining influences of education and a literary standard, it was natural that many speakers should wrongly apply the pattern of weak verbs to some which should have been strong. The tendency was not unknown even in Old English. Thus *rǣdan* (to advise) and *sceððan* (an injure) had already become weak in Old English, while other verbs show occasional weak forms. In the thirteenth century the trend becomes clear in the written literature. Such verbs as burn, brew, bow, climb, flee, flow, help, mourn, row, step, walk, weep were then undergoing change. By the fourteenth century the movement was at its height. No less than thirty-two verbs in addition to those already mentioned now show weak forms. After this there are fewer changes. The impulse seems to have been checked, possibly by the steady rise of English in the social scale and later by the stabilizing effect of printing. At all events the fifteenth century shows only about a dozen new weak formations.

In none of the many verbs which have thus become weak was the change from the strong conjugation a sudden one. Strong forms continued to be used while the weak ones were growing up, and in many cases they continued in use long after the weak inflection had become well established. Thus *oke* as the past tense of *ache* was still written throughout the fifteenth century although the weak form *ached* had been current for a hundred years. In the same way we find *stope* beside *stepped*, *rewe* beside *rowed*, *clew* beside *clawed*. In a good many cases the strong forms remained in the language well into modern times. Climb, which was conjugated as a weak verb as early as the thirteenth century, still has an alternative past tense clomb not only in Chaucer and Spenser but in Dryden, and the strong past tense *crope* was more common than crept down to Shakespeare's day. *Low* for *laughed*, *shove* for *shaved*, *yold* for *yielded*, etc., were still used in the sixteenth century although these verbs were already passing over to the weak conjugation two centuries before. While the weak forms commonly worn out, this was not always the case. Many strong verbs also had weak forms (*blowed* for *blew*, *knowed* for *knew*, *teared* for *tore*) which did not survive in the standard speech, while in other cases both forms have continued in use *(cleft–clove, crowed–crew, heaved–hove, sheared–shore, shrived–shrove)*.

Survival of Strong Participles. For some reason the past participle of strong verbs seems to have been more tenacious than the past tense. In a number of verbs weak participles are later on appearing and the strong form often continued in use after the verb had definitely become weak. In the verb *beat* the participle beaten has remained the standard form, while in a number of other verbs the strong participle (*cloven, graven, hewn, laden, molten, mown, (mis) shapen, shaven, sodden, swollen*) are still used, especially as adjectives.

OCCURRED IN PRONUNCIATION OF ENGLISH

In considering the changes in pronunciation which English words underwent in passing from Old to Middle English we may say that qualitatively they were slight, at least in comparison with those that occurred later. Changes in the consonants were rather insignificant, as they have always been in English. Some voiced consonants became voiceless, and vice versa, and consonants were occasionally lost. Thus w before a following o was lost when it followed another consonant: sö (O.E. swä), hö (who, O.E. hwä). Sc became sh (O.E. Scip>M.E. ship or schip), or had already done so in Old English. But we do not expect much change in the consonantal framework of words. Nor was there much alteration in the quality of vowels in accented syllables. Most of the short vowels, unless lengthened, passed over into Middle English unaltered. But short æ became a, and y [Y] was unrounded to i in most districts, either early or eventually (O.E. cræft > M.E. craft; brycg > brigge). The other short vowels, ä, ë, ï, ö, ü, remained (O.E. catte > cat, bedd > bed, scip > schip, folc > folk, full > ful). Among the long vowels the most important change was that of ä to Q̈ mentioned in the preceding paragraph (O.E. bän >bQ̈n, bone; bät > bQ̈t, boat). the long ÿ developed in the same way as short ÿ (O.E. brÿd > bride, bride; fÿr > fir, fire). The long ǣ, so characteristic a feature of old English spelling, represented two sounds. In some words it stood for an ä in West Germanic. This sound appears as a close ë outside the West Saxon area and remains ë in Middle English (Non-W.S. dëd > dëd, deed; slëpan > slëpen, sleep). In many words O.E. ǣ was a sound resulting from the i-umlaut of ä[-1]. This was a more open vowel and appears as ë in Middle English (O.E. clǣne > clëne, clean; dǣlan > dëlan > deal). These two sounds have now become identical (of. deed and clean). The other long vowels of Old English preserved their original quality in Middle English (mëd > mëde, meed ; fif > fif, five; böc > bök, book, hüs > hüs, house, often written hous through the influence of Anglo-Norman scribes). The Old English diphthongs were all simplified, and all diphthongs in Middle English are new formations resulting chiefly from the combination of a simple vowel with a following consonant (3, w) which vocalized.

If the quality of Old English vowels did not change much in passing into Middle English, their quantity or length was subject to considerable alteration. For example, Old English long vowels were shortened late in the Old English period or early in Middle English when followed by a double consonant or by most combinations of consonants (grëtter, comparative of grët < O.E. grëat; äsken < O.E. äxian, ask). Conversely, short vowels in open syllables were lengthened in Middle English (O.E. bäcan > M.E. bäken, bake; ëtan > ëten, eat). Such changes in length are little noticeable in the spelling, but they are of great importance since they determine the course which these vowels pursue in their subsequent development.

From Middle English to Modern

When we come to the vowel changes in Modern English we see the importance of the factors that determined the length of vowels in Middle English. All Middle English long vowels underwent extensive alteration in passing into Modern English, but the short vowels, in accented syllables, remained comparatively stable. If we compare Chaucer's pronunciation of the short vowels with ours, we note only two changes of importance, those of a and u. By Shakespeare's day (*i.e.* at the close of the sixteenth century) Chaucer's a had become an [æ] in pronunciation (cat, thank, flax). In some cases this M.E. a represented an O.E. æ (at, apple, back) and the new pronunciation was therefore a return to approximately the form which the word had in Old English. It is the usual pronunciation in American and a considerable part of southern England today. The change which the u underwent was what is known as unrounding. In Chaucer's pronunciation this vowel was like the u in full. By the sixteenth century it seems to have become in most words the sound which we have in but (*e.g.*, cut, sun; love, with the Anglo-Norman spelling of o for u). So far as the short vowels are concerned it is clear that a person today would have tittle difficulty in understanding the English of any period of the language.

GRAMMATICAL FEATURES OF ENGLISH IN RENAISSANCE PERIOD

English grammar in the sixteenth and early seventeenth century is marked more by the survival of certain forms and usages that have since disappeared than by any fundamental developments. The great changes which reduced the inflections of Old English to their modern proportions had already taken place. In the few parts of speech which retain some of their original inflections of the reader of Shakespeare or the Authorized Version is conscious of minor differences of form, and in the framing of sentences he may note differences of syntax and idiom which, while they attract attention, are not sufficient to interfere seriously with understanding. The more important of these differences we may pass briefly in review:

The Noun. The only inflections retained in the noun were, those marking the plural and the possessive singular. In the former the s–plural had become so generalized that except for a few nouns like sheep and swine with unchanged plurals and a few others like mice and feet with mutated vowels we are scarcely conscious of any other forms. In the sixteenth century, however, there are certain survivals of the old weak plural in –n. Most of these had given way before the usual s–forms; fon (foes), kneen (knees), fleen (fleas). But beside the more modern forms Shakespeare occasionally has eyen (eyes), shoon (shoes), and kine, while the plural hosen is occasionally found in other writers. Today, except for the poetical kine and mixed plurals like children and brethren, the only plural of this type in general use is oxen.

An interesting peculiarity of this period, and indeed later, is the his-genitive. In Middle English the –es of the genitive, being unaccented, was frequently written and pronounced –is, –ys. The ending was thus often identical with the pronoun his, which commonly lost its h when unstressed. Thus there was no difference in pronounciation between stonis and ston is (his), and as early as the thirteenth century the ending was sometimes written separately as though the possessive case were a contraction of a noun and the pronoun his. This notion was long prevalent and Shakespeare writes 'Gainst the count his galleys I did some service and In characters as red as Mars his heart. Until well into the eighteenth century people were troubled by the illogical consequences of this usage; Dr. Johnson points out that one can hardly believe that the possessive ending is a contraction of his in such expressions as a woman's beauty or a virgin's delicacy. He, himself, seems to have been aware that its true source was the Old English genitive, but the error has left its trace in the apostrophe which we still retain as a graphic convenience to mark the possessive.

One other construction affecting the noun becomes established during this period, the group possessive: the Duke of Gloucester's niece, the King of England's nose, somebody else's hat. The construction is perhaps illogical, since even a king may be considered to have some rights in his nose, and the earlier construction was the Duke's niece of Gloucester, etc. But the expressions Duke of Gloucester, King of England, and the like, occurred so commonly as a unit that in the fifteenth century we begin to get the sign of the possessive added to the group. Instances are not common before the sixteenth century, and the construction may be thought of properly as belonging to the modern period. Nowadays we may say the writer of the book's ambition or the chief actor in the play's illness.

The Adjective. Since the adjective had already lost all its endings, so that it no longer expressed distinctions of gender, number, and case, the chief interest of this part of speech in the modern period is in the forms of the comparative and superlative degrees. In the sixteenth century these were not always precisely those now in use. For example, comparatives such as lenger, strenger remind us that forms like our elder were once more common in the language. The two methods commonly used to form the comparative and superlative, by the endings –er, –est and with the adverbs more and most, had been customary since Old English times. But there was more variation in their use. Shakespearian comparisons like honester, violentest are now replaced by the analytical forms. A double comparative or superlative is also fairly frequent in the work of Shakespeare and his contemporaries: more larger, most boldest, or Mark Antony's This was the most unkindest cut of all. The chief development affecting the adjective in modern times has been the gradual settling down of usage so that monosyllables take –er and –est while most adjective of two or more syllables (especially those with suffixes like those in frugal, learned, careful, poetic, active, famous) take more and most.

The Pronoun. The sixteenth century saw the establishment of the personal pronoun in the form which it has had ever since. In attaining this result three changes were involved: the disuse of thou, thy, thee; the substitution of you for ye as a nominative case; and the introduction of its as the possessive of it.

(1) In the earliest period of English the distinction between thou and ye was simple one of number; thou was the singular and ye the plural form for the second person pronoun. In time, however, a quite different distinction grew up. In the thirteenth century the singular forms (thou, thy, thee) were used among familiars and in addressing children or persons of inferior rank, while the plural forms (ye, your, you) began to be used as a mark of respect in addressing a superior. In England the practice seems to have been suggested by French usage in court circles, but it finds a parallel in many other modern languages. In any case, the usage

spread as a general concession to courtesy until ye, your, and you became the usual pronoun of direct address irrespective of rank or intimacy. By the sixteenth century the singular forms had all but disappeared from polite speech and are in ordinary use today only among the Quakers.

(2) Originally a clear distinction was made between the nominative ye and the objective you. But since both forms are so frequently unstressed, they were often pronounced alike. A tendency to confuse the nominative and the accusative forms can be observed fairly early, and in the fourteenth century you began to be used as a nominative. By a similar substitution ye appears in the following century for the objective case, and from this time on the two forms seem to have been used pretty indiscriminately until ye finally disappeared. It is true that in the early part of the sixteenth century some men (Lord Berners, for example) were careful to distinguish the two forms, and in the Authorized Version of the Bible (1611) they are often nicely differentiated: No doubt but ye are the people, and wisdom shall die with you (Job). On the other hand Ascham and Sir Thomas Elyot appear to make no distinction in the nominative, while Shakespeare says A southwest wind blow on ye and blister you all over! In The Two Gentlemen of Verona occurs the line Stand, sirs, and throw us that you have about ye, where the two pronouns represent the exact reverse of their historical use. Although in the latter instance, ye may owe something to its unemphatic position, as in similar cases it does in Milton, it is evident that there was very little feeling any more for the different functions of the two words, and in the course of the seventeenth century you becomes of the regular form for both cases.

(3) In some ways the most interesting development in the pronoun at this time was the formation of a new possessive neuter, its. As we have seen above, the neuter pronoun in Old English was declined hit, his, him, hit, which by the merging of the dative and accusative under hit in Middle English became hit, his, hit. In unstressed positions hit weakened to it, and at the beginning of the modern period it was the usual form for the subject and object. His, however, remained the proper form of the possessive. Although it was thus identical with the possessive case of he its occurrence where we should now use its is very common in written English down to the middle of the seventeenth century.

If grammatical gender had survived in English the continued use of his when referring to neuter nouns would probably never have seemed strange. But when, with the substitution of natural gender, meaning came to be the determining factor in the gender of nouns, and all lifeless objects were thought of as neuter, the situation was somewhat different. The personal pronouns of the third person singular, he, she, it, had a distinctive form for each gender in the nominative and objective cases, and a need seems to have been felt for some distinctive form in the possessive case as well. Various substitutes were tried, clearly indicating a desire, conscious or unconscious, to avoid the use of his in the neuter.

The Verb. Even the casual reader of Elizabethan English is aware of certain differences of usage in the verb which distinguish this part of speech from its form in later times. These differences are sometimes so slight as to give only a mildly unfamiliar tinge to the construction. When Lennox asks in Macbeth, Goes the King hence today? we have merely an instance of the more common interrogative form without an auxiliary, where we should say Does the king go? or Is the king leaving today? A very noticeable difference is the scarcity of progressive forms. Polonius asks, What do you read, my Lord?–*i.e.*, What are you reading? The large increase in the use of the progressive froms is one of the important developments of later times . Likewise the compound participle, having spoken thus, having decided to make the attempt, etc., is conspicuous by its infrequency. There are only three instances in Shakespeare and less than three score in the Bible. The constructions arose in the sixteenth century. On the other hand, impersonal uses of the verb were much more common than they are today. In addition to such features of Elizabethan verbal usage, there are certain differences in inflection which are more noticeable, particularly the ending of the third person singular of the present indicative, an occasional –s in the third person plural, and many forms of the past tense and past participle, especially of strong verbs.

The regular ending of the third person singular in the whole south and southeastern part of England–that is, the district most influential in the formation of the standard speech– was –eth all through the Middle English period. It is universal in Chaucer: *telleth, giveth, saith, doth,* etc. In the fifteenth century forms with –s occasionally appear. These are difficult to account for, since it is not easy to see how the Northern dialect, where they were normal, could have exerted so important an influence upon the language of London and the south. But in the course of the sixteenth century their number increases, especially in writings which seem to reflect the colloquial usage. By the end of this century forms like tells, gives, says predominate, though in some words, such as doth and hath, the older usage may have been the commoner. One was free to use either.

Usage and Idiom. Language is not merely a matter of words and inflections. We should neglect a very essential element if we failed to take account of the many conventional features–matters of idiom and usage–that often defy explanation or logical classification but are nevertheless characteristic of the language at a given time, and like other conventions, subject to change. Such a matter as the omission of the article where we customarily put it in is an illustration in point. Shakespeare says creeping like snail, with as big heart as thou, in number of our friends, within this mile and half, thy beauty's form in table of my heart, where modern idiom requires an article in all these cases. On the other hand, where we say at lenght, at last. Shakespeare says at the length, at the last. Again, usage permitted a different placing of the negative–before the verb–as in such expressions as I not doubt, it not appears to me, she not denies it. For a long time English permitted the use of a double negative. We have now discarded it through a false application of mathematical logic to language; but in Elizabethan times it was felt merely as a stronger negative, as indeed it is today in the instinct of the uneducated. So Shakespeare could say Thou hast spoken no word all this while–nor understood none neither; First he denied you had in him no right; My father hath no child but I, nor none is like to have; I know not, nor I greatly care not; Nor this is not my nose neither; Nor never none shall mistress be of it, save I alone. It is a pity we have lost so useful an intensive.

Perhaps nothing illustrates so richly the idiomatic changes in a language from one age to another as the uses of prepositions. When Shakespeare says I'll rent the fairest house in it after three-pence a bay we should say at; in Our fears in Banquo stick deep, we should say about. The single preposition of shows how many changes in common idioms have come about since 1600; One that I brought up of (from) a puppy; he came of (on) an errand to me; 'Tis pity of (about) him; your name. ... I know not, nor by what wonder you do hit of (upon) mine; And not be seen to wink of (during) all the day; it was well done of (by) you; I wonder of (at) their being here together; I am provided of (with) a torch-bearer; I have no mind of (for) feasting forth tonight; I were better to be married of (by) him than of another; That did but show thee of (as) a fool. Many more examples could be added. While matters of idiom and usage generally claim less attention from students of the language than sounds and inflections or additions to the vocabulary, no picture of Elizabethan English would be adequate which did not give them a fair measure of recognition.

CONTRIBUTION OF CHAUCER

Chaucer who was born in London, spent most of his time there. So by birth and surroundings he was confined to the language spoken in the neighbourhood of London, the Midland dialect, which was then also the language of the court the "King's English", and which was to become mainly through his efforts, the sole literary language of the whole of England–the English literature. When Chaucer took it up, it was poor and barren. No real poetry had so far appeared in the dialect. Chaucer's aim was to breathe into this dialect a higher poetical life, and in this aim he was definite and unswerving.

Chaucer deliberately chose the Midland dialect, because he found that it was really living, and because it had spread up to the upper classes of people. He wrote this dialect with an ease, a polish, and a regularity which commanded immediate and unanimous admiration, and used it as the vehicle for first rate poetry. During the previous three centuries and even in Chaucer's life-time there were people who wrote in the London dialect, but they belonged to countries where the dialect was already archaic, and they clung to obsolete poetical modes. Chaucer had come at the psychological moment. He found that most of the nobles read the French poets and that the English which was then coming into use at Court was full of fresh forms and words. He therefore found it much easier to adopt the French verse-forms to English use. He endowed the London dialect with all the grace and refinement which instinct and knowledge enabled him to detect in French poetry. He infused into native vocabulary the courtliness of France, and expressed in English all the graces and delicate shades of meaning which he found in French poetry. So, whereas he enriched the particular English of his district and gave it the status of the literary language of England, he also broke away from the literary past of England and thus by throwing the weight of his genius into the balance decided the future. Chaucer thus became the founder of modern English, and he gave to the poets of succeeding generations a ready and well-formed medium to express themselves. Nothing more was needed. Those who came after him had now an accepted standard. In this way Chaucer did for the English language what Dante had done for the Italian language.

Chaucer's Versification

Chaucer paid particular attention to versification. Except for the octosyllabic verse, which was already in use, he had to fashion for himself all the other metres he used. He had doubtless read all the rude masterpieces which had hitherto been introduced in the English tongue.

On the other hand the lawless treatment of rhyming verse, by poets who had almost got rid of inflections, was displeasing to a fastidious ear which required the accent to be regularly distributed in lines measured by an equal number of syllables. Chaucer resolved accordingly, to look exclusively to France for his metrical models.

The study of the literature of this century is therefore essentially fragmentary. The progress in the north, and more especially in the west, had been far slower than in the rest of the country. These districts remained attached to the forms of the past. They kept their taste for alliteration.

The provincialism of a backward district does not, however, by itself explain the return of this old verse-form. It was due also to the failure of the new versification to fill the place of the old epic verse. Chaucer had not yet imported from France the decasyllabic or heroic line which was to take precedence of all others. The prevalent short and slight rhythms could not satisfy men in whose-ears the last echoes of the epic verse of their ancestors were still singing. Moreover, the versification derived from France lacked an assured prosody. Accent hovered, doubtfull, over the different syllables of words of French origin, and even Germanic words were infected by the uncertainty. The relation between rhythm and tonic accent was in consequence, not clearly perceived.

His Diction

His Diction has an elegant simplicity which produces the deceptive effect of artlessness. "It achieves decorum with apparent effort and with no suggestion of formality. Its freedom from puns. Conceits jingles, and antithetic affections moved the admiration of Dryden, who found in Chaucer a "continence, which is practised by few writers,and scarcely by any of the ancients excepting Virgil and Horace."

"In one sense", says Courthope, "he is the poet of the schools. Brought up in the nature of encyclopaedia learning, an intense intellecutual curiosity carried him into studies which must have crushed a feebler mind, equipped with a necessarily imperfect instrument of expression. But the treasures that he drew from theology, astronomy, and alchemy were seldom used, as is so often the case in the *Romance of the Rose* and other poems of the medieval period, for the mere purpose of display, but were devoted to the enrichment and illustration of his art. Again, there is a sense in which Chaucer is an imitative poet. He admired with all the enthusiasm of fine taste the more finished art of the poets of France and Italy, and felt no scruple in transferring bodily many of their thoughts and sentiments into the English tongue; he borrowed, however not from poverty but from enterprise, and used the poems of his contemporaries or predecessors.

Alliterative Verse

When William Langland's Piers Plowman appeared in 1362, the vocabulary which he drove belonged to the West–the West Midlands. the verse is purely alliterative, it is quite uncontaminated by French versification and makes no concession to rhyme. When the language came into Chaucer's hands, it was rude and inharmonious, inadequate to express either the complex ideas of philosophy or the finer shades of character, when he left it, it had been endowed with a copious vocabulary, refined syntax, musical numbers which was fitted to become a vehicle of noble literature.

That chaucer was a pioneer in many respect should be readily granted. "With him is born our real poetry" says Mathew Arnold. He has been acclaimed as the first realist, as the first humorist, the first narrative artist, the first great character-painter and the first great metrical artist in English literature. Further, he has been credited not only with the "fatherhood" of English poetry but has also been hailed as the father of English drama before the drama was born, and the father of English novel before the novel was born. And what is more, Chaucer's importance is not due to precedence alone, but, due to excellence. He is not only the first English poet, but a great poet in his own right. Justly has he been called "the fountain-source of the vast stream of English literature."

Dialect and Language

"Chaucer found English a dialect and left it a language." Borrowing Saintshbury's words about the transformation which Dryden effected in English poetry, we may justly say that Chaucer found the English language brick and left it marble. When Chaucer started his literary career, the English speech, and still less, the English of writing, was confusingly fluid and unsettled. The English language was divided into a number of dailects which were employed in d[illegible] parts of the country. The four of them vastly more prom[illegible]nt than the others were:

(i) The Southern

(ii) The Midland

(iii) The Northern of Northumbrian

(iv) The Kentish

Out of these four the Midland or the East Midland dialect, which was spoken in London and its surrounding areas, was the simplest on grammar and syntax. Moreover, it was patronised by the aristocratic and literary circles of the country. Gower used this dialect for his poem *Confessio Amantis*, and Wyclif for his translation of the Bible. But his dialect was not the vehicle of all literary work. Other dialects had their votaries too. Langland in his *Piers Plowman* to quote an instance, used a mixture of the Southern and Midland dialects. Chaucer employed in his work the East Midland dialect, and by casting the enormous weight of his genious in balance decided once for all which dialect was going to be the standard literary language of the whole of the country. None after him thought of using any dialect.

TO REFINE ENGLISH LANGUAGE

According to Edgar H. Schuster "TODAY MAN'S knowledge and achievements are increasing at a tremendously rapid rate: Astronauts soar through space at incredible speeds, television broadcasts are made directly from continent to continent via Telstar, and problems that would have taken centuries to solve are handled by computers in a matter of minutes. The advance of the recent past are aptly described as a "knowledge explosion."

The physical science are such dynamic fields that we take their progress for ganted; we assume that advances are going to be made almost every day. When it comes to grammar, however, the attitude of most persons is quite diferent. Many believe that grammar never changes and that it is not possible to know anything more [illegible] language than was known centuries ago.

Language is not static; it has changed a great deal over the centuries and it is continuing to change. The language you speak is in certain ways different from language your grandparents spoke. What was "correct" in the past may not neessarily be correct in the future.

Although some persons tend to feel that change corrupts a language, this would be hard to prove by studying our language historically. While some may not consider this an improvement, it certainly simplifies the language, and it does so without any signficant loss of precison. Not only has the language changed, but our knowledge of its changes, of its basic structure, and our system for classifying these has improved considerably. Although the study of the English language is several hundred years old, only within the last forty years or so has it become possible to speak of that study as scientific. During those forty years, those who have been studying English, men called linguistic scientists or linguists, have advanced language study singficantly. So significant has been their work that it is possible to say that there has been a knowledge explosion in linguistic science equal to the "explosion" in the physical sciences.

What Is Grammar?

The word grammar is used in a number of different senses. In one sense, a grammar is merely a description of a language. A scientist interested in describing a language works in the same ways that other scientists do. Like other scientists, he will want to gather a great deal of data. If he is studying the English language, he will be interested in the English used in all sections of our country and in all sections of the world. He will be interested in the English spoken by cardrivers and in the English spoken by college professors. As a scientist he may note that a majority of well-educated speakers say, "They don't have any money," and a majority of uneducated speakers say, "They don't have no money," but he will not say that one form is better than the other. A botanist would not say that a birch tree is "better" than a ginkgo tree.

Although many persons would condemn an expression such as, "They dont't have no money," everyone would have to admit that it is English and every native speaker of English would have no difficulty in understanding it perfectly. They would also understand "He ain't gone nowheres," He run more better than me," and other sentences usually regarded as incorrect. For the linguistic scientist, "bad" English is still English, and it is even grammatical, at least in the sense that it can be understood by native speakers.

But if both "They don't have any money" and "They don't have no from money" are "grammatical" from the point of view of the scientific grammarian, what is ungrammatical? Are there any rules that all speakers of English observe?

Any person who has studied English as a foreign language would be very quick to answer this last question with a strong "Yes?" There are in fact a very large number of rules that all native speakers of English use. They learn most of these rules painlessly, through imitation, by the time they enter first grade. When you went to first grade, you might have said, "they don't have any money" or "They don't have no money," but you did not say, "Have any don't money they."

It you think of grammar as the way that words are put together to make meaningful structures in speech or writing, you will see that you already know a great deal about English grammar. Your knowledge may not be conscious, but knowledge you have. You are in fact a walking grammar book. To prove this for yourself, try to make a meaningful English sentence out of the following words: friends, there worked, odd, could, have, his.

Most of the possible combinations of these words would not give you an English sentence.

Here are some examples of combinations that add up to somethings that is not English:

worked old could friend his there have

friend there have could old worked his

thère friend worked have could his old

have his could worked old there friend

You did not choose any of these combinations because your knowledge of English grammar made you realize that they were not English sentences.

At this point you might wish to ask a question. If grammar means the study of the way words are put together to make meaningful structures in speech and writing and if a person already knows how to make such structures, why should he study grammar? This is an intelligent question and it deserves a thoughtful answer. Anyone who graduates from high school will have studied many things that will be of little or no practical value to him later in life. He will have studied art and music, for example, even though he has no intention of becoming an artist or a musician. He will probably have studied much more science math, and history than will be of use to him. But thought he may not use much of what he learned in school for any practical purpose, it has helped to make him an educated person. It has made him better able to appreciate the world around him. If he were to have studied only subjects that had a practical value, he would have been a limited person. In general, he would be less interesting to talk to and to be with than a person who had a wide variety of knowledge and interests.

One reason for studying grammar, then, is for its own sake. The study of grammar contributes to one's education ; it is simply interesting to know how language works.

A second reason for studying grammar is more practical. When a person studies any subject, he learns the vocabularly of that subject. A person studying auto mechanics, for example, is expected to know what such words as piston, transmission, camshaft, and carburetor mean. Someone studying electricity is expected to know the meaning of words like ampere, transformer, electrode, and ohm. Knowing the meaning of these words will not guarantee that a person will be an expert in his field, but mastering the vocabulary will make it easier for him to become a good mechanic or electrical engineer.

Similarly, if a student knows the meaning of terms like verb, phrase, subordinate clause, and sentence, it will be easier for him to learn how to write effectively. If he understands a comment like "Make your first sentence into a subordinate clause," he will learn more efficiently than someone who doesn't. Because the mastery of grammatical terms is so helpful in improving style, the style chapters in this book always follow the discussions of grammatical principles and terms.

In conclusion, grammar may be defined as the study of the way words are put together to make meaningful structures in speech and writing. Grammar, in this sense, has little to do with "correct" speech or writing.

Speech has dimensions unknown to written language. Written language operates with the choice and arrangement of words. Speech operates not with these devices but also with features unrecorded in writing, such as tempo, dynamic range, voice quality and speech melody.

The different kinds of radio commentary provide an interesting study in tempo, or rate of utternance. At one end of the range lies the slow sombre gravity of the spoken royal or religious occasion. Sports commentaries require greater flexibility, as excitement mounts and dies away. Different sports are themselves graded: the climax of a horse race; the bursts of savage energy in a boxing match; the sustained speed and high-pressure excitement of Cup Final. Each has its own appropriate tempo, form which lone the sport can be identified given even a small smple.

In addition to changes in tempo, variations in overall loudness and dynamic range can be used to distinguish, say, the principle from the example, or the essential from the marginal. As such it may be used by a lecturer to indicate careful formulation, which should be noted verbatim, as opposed to glosses, which need only be followed and understood. The most effective examples of the use of the device are found in oratory, while in the mouth of an unscrupulous judges, the device could be used in a summing-up to combine an impression of impeccable verbal impartiality with a clear directive to a jury.

Voice quality can be varied, amplifying higher harmonics to achieve clarity and audibility at a distance, or suppressing them to achieve a cosy intimacy. There are many other effects which though well appreciated are but little investigated: the icy, the convivial, the edgy, the rasping, the brassy, the reassuring, the soothing. All these are powerful in their effect in the proper context; it is when we allow ourselves to become fixed permanently in one mode, that we lose effectiveness and degenerate into caricatures. Penetrating audibility in a public speaker is one thing: in a woman companion it is quite another. And, as for the icy voice, it repels unwelcome strangers and welcome vistors alike.

Chief among these means of expression specific to speech is intonation, compound of rythm and melodic patterns. It is still not generally realised that in English we have a regular, ordered, closely structured system of intonation patterns which we apply to the various sentence structures to get fine distinction of meaning. They are hinted at in punctuation, but are otherwise unrecorded in normal orthography. Let me illustrate briefly the effect of some patterns by attaching them to sentence, It's not bad:

It's not bad.—(a plain statement)

It's not bad.—(enthusiastic)

It's not bad.—(surely)

It's not bad.—(querying...Do you mean to say that...)

It's not bad.—(reassuring)

It's not bad.—(hesitant, insinuating that it is not very good)

That's not a style I've ever worn, pronounced as in the first of the above examples, in final, and will send a salesman off looking for another dress. But That's not a style I've ever worn, uttered with the intonation pattern of the last examples, sounds uncertain, and no self-respecting salesman would stop short of a sale. Like the other direct phonic means of communication, intonation is not available for use in written language and instead we have resource to lexical and syntactical devices. I have heard a 'linguistic philosopher's complain that English has no explicit mean of conveying distinctions of attitude because it does not employ special words for the purpose, and dismiss 'tone of voice' as primitive clumsy and inexact. In fact, intonation patterns are ideally suited to convey such distinctions, which cannot readily be fitted into a number of discrete categories. The fact that we find it difficult to formulate the meaning of a given intonation simply shows that words cannnot do the same job, not that intonation is imprecise. Admittedly, a large proportion of misunderstandings and intuitive dislikes, both individual and international, are due to an incongruence, incomptability, failure to communicate, on this level. The principal reason is our ignorance of the intonation systems of other dialects and other languages, which we have not yet learned to translate. Within the same speech community, however, while a certain number of speakers do deviate widely in their use and evaluaton of intonation patterns, and a very few are quite insensitive to them, there is close agreement on the force of these intonations among most speakers.

In recent years many phoneticians have devoted close attention to this fascinating and rewarding study. As a result, the main features of English intonation have now been codified, and a suitable notation evolved. Some modern grammaers of English are incorporating discriptions of intonation, though as yet the treatment is generally confined to an appendix or special section. The stage has been reached where no English specialist can regard himself as fully competent if he lacks a thorough understanding and command of this fundamental resource of the English language.

INFLUENCE OF FRENCH OVER ENGLISH LANGUAGE

The most important event of far-reaching consequences in the history of England was the Norman Conquest. The Conquest of England by William, the Conqueror in 1066 changed the whole course of the English language. Even before the Norman conquest the English had become acquainted with the Norman culture and way of life because of the social, political and ecclesiastical intercourse between the two nations, following upon the marriage of the English king, Ethetred the Unready to a Norman princess. During the reign of Edward the Confessor, several Norman nobles were placed in important positions in England and the fortified buildings in which they stayed were known as 'castles' Capun (capon) and bacun (bacon) are two other words introduced at the time and they serve to suggest the greater luxury of French cooking which was new to the English.

The Normans were Northmen, a race of the Scandinavians who settled in along the Northern coast of France in the ninth and tenth centuries. Having settled in France, these Scandinavians like their Kinsmen in England showed remarkable adaptability and soon absorbed the most important elements of the French civilization. They accepted christianity and gave up their own language and learned French. The French spoken by this alien race was not the same as the French spoken by the people of France and is known as Norman French. The French of Paus is known as Central French of Parsian French.

A district of France named Normandy was occupied by the West Teutonic Franks in the fifth century when Great Britain was occupied by three other West Teutonics tribes Angles, Saxons, and Jutes. The Franks mingled and merged with the local Gallo-Roman population and accepted the language of the conquered people and embraced christianity. In the ninth century, Danes settled in Normandy as well as in England. The Normans adopted christianity, the local language and the ideas, customs and the most important elements of French civilization. It will be evident that the Normans were closely related both to the English and to their Scandinavian conquerors.

William the Conqueror, was a Norman. This victory at Hastings after fierce fight with the English and his subsequent coronation in London marked the beginning of the Norman influence on the English way of life and on the English language. Many of the English higher class had been killed in the battle field at Hastings and those who escaped were treated as traitors. Their places were filled by William's Normans followers. Thus one most important result of the Norman conquest was the introduction of the new nobility in England. Many key positions such as bishopies and abbacies were also given to Normans. French become the language of upper classes and the court in England chiefly because it was the language of the conquerors. Since the church and education were dominated by Normans, French become also the language of the lower classes of the conquered. Even some of the Englishmen who wanted to get on in the world learned French. In the following years peoples accepted the new order as an accomplished fact to which they had to adjust themselves. The fusion of Normans and the English was rapid. There is plenty of evidence of mutual respect, peaceful cooperation and even intermarriage between the Normans and English.

French became the language of the church, scholarship and administration. This supremacy of French on English soil continued for about three hundred years. English remained the language of masses. But in the thirteenth century there was a shifting of emphasis. The tipping of the balance started moving away from French back to English. National feeling was beginning to arise in England and this contributed to rise of the prestige of the English language. The definite triumph of English however came in the fourteenth century. French was gradually ceasing to be the mother tongue of even the nobility. More and more literature was written in language. The second half of the fourteenth century experienced a kind of literary upsurge in English, with Chaucer as the central figure and guiding spirit. In 1362 the kings speech of at the opening of parliament was made in English. In the same year, an Act making English the official language of the land was passed. Therefore, the three hundred year old supremacy of French came to an end.

The Anglo-Saxons did not adopt the language of conquered people. The Scandinavians who invaded English mingled with the Anglo-Saxons. And the language that resulted from the fusion was highly Teutonic. But the Franks and the Scandinavians who settled in Normandy adopted French, the language of the conquered people. And the Normans were mostly Norsemen who had completely shed their Scandinavian speech and become comments to Latin culture. At that time there was no standard French language and there were only a number of dialects among which that of Normandy was one which was introduced into England after the Norman Conquest. These French dialects among which that of Normandy was one which was spoken in different Roman Provinces. The colloquial Latin underwent diverse changes in various regions, producing different languages French, Italian, Spanish, Portugues etc. which are known as Romance languages. Evidentally, the Normans went to England as Frenchmen and they took with them a different language and a different and superior civilization.

During the long period French rule of the French language greatly influenced the English language. Indeed its effect on English was so great that when English again become the language of literature it was very much changed and was called by new term, Middle English. For about two centuries in England French enjoyed greater prestige and higher social status and it tremendously influenced English, but because English was spoken by ninety per cent of the population it remained predominantly Teutonic even after the long impact of a vastly superior tongue. The conquest did not effect the French influence on English. But with Edward the Confessor who ascended the English throne in 1042, the son of a French mother Edward was educated in France and when he ascended the throne he was brought to England. It was from this time that French words began to enter the English language.

The events rapidly show the introduction, growth and eclipse of French in England. By the fourteenth century there was a complete switch over from French to English, in the church education and in the court. Although French died out in England it left its deep marks on the English language. The influx of French words brought about by the Norman conquest has continued with varying tempo upto the present day. And the number of French words that have poured into English is unbelievably great. French civilization and culture have exerted a profound influence on the English. Indeed there is scarcely any department of English life which has remained unaffected by the activities of the French. This influence is clearly mirrored in the English vocabulary. Most of the French words borrowed before 1650 were thoroughly naturalised in English and were made to conform to English pronounciation and accent. But French words borrowed in the modern period are after pronounced in the French fashion. The influence of French was the greatest on the English vocabulary. It is natural when two language-communities co-exist with intimate relations for a long time a considerable flow of words from one language to another takes place. It is possible to arrange the French loan words in groups classified according to the ideas they express. A large number of words relating to government and administration, ecclesiastical, legal and military matters, fashion, food, art, science and philosophy have been appropriated from French.

The enormous number of French words came into the English language. This flux of French words was neither sudden nor immediate. French words poured into English fastest when French was dying out. It may be noticed that the eleventh and twelfth centuries, when French was the unchallenged language of the upper classes, the stream of French words into English was thin. But in the thirteenth and fourteenth centuries there was a flood of them, perhaps because when bilingual speakers were changing over from French to English they felt the need for some specialized terms and therefore imported them fastest just before the switch over.

One interesting difference between the flux of Scandinavian words and that of French words is that the former came from the Danelaw and the latter came from London and the court. The

Scandinavians mixed with the people on more or less equal terms and so their words were common, familiar and homely. But, on the other hand, French words reflect the cultural and political dominance. They were the words tended to penetrate downwards in society, imposed from above. They are connected with the law, hunting, arts, fashions war and ecclesiastical matters. They bear the stamp of aristocracy and of the superior French culture and civilization.

French influence on the language was general and widespread during the Middle English period it was no longer so after the beginning of the 16th century. Though like Latin, French continued to be the source of the words the French loans after the 15th century were confined to particular classes of technical words restricted in use to the better educated people. The 16th century borrowings for instance were mostly technical terms relating to war, and the common war had little to do with these.

The 17th century is significant in the history of the French loans and as it was a period of very close contact between the English and the French in matters of literature and social intercourse. One of the subjects which engaged the attention of the satirist and playwrights of the Restoration period was the indiscriminate imitation of all things French by the smart set in London. Dryden's play *Marriage a la mode* is entirely devoted to satirising of the Frenchified fashionable woman of the age, words like 'dragoon, slockade, reprimand, ballet, burlesque, tablean, chagrin champagne, coquette, Liaison verve, cortege native, decor, forte, soup and quart' are representative of the 17th century borrowings from French.

The English language owes many of its words dealing with government, administration and nobility to the French language. While the old words like, king, queen, earl, lord, and lady are intact, French words like government, govern, administration, crown, state, real in, reign empire, authority, majesty, usurp sovereign, country, power, court, council, parliament, assembly, public liberty and many such other words were imported from French. Words relating to

French nobility are noble, nobility, prince, peer, princess, court, duke, duchess squire are French. French words relating to court life are courteous, fine, refined, honour, glory, heraldry and so on.

Feudalism and manorial system were imported from France and a number of words relating to it entered the English language fief, feudal, vassal, liage. The French word court was used only in speaking of foreigners. Ecclesiastical matters were for long under the control of the Normans and hence we find in English such French words as religion theology, service, sermon, baptism, trinity, saviour, confession, prayer, penance, clergy, altar, serman, parish, angel, curate, cardinal, firer, deacon, virgin, alter, convent etc.

All military matters were managed by the French upper classes and as a result the English language has a host of French words relating to war. They are army, navy, peace, arms combat, skirmish, defense, strategem, soldier, garrison, lance, bamer, assault, and so on. Names of military officers like officer, chieftain, lieutenant, sergeant, admiral and many other are of French source. Some words which were first military in nature are now extensively used in ordinary life. They are enemy, challenge, danger, escape, perison, gallant and so on.

As a natural consequence of French being so long the language of the law courts, the English legal vocabulary was flooded with French words. The old words of Scandinavian origin, law, out-law, by-law were retained. But words like justice, just, judge, jury, court, equity, crime, punishment, attorney, plea, plaintiff defendant, to summon, session, accuse, felony, heritage, property, estate, feume, innocent, culpable and host of many others are of French source.

As had been already mentioned high offices of wealth and power in religion were all occupied by Normans. In monasteries and religious house, French was the usual language for a long time. As a result we find a great many French words connected with the church, such as religion, service, trinity, virgin, angel, theology, sacrament sermon, baptism, confession penance prayer. Words like clergy, clerk, prelate, cardinal, dean, parson, paster, vicar, friar indicate ranks in religion. As the clergy were also teachers of religion, a number of words connected with moral ideas were introduced into English. Vice and virtue themselves are of French source. Others include duty, conscience, grace, chairity, faith, chaste, cruel temptation and so on.

The French upper classes led the fashion in the Middle ages and no wonder that a good many French words belonging to this sphere of life entered English. The words fashions and dress are themselves French words and others are apparel, habit, gown, robe, garment, coat, frock, lace, ambroidary, buckle, button, verbs, like embellish, adorn; colours, like blue, brown, scarlet, veumillar, names of articles, and precious stones like ornaments, broach, ivory, jewel, ruby, emerald, sapphirepeal, diamond and many others bearu linguistic evidence for the wealthy and luxuriance life the French must have lived in England. Joy, pleasure, delight, flowers and fruits and such enviable things were theirs. Sports and hunting were then past time and so words like couple, leash, falcon, chase, track, cards, dice came from French. The words dinner and supper are French feast, appetite, taste victuals Ivawhoe are French. Thus many animals like sheeps, ox, calf, swine live English life and die French death when they appear as mutton, beef, veal, pork and so on.

The cultural and intellectual interests of the French ruling class were reflected in words relating to art, literature, and science. The words art, painting, sculpture, music, beauty, colour, image belong to French. Cathedral, place, mansion, Chamber Ceiling, tower, pinnacle, pillar belong to the sphere of architecture, and words such as poet, prose, poem, romance, tragedy, preface, volume and so on represent the literary interests of the French. Among sciences medicine, is represented by words like medium, physician, debility, distemper, pain, jaundice, plague, paralysis, anatomy, pulse and so on.

Now, all these classes of words that have been discussed indicate the nature and breadth of the French influence on the vocabulary of the English language. Many of these words have become indispensible elements in English vocabulary.

The French had plenty of leisure, and various pastimes and entertainments to amuse themselves. This is revealed by the French word like recreation, dance, leisure, music, melody.

Norman French was a variety of French spoken by the Normons in England. It is also called Anglo-Norman. Naturally, it may be expected that Norman French differed in many respects especially in pronounciation, from the French spoken by the natives of France, particularly in Paris, French spoken by the French people is a sort of standard French and is called central French and Parisian French. Whatever English borrowed in the Middle ages was mostly from Norman French. Some words, however, were borrowed from the standard central French in more recent times. The difference between Norman French and Central French is reflected in the words that came into English. Most of the terms of family relationship outside the immediate circle of the household are of French origin. Soon after the conquest uncle, aunt, nephew, niece, cousin replaced their English counterparts.

IMPORTANCE OF LANGUAGE

A language lives only so long as there are people who speak it and use it as their native tongue, and its greatness is only that given to it by these people. A language is important because the people who speak it are important–politically, economically, commercially, socially, culturally. English, French, and German are great and important languages because they are the languages of great and important peoples; for this reason they are widely studied outside the country of their use. But Romanian and Serbian and Malay are seldom learned by any save the native population. Sometimes the cultural importance of a race or nation has at some former time been so great that their language remains important among cultivated people long after it has ceased to represent political, commercial, or other greatness. Greek, for example, it studied in its classical form because of the great civilization which its literature preserves the most complete record of; but in its modern form as spoken in Greece today the Greek language is wholly neglected by the outside world.

The importance of the English language is naturally very great. English is the language not only of England but of the extensive dominions and colonies associated in the British Empire, and it is the language of the United States. Spoken by over 260 million people, it is in the number who speak it the largest of the occidental languages. English-speaking people constitute about one tenth of the world's population. English, however, is not the largest language in the world. The more conservative estimates of the population of China would indicate that Chinese is spoken by about 450 million people. But the numerical ascendancy of English among European languages can be seen by a few comparative figures. Russian, next in size to English, is spoken by about 140 million people; Spanish by 135 millions; German by 90 millions; Portuguese by 63 millions; French by 60 millions; Italian by 50 millions. Thus at the present time English has the advantage in numbers over all other western languages. But the importance of a language is not alone a matter of numbers of territory; as we have said, it depends also on the importance of the people who speak it. The importance of a language is inevitably associated in the mind of the world with the political role played by the nations using it and their influence in international affairs; with the confidence people feel in their financial position and the certainity with which they will meet their obligations–*i.e.*, pay their debts to other nations, meet the interest on their bonds, maintain the gold or other basis of their currency, control their expenditures; with the extent of their business enterprise and the international scope of their commerce; with the conditions of life under which the great mass of their people live; and with the part played by them in art and literature and music, in science and invention, in exploration and discovery–in short, with their contribution to the material and spiritual progress of the world. English is the mother tongue of nations whose combined political influence, economic soundness, commercial activity, social well-being, and scientific and cultural contributions to civilization give impressive support to its numerical precedence.

The Future of the English Languages

The extent and importance of the Englsih language today are such as to make it reasonable to ask whether we cannot attempt an intelligent speculation as to the probable position which it will occupy in the future. It is admittedly hazardous to predict the future of nations; there are individuals who doubt even the permanence of our present civilization. But, assuming that a people's past is to some extent an index of its future, at least over a moderate period of time, and that the future development of Europe (and its colonial extensions) will continue more or less along the lines which that development has pursued in recent centuries, some speculation seems justifiable at least concerning the growth and possible spread of the European languages. Growth in language is primarily a matter of population. Consequently the most important questions affecting the future size of a language is, how much undeveloped territory does it have in which to expand? A second and almost equally important consideration is the climate and fertility of that territory. Civilization today thrives best in the temperate zones. It would obviously be of little value to a language to possess vast territory at the North Pole. What then is the territorial position of the principal European languages?

Among the seven languages English, Russian, and Spanish possess the largest areas. As a result of the colonial expansion of England in the seventeenth and eighteenth centuries, the English-speaking nations today control about a quarter of the earth's surface, while Russian controls a sixth and Spanish a ninth. French in the colonial possessions of France and Belgium, and Portuguese as the language of Brazil, have opportunities, though more limited, for growth. On the other hand, any growth in German or Italian will apparently now be confined chiefly to the areas in which these languages are spoken in Europe. It would seem then that, numerically speaking, the three great languages of the future should be English, Russian, and Spanish. Among the English-speaking territories, those offering the greatest opportunity for growth of population are the United States and Canada, Australia, New Zealand, and South Africa. The political changes in India and Egypt since World War II are not favourable to the expansion of English in these areas. Russia is capable of great increase in population, and at the present time the Slavic race shows a fairly rapid rate of growth. On the other hand, a considerable part of Russian territory in Asia is in or near the Arctic zone, obviously an unfavorable factor. The opportunities for growth which Spanish has center in Spanish America, and not a little of this territory is in the tropics. All in all, we may conclude that the English language is best provided with the facilities for expansion. Such expansion will come partly from the natural growth of the present population, partly from immigration. Between 1901 and 1910 over thirteen million people emigrated from Europe. While the world wars have brought about important changes in this movement of people, both in the countries from which and the areas to which population is flowing, humanity still seeks and will probably continue to seek the opportunities and advantages offered by those districts in which a favourable soil and climate, abundance of natural resources, and populations of lesser density prevail. English, Russian, and Spanish are, in varying degrees, in a position to benefit by this transfer. On the basis of territorial control it is probable that at no very distant time the English language will be spoken by a fifth, perhaps even a quarter, of the population of the world.

Less than a century ago French would have appeared to have attained an undisputed claim to such employment. It was then widely cultivated throughout Europe as the language of polite society, it was the diplomatic language of the world, and it enjoyed considerable popularity in literary and scientific circles. During the nineteenth century its prestige, though still great, gradually declined. The prominence of Germany in all fields of scientific and scholarly activity made German a serious competitor. And the rapid expansion of English and its growing influence in political and commercial affairs have raised a second great competitor. Today it would seem as though English were in the ascendant. Its pre-eminence in commercial use is undoubted. Its employment for purposes of science and research has increased notably of late, especially in Scandinavian countries and among the smaller nationalities of Europe. Its influence is dominant in the East; cultivated Chinese and Japanese have adopted it as a second language. It is nowhere a question of substituting English for the native speech. Nothing is a matter of greater patriotic feeling than the mother tongue. The question simply concerns the use of English, or some other widely known idiom, for international communication.

The probable extension of English in the future, thus indicated, leads many people to wonder whether English will some day become the language of all the world, or at least its civilized portions. In many cases the wish is farther to the thought, and the wish springs partly from considerations of national pride, partly from a consciousness of the many disadvantages that result from a multiplicity of tongues. That the world is fully alive to the need for an international language is evident from the number of attempts that have been made to supply that need artificially. Between 1880 and 1907 fifty- three univeral languages were proposed. Some of these enjoyed an amazing, if temporary, vogue. An artificial language might serve sufficiently the needs of business and travel, but no one has proved willing to make it the medium of political, historical, or scientific thought, to say nothing of the impossibility of making it serve the purposes of pure literature, involving sustained emotion and creative imagination. It would seem as though the hope of the world for intellectual community lay in the eventual employment of one or a few widely known languages whose importance is universally recognized.

❒

6

Spelling and Pronunciation

It is widely accepted that English spelling is notoriously' irrational and, therefore, difficult. Nesfield describes English spelling as a little less than chaotic. Foreign students of English are bewildered by the gulf of discrepancy between spelling and pronunciation. Those whose native language is English have been sor much accustomed to the vagaries of English spelling that they take them for granted. Some of them, however, admit cheerfully and perhaps with a touch of naive pride, that they can not spell correctly. While some advocate spelling reform, others resist it ferociously. The story of the controversy of spelling is interesting to the student of language. We shall see here the nature of English spelling, its historical background and arguments in favour of and against the spelling reform.

In a perfectly consistent system of spelling there would be one symbol for each sound in the language, and each sound would be always represented by one symbol. This sort of ideal relation between the symbol and the sound is called phonetic spelling. It is immediately obvious that the English language is unphonetic in its spelling. For example the vowel sound ə is represented by many different symbols in convential spelling as illustrated in the words *about, father, neighbour, pleasure, the, theatre*. That is to say, one sound is represented by more than one symbol. On the other hand, the symbol *a* is made to represent several distinctly different sounds as in *about, gate, cat, father, talk*. The notorious *-ough* group of words have been often made the butt end of scorn and obloquy. The same set of symbols represent several different pronunciations as illustrated in the words, *plough, trough, rough, thought, through, though, thorough*.

One reason for such irrationality is that in English the alphabet are made to overwork. Nesfield mentions that there are 180 spellings for 25 consonantal sounds, and about 200 spellings for 20 vowel sounds. This gives us an idea of the magnitude of the problem of symbol and sound or spelling and pronunciation.

Old English Period. Anglo-Saxon Alphabet was by and large phonetic. It was an adoption of the Roman letters by early Christian missonaries from Ireland so as to make it roughly a phonetic representation of the vernacular of their converts. Sounds which did not exist in Latin were improvised by using runic letters which the Germanic peoples had among their priests for religious and magical purposes. Thus p̄ was runic letter for Old English *th* sound. Its corresponding voiced sound was represented by an, invented symbol ð. Among the Old English consonants the chief defects were the double use of f for *f* and *v* and the double use of s for *s* and *z*. In most cases in Old English *c* represented the *k* sound, and so the letter k remains idle and superfluous. Again, by the end of the Old English Period *c* came to represent also *ch* sound as in *ceason* (choose). Another important feature of Old English was that there were no silent consonants. In a word like *cniht* all the four consonants were pronounced instead of only two as in its Modern English equivalent, knight.

Middle English. The transition from Old English to Middle-English was marked, among other things, by change in spelling conventions. In the thirteenth and fourteenth centuries, the English language was respelt according to the Anglo-French method, by scribes who were familiar with Norman French and not with Old English. French spelling conventions were introduced into English. One reason for the change was, perhaps, that the French scribes represented more or less phonetically the sounds that they heard, whereas Old English scribes were influenced by West Saxon spelling conventions. In Middle English the symbol *æ* was lost. The Old English c pronounced *k* was replaced by the symbol *k* as in *cyn* becoming *kin*. On the other hand, where *c* had the sound of ch as *ceason, ch* group was introduced in Middle English. It is neither possible nor desirable to go into the details of this topic here. Suffice it to say, that the phonetic: system which characterised the early phase of English started to disappear from the Middle English Period.

Modern English. There have been hardly any striking innovations in English spelling since the Middle English Period. The most marked feature of Modern English spelling is that it permits no freedom of choice as generously as it used to be in earlier phases. But there are a few words where such freedom still exists, such as *show* and *shew, grey and gray, wagon* and *waggon*. Sometimes the same word alternately spelt came to be regarded as two different words, as for instance, *metal and mettle, flour* and *flower*. During the sixteenth and seventeenth centuries, the printing press stabilised English spelling to a large extent. Caxton himself exercised some influence on English spelling. But in his times books did not become so widespread as to influence the whole country, till in the eighteenth century Dr. Johnson's Dictionary was accepted as the arbiter of usage and spelling. All dictionaries for the next century more or less imitated it.

It is not out of place here to consider briefly the relation between spelling and rhyme, ever since poetry came to be printed by the end of the 17th century. Poetry had hitherto been written to be recited and heard. But the emergence of the printing press made it possible to address the readers of poetry through the printed word. As C. L. Wren remarks, "Milton was probably the last great poet who wrote with deliberate aim of being read aloud." Now, since rhymes are to be seen in print, a new relation has come up between spelling and rhyme. The whole craft of verse and the poet's relation with his reader has changed with the spread of printing. While rhymes were auditory earlier, now, a new class of rhymes called visual rhymes have come up. C. L. Wren distinguishes five types of rhymes:

(a) *true rhymes* which still sound exactly alike,

(b) *traditional rhymes* which once had the same pronunciation but now do not rhyme in sound as in *hand* and *wand*,

(c) *eye rhymes* or *visual rhymes* which depend entirely on the agreement of spelling, as in *foul* and *soul*,

(d) *traditional spelling rhymes* used by great poets of the past which are similar not in sound but in spelling as in *love* and *grove*, and

(e) *true-plus rhymes* where the spelling of one of the rhyming words is adjusted so as to make it an eye-rhyme, even though rhyme was already perfect, for example Spenser's *arre* (for are) to rhyme with *farre*.

Back to spelling, the decay of phonetic nature of Old English spelling can be traced back to many historical factors. One reason for the variety of English spelling is the mixture of Fresh words with English and the introduction of Fresh conventions into English spelling. More important reason is, that for the last three centuries or more, English spelling has changed little-whereas pronunciation is constantly changing. In any living language change is inevitable. But changes in pronunciation are always ahead of changes in spelling. The present day English spelling, therefore, represents pronunciation as it used to be rather than as it is today. It is said that Modern English has still retained the spelling habits of the days of James I. In the words of Skeat, "Practically we retain a Tudor system of symbols with a Victorian pronunciation". And hence the ever widening gulf between spelling and pronunciation.

Sometimes, a word acquires the pronunciation of Standard English, but retains its dialectical spelling. Thus, the word *busy* has the South-Western spelling with the Standard English pronunciation. On the other hand, the word *bury* has the South-Western spelling with the South-Eastern pronunciation. Sometimes faulty and inadequate scholarship of earlier periods contributed in some measure to the confusion of English spelling. Thus, the words like *island, posthumous, style, scythe* and *scent* were respelt on the analogy with some Latin words. Thus, several contributory causes have made English spelling what it is today, while there were no such forces working on pronunciation to check its change. So it is rightly said that English spelling has its roots in history.

Several spelling reforms that have been attempted so far, have merely touched the fringe of the problem; that is they have changed the spelling of certain individual words. Advantages of spelling reform are obvious although they are magnified by its champions. A consistent spelling convention will make the language easier than what it is now. It bridges the gulf between speech and writing and the learner of English saves a lot of time and energy wasted on trying to remember the present capricious system.

One of the earliest spelling reformers was Orm, a versifier of the thirteenth century. He used several devices and concentrated more on doubling of consonants. But his spelling system remained entirely his, but did not reach the public. The Renaissance spelling reformers too did not leave any indelible mark on the spelling convention. In recent times Noah Webster, on the other side of the Atlantic, tried to bring drastic changes in English spelling. Though he made some mark in this field, he could not carry out all the changes he advocated. He was conscious that his dictionary would not find market, if all the changes were made. Some of the American spelling conventions have been accepted by the English. But present day swing in matters of spelling seems to be towards European conventions.

One important objection to phonetic reform of English spelling is in the lack of uniformity and in the changing nature of spoken language. With English pronunciation ever changing, any 'reformed spelling' of the present century may not represent the pronunciation of the language, say a hundred years hence. Then a new reform will have to be attempted. The process goes on endlessly but the energy and thought spent on it would be fit for a better cause.

Another important objection to spelling reform is that it results in the loss of continuity with the past and contact with older literature. As Sir William Craigie pointed out in his S.P.E. tract on "Problems of Spelling Reform" (1944), the crux of the problem is that if native spelling were retained much of the Latin and French elements would become unrecognisable. Phonetic spelling would obscure the connexion between *nation* and *national* by spelling them *nei ʃ ∂n*, *nei ʃ ∂n∂l* and similarly the relation between *photographic* and *photographer* might be disguised. On the other hand, it may introduce misleading identity between *cession* and *session*, *symbol* and *cymbal, allowed* and *aloud, seed* and *cede.*

However, inspite of innate conservatism and logical objections, some of the enterprising attempts at spelling reform in the past have changed at least some individual words. Some attempts, however, have given rise to permissible variations, as in the Oxford manner of writing abridgement, acknowledgement and Judgement and Cambridge fashion of writing them without e following g. Similarly, there is no use denying others their right to spell *biassed, focussing, civilization* and *connection* instead of your own *biased, focusing, civilisation* and *connexion*. If the reader of English shows some tolerance of alternate forms of spelling and if he welcomes attempts at improvements and encourages writers to be enterprising, then English spelling can take its own course. It needs neither a champion or reform measures nor a guardian of ancient orthography.

SLANG AND DIALECT

Slang and dialect are departure from standard speech. If we take standard speech as an ideal form of speech to be emulated by all, slang and dialect are other levels—lower levels of speech. Standard speech is polite, literary, rhetorical and at the same time artificial and monotonous. In order to relieve itself of the monotony of "speaking like a book", every language-community invents and practices a slang ef its own. It may be said that slang springs as a reaction against the monotony of the standard form of speech. Once a slang word is born, it hovers in the outskirts of respectable speech continually trying to force its way into it.

A good number of writers in the past looked at slang with contempt, which was generally based on misconception. In modern times, however, slang has been recognised as one of the various levels of speech. A lively speaker should be able to express himself at each of the levles, as the occasion demands. Slang and other levels of speech like colloquialism, cant, dialect deserve as much tolerance, if not respect, from language-lovers, as light music from the unprejudiced music-lovers. Slang is not altogether devoid of virtues. It is racy, sparkling, vivacious and picturesque, though odd and grotesque. Before we pass on to discuss the birth, growth and virtues of slang, it would be worthwhile to define terms like vulgarism, cant, slang, colloquialism and dialect. These are all various levels of speech. They have one common characteristic—they are all deviations from standard speech. The degree of deviation varies from one level to another. The lines of distinction among them are vague and uncertain. Dialect is simply a way of speaking, of pepole belonging to particular region or to particular class, or occupation. For example, as one travels to different parts of England, from South to North, or from the Centre of the country to the extreme West, one is struck with the great differences between speech of Sussex and that of Yorkshire, or between the speech of Oxfordshire and that of Cornwall. The differences are due to geographical separation of one region from the other and due to lack of free intercourse between the inhabitants of one region and those of the other. Varieties of speech of this kind are called regional dialects because, they are peculiar to particular regions. Besides regional dialects, there are what are called *class dialects*. They are chiefly due to occupational differences *with a problem*, to lose *track* of a subject, *crestfallen*, to show *white feather*.

One interesting slang coming from games is 'Love All' used in Tennis when there is no score. Many of us in fact do not know its origin, nor do we know that it is a slang. The explanation of such queer expression is that the match begins with the 'Love-All', because playing for love means playing for no stakes and with no bet on the result of the game. Hence Love came to mean 'nothing'. Similarly, Cricket has given some curious slang terms to the English language. "Till sometime ago, journalists employed alternative names for various items of the game. Thus, they would call the wickets the timber-yard, and the wicket-keeper was called timber-watcher. These are not, however, happy expressions and so are not in current use. Bat and ball were called *willow* and *leather* and by a touch of fancy, a ball that kept low and shot along the ground was called a daisy-cutter.

Another variety of slang is called rhyming slang. This is a pointless and cumbersome trick using a word that rhymes with the name of the article or thing in mind. That is, if you want to speak of *money*, find a rhyming word like *honey* and use it for money. Sometimes this slang is expanded by adding something to the rhyme word. Thus, money is called in slang *bees* and *honey*. By a similar trick wife is described as *trouble* and *strife*. Slang terms created in this process are not, however, in extensive use.

It has been mentioned that *exam* is slang term for examination and is made by clipping the latter form. The clipping process is quite extensively used and some of the terms came into use by this process have been accepted by Standard English. Familiar examples are *bus* from *omnibus, phone* from *telephone*. We find this clipping often in pet-names as *Bill* for William, *Jack* for John, *Dick* for Richard, *Tom* for Thomas. Pet-name clippings imply familiarity and intimacy. Some terms like *doc* for doctor, *prof* for professor have not gained currency in respectable circles. One of the interesting examples is *down*. This is made by clipping the word *adown* which is itself a corruption of the Old English phrase of *dune* (from the hill). From this, the English language has earned two words, the noun down meaning 'a hill' and the adverb *down* which is the opposite of hill. The word *size* is derived by clipping the word assize; back from *aback, wayward* from *away-ward* and so on.

Political events and personalities are not lagging behind in supplying slang terms to the English language. For example, the word *cabal* in the sense of 'intriguing clique' comes from the Hebrew word for tradition. But, its meaning was strengthened and it came into wider use, when it was applied for Charles II's Committee for

Foreign Affairs. The term was applied in particular to five members of that 'cabinet council' whose names, by a stroke of accident, begin with C, A, B, A, L (*Clifford, Arlington, Buckingham, Ashley, Landerdale*). From this event the word came to mean 'Political machination'. Another interesting slang with political background is *gerrymander*. In 1812, Elbridge Gerry, Governor of the Commonwealth "redistricted" Massachusetts, to insure the success of his party in an election. Some clever person discovered that one of the newly formed districts took the shape of a fantastic monster. The map of the district was published with the caption 'gerrymander (Gerry and Salamander) to the monster-shape of the district. This tickled the fancy of Americans and the word is still in use both in America and Canada. Similarly, *bunkum* and *bunk* has an interesting political origin. Buncombe was a country in North Carolina. In the sixteenth Congress, when the debate on the Missouri Question was nearing its close, the member from Buncombe insisted on making long and factuous speech, just because the people of his district expected it of him.

Slang is not a permanent element in language. Many of the slang terms have had their day and are beard no more. For example, police was called for some time *peeler*, for sometime *bobby, body-snatcher, the arm of the law,* and so on. But the present fashion is to call him *cops*. Similarly *beak* or *beck* was used for sometime to police, then for magistrate and then a teacher — all because police, magistrate or teacher 'pokes his nose (beak) into the affairs of others, particularly thieves and students.' A great number of slang substitutes were in use for the word money. It was once called *tin, brass, coppers, boodle, spondulics,* the *dibs,* the *ready,* the *first quids* and *nickets* and so on. The term lolly is favourite slang for money in modern times. In India *chips* is often heard. Many slang-names for being drunk came into use and then disappeared, So, the among men. The country gentry, the clergy, the professional classes, military men, shopkeepers, farmer, labourers, politicians and tramps—each of these is a class by itself and members of each class more frequently associate together than with the members of any other group. Each class has its own problems, its own interests and so on. So, naturally each class develops a way of speaking of its own, which is different from that of other classes. But it should not be taken to mean that each class is completely isolated from the other. On the other hand, all these classes speak a form of English, each understands the other quite well, and yet in pronunciation, vocabulary and grammatical forms each differs from the other. When these differences are sufficiently great, *class dialects* arise. When each class-dialect develops a way of speech of its own in vocabulary and in grammar, to such an extent as is not easily intelligible to any other class, it becomes a jargon. Thus, the language of science is a kind of jargon to a man of letters, and similarly, the langauge of literature is a jargon to an economist.

Vulgarism is a bad variety of English imported from a class dialect—dialect of low and uneducated speakers. For example, if one pronounces *tape* as *type* or *hours* as *orse*, it can be called vulgarism. Vulgarism does not seem so in the company of vulgarisms. But when it intrudes itself into standard speech, by mistake or carelessness of the speaker, it would certainly produce the effect of greater vulgarity. That is, when a speaker is attempting to speak standard English, but, by force of habit or negligence, lapses into his regional or class dialect, his speech is liable to sound vulgar.

Cant is a bad variety of slang, like the catch-phrases of political slogans, those vote-catching half-truths "which are framed to play upon the emotions of an undiscerning section of the community." It is, however, difficult to define the boundaries between slang and cant. Simeon Potter observes, "public school slang is a form of cant. It is an inherited esoteric lingo changing from school to school, from Westminster to Winchester and from Rugby to Shrewsbury."

Colloquialism is a spoken variety of language. It is usually a respectable variety of slang. It takes position between slang and standard form of language. Spoken conversation which is easy but not slovenly, conventional but not formal and pedantic can is simpler than its counterpart in England, but it is not entirely phonetic. If its aim is to spell as we prouounce, why *check* and not *chek*; why *public* and *not publik* and why two consonants in *offence*, while there is only one in defense? Again, present-day American spelling is not what Noah Webster originally planned it to be. Webster would have liked to be *hed* (head), *proov* (prove), *hiz* (his), *giv* (give), *det* (debt), *dout* (doubt), *ruf* (rough), and so on. American spelling is not dnistically different. Obviously it is mid-way between the ideal and the real, it is neither extremely unphonetic, nor is it absolutely phonetic.

Vocabulary. The largest divergences between King's English and American English are in vocabulary. In the great mainstream of the English language, American English acts as an important tributory, in the sphere of vocabulary. As Lincoln Barret puts it, "in Colonial America, as elsewhere in the expanding British Empire, new words were invented, improvised, borrowed and translated from native lexicons to describe new things, experiences, flora and fauna, occupations and activities for which no countepart existed in England. New and special vocabularies came into being and, as they circulated, many words worked back into the central treasury of the English tongue". (Span, October, 1963). Red Indian words, terms from the French, Dutch, Spanish were freely borrowed and assimilated into American English. Thus, Red Indian word *seganku* was borrowed as skunk. Other Red Indian words are *woodchunk, terrapin, chipmunk, kicory, caucus* and so on.

Other interesting differences are noticed in more familiar words. English *rail* is American *railroad*; English *lugguage* is American *baggage* and the *luggage-van* is *baggage-car*. A goods train in America is often called a *freight-van*, and a *break-van* is referred as a *caboose*. English *lift* is an American *elevator*, and English *groundfloor* is American *firstfloor*, and as a result what is fifth floor in America turns out to be fourth floor in England. English *driver* is American *Engineer* and English *undertakers* are *morticians*. Some Americans do not hesitate to use words like healthatorium, shavatorium and such other strange compound terms. Number of such differences can be multiplied.

In idiom too, there are characteristic features in American English. As Shakespeare did, Americans verbed nouns frequently and very casually. Thus, expressions like *to audition, to park, to service, to orbit* are quite popular in America. Similarly verbs are converted into nouns as in, *a dump, a strike, a probe.* As if it were by a verbal jugglery, in America, nouns are converted into adjectives, *space age, skin diver, summit-meeting, London-correspondent;* and adjectives are transformed into nouns, as for example in *basics, briefs, compacts, wets* and *drys*. Expressions like *check-up drive-in, feed-back, slow-down, pullover, pushover* and such others were originally coined in America, but now have become proud possessions of English. Some of the scientific and technological words that are very indispensable to English were originally made in U.S.A. by dropping either the initial syllable or the trail-end syllable of the word. Words like *phone* (from telephone), *plane* (from aeroplane), *gas* (from gasoline), *memo* (from memorandum), *movie* (from moving pictures) belong to this group.

It is clear by now that there are quite a number of divergences between American English and British English. But the divergences are not so great as to progressively differentiate these two varieties of English into two different languages. Many modern factors like, the radio, television, swift means of travel and communication and above all man's ambition to overleap national boundaries are working against any such possibilities. Today forces are at work to converge and unify the two varieties .of English. In spite of the apparent diversity the essential unity has not been destroyed. Thus, underlying architecture of the language remains the same. It is vain to discuss the relative merits of American English and British English; both of them are one language—English. For, to Lincoln Barrett again, "the life of a great language is rather like that of some giant tree in the ever green rain forests of the tropics. It knows no seasons. Around the year random leaves detach themselves and flutter to the forest floor, and as they fall new ones appear.

ENGLISH AS A WORLD LANGUAGE

Lewis Mumford observes, "a world language is mere important for mankind at the present moment than any conceivable advance in television or telephony." Many eminent statesmen, philosophers and intellectuals of international reputation have, by and large, unanimity about the desirability of an international world language. If at all an international medium is desirable perhaps it is never more dreadfully needed than now. However it is not proposed to discuss here the pros and cons of the problem of desirability of a world language; it perhaps concerns, the anthropologists and students of other social sciences rather than the student of the English language. Starting with the basic assumption that a common link language is necessary, it is the object of this chapter to see the requirements of a good world language, and the possible candidates for the position and to examine how far the English language is suitable to play the role of a world language.

Many attempts were made in the past to devise universal languages which would be adapted without prejudice and learned without trouble. Artificial languages like Esperanto, novial and hundreds of such others were invented with this noble intention Their failure is chiefly due to the fact that they are not living languages, in the sense, that they have no living core of speakers. So it dawned upon many linguists that any world language must be a living language. Basic English was invented and abortive attempts were made to make it a language of international communication.

One of the forces that might make a language a world language is Power—power of all kinds, political, economic and military. History tells us that French became almost a world language in the seven teenth and eighteenth centuries, "because France was the nearest Europe had to a dominant military and social power." (Charlton Laird). Similarly, in recent years, during the hey-day of Hitler German was well-high a world language. Had Hitler succeeded in his plans, German would have increased hundred fold in importance. But, today English has, by all odds, the best prospect of becoming a world language, because it is the native tongue of the United States and is known in all the British Commonwealth of Nations. T.hese countries have now great power, political and military, great wealth, international trade and great productive potential. But the political, economic and military power of the countries is not the only requirement of a good world language. The principal requisites of a good world language fall under several items like:

(a) number of speakers of the language,

(b) distribution of speakers,

(c) linguistic adequacy of the language,

(d) easy availability of the language, as world medium.

Now, in the light of these requisites, let us examine the suitability of the English language for this role.

(a) Number of Speakers of the Language. Of the possible candidates for the position of a world language, French is spoken by a little more than 50 millions, Spanish by little more than 75 millions. German has perhaps crossed one hundred million. Russian is spoken by about a hundred and forty million people. But some of the dialects of Russian are mutually unintelligible. Hindi is spoken by about one hundred and sixty million people, but it has its own dialectal differences. Of all languages, Chinese is spoken by more than a four hundred million, But it is a welter of many unintelligible dialects which can be regarded as languages.

(b) Distribution of Speakers. We have seen that English gets the second place among the rivals, from the point of view of number of speakers of the language. But here. English gets the first position. No other language in the world had spread so widely as English. French is the language of France, part of Switzerland and Belgium, the Belgian and French colonial empires. It is also widely spoken in Haiti and the province of Quebec in the Western Hemisphere. It is widely used as a cultural tongue in Europe, Asia, Africa and Latin America and it is estimated that in Europe alone over a million people outside of France speak French besides their mother tongues. But in recent times French seems to be slowly declining.

Spanish is spoken in its homeland, Spain, and in the Canary islands and in Spanish colonies. But the distribution of Spanish is unequal. Only less than one fourth of its total number of speakers are located in Canary islands and Spanish colonies and three-fourths are in Western Hemisphere, where Spanish is second to English, in regions covering Mexico, Central America, Cuba, Puerto Rico, the Dominican Republic and a good part of South America.

German is mostly confined to Europe; it is spoken in Germany, Austria and a large part of Switzerland. It is also spoken in the neighbouring Central European countries like Czechoslovakia, Poland, Netherlands, Yugoslavia, Sweden, Hungary and so on.

Russian seems to be expanding with the expansion of the Soviet. At present it is spoken over one sixth of the earth's land surface. It is a predominant language of the Soviet Union, a "binding tongue", joining the far-flung distances of the country. But it is used as native tongue only by hundred and forty million people while the rest of the people in Soviet Union speak as many as hundred and forty languages-like Ukranian, Georgian, and many Turkish tongues.

India's over four hundred million inhabitants speak a little more than thirty major dialects and a host of minor dialects. It is estimated that more than two hundred languages are spoken in different regions in India. Hindi with its 160 million, is the leading language in India. But, as native language, it is largely restricted to Northern and Central India. It has little currency outside India. As a candidate in world-language contest, Hindi is outnumbered by Chinese, another candidate from the same continent—Asia. Russian speakers are divided between Europe and Asia and in both the continents Russian is outnumbered by Hindi and Chinese in Asia any by German in Europe.

That Leaves English. It is the native speech of more than 50 million in Europe. It holds undisputed control over the United States, the British Isles, Canada, Australia, New Zealand, and parts of South

Africa. It is current in aB British and American colonies or possessions. Besides the fifty million in Europe, about 150 million speak English in the Western Hemisphere, over 25 million in Asia, over 5 million in Africa and about 10 million in Australia and New Zealand. A few more million people speak English in addition to their mother tongue. Speakers of a variety of English called Pidgin English which has spread widely through the world in areas, are not included here. As a native or colonial language, English covers one fifths of the land surface. So from the point of view of distribution of speakers all over the world, English beats all other languages in competition.

(c) Adequacy of the Language from Linguistic View Point. This is a complicated aspect, because every language has one merit or the other. It is all the more complicated when everyone starts claiming that his language is superior to any other language. However, viewed from linguistic point of view it can be said that Russian has difficult grammar and different scripts. Chinese is not an Indo-European language and so would be difficult for Europeans and many Asians to learn. German, too, has complicated grammar. Spanish seems promising because its inflexional system is simple, its vocabulary is considerably large and its spelling is phonetic to some extent. English has prodigiously rich vocabulary and a simple grammar. Since it is a member of Germanic group of Indo-European family of languages and since it has borrowed words extensively from Romanic languages, it would be easy for foreigners, especially Europeans, to learn it. Its alphabet (Roman script) is widely spread in Europe. But it has its own weak points; its spelling is chaotic. We have seen in early chapters the difficulty of English spelling system. Unless some drastic measures are taken to reform spelling it would not be easier for foreigners to learn it. But, measures against any spelling reform are equally strong and valid.

(d) Availability of the language. World medium involves human mechanical and technological problems. Any language cannot be as good as any other to become a world language. If any obscure language is suddenly enthroned as an international auxiliary, it would fail to work because there was no technological advance like Printing, broad-casting in that language. English has a tremendous publishing industry behind it and the ability to print and broadcast English is scattered all over the globe. It is said that three-fourths of the world's mail is written in English. More than half of the world's newspapers are printed in English and English is heard in from more than three-fifths of the world radio-stations. English is the most uniform of all the great languages. It is spoken in all parts of the world in a mutually intelligible manner. It has the best and most numerous dictionaries and more than half of the world's scientific and technical periodicals are printed either entirely or partly in English. It has a flourishing literature and in recent times has become one of the leading tongues of international scholarship and research in all branches of knowledge.

Another important claim of English in aspiring to the honour of becoming a world-language is, that the best of world's literature, cultural heritage and civilization of mankind have been well translated from many languages, printed, bound and catalogued in libraries. Thus, continuity of mankind's heritage is preserved in English. It can, perhaps, be said that no other language has been the medium of such staggering widespread translation and publication as English. Yet, one more virtue English has; it comes from a democratic and relatively free world. So, if there is to be a world language in the near future, there is scarcely any close competitor to English, in spite of the serious limitations of it, especially in its spelling.

❒

7

English Grammer

TENSE

Tense does not directly situate the associated process in time, but rather orders it with respect to some point of reference, which may be called the axis (of orientation). Hence, past, present, and future mean before, simultaneous with, and after the axis, respectively. The axis, therefore, is the situation of utterance, and tense obvisouly a deictic category /zȯɳAciei/ '(The) monkey goes' reflects the present situation while /zȯ Anā cieī/ '(The) monkey want is the past tense telling about the events which has taken place before now. Future tense /zȯɳĀcie diɳAhi/ '(The) monkey will go' denotes about the event which is going to take place beyond now. Int he present study all the three tenses are denoted by different affixes used with the main verb in a grammatical construction.

TENSE MARKERS

Present Tense. The Present Tense is expressed with a zero (ϕ) marker. It takes the *-è* auxiliary after the main verb but -Āhi in case of progressive constructions. e.g.,

kĀ-nĕ-ė	=	'I eat'
pĀsĀlin kȯltù-Ā-né-é	=	'(The) man eats (the maize)'
kÀnĕ-pèt-tà ?-Ahi	=	'I am eating (just now)'

Past Tense. *n*Ā- as noted about is the past marker occurring as a prefix to the main verb which is turn is followed by an obligatory auxiliary -é. The personal prefix occurs before the tense marker and not before the main verb in the past tense (see diagram on page 58)

kĀ-nĀ-cèp-mè	=	'I smoked'
nĀ-nĀ-cèp-mè	=	'you smoked'
Ā-nĀ-cèp-mè	=	'he smoked'
Ā-nĀ-cėp-hlȯn-ė	=	'they (two) smoked'

Future Tense. *diη*, the future tense marker occurs as suffix to the main verb. The suffix shows that the action has not yet started but is to take place sometime after now. It is always followed by the auxiliary -Ā*hi*. The auxiliary optionally takes the personal suffix as an agreement with the subject, in such cases the main verb will not take the personal suffix:

cèp-diη-nAhi		
nĀ-cèp-diη-Āhi	=	'you will smoke'
kĀ-vė-diη-Ahi	=	'I will see'

-*η* an allomorph of -*diη* occurs interchangeably in case of 1st person singular as a free varient do *diη*. While it is used in the utterence neither the main verb nor the auxiliary takes the personal suffix. It is always followed by the obligatory auxiliary, -ė and never with -Ā*hi*.

kĀ-cie-diη Ahi		
cie ηė	=	'I shall go'
nė ηė	=	'I shall eat'
nėi ηė	=	'I shall take'

The -*η* become -*iη* while occurring after a consonant final verb.

cėp-miηė[6]	=	'I shall smoke'
vėt-iηė	=	'I shall see'
bȯl-iηė	=	'I shall do'

ASPECT

The category of aspect covers a vide range of distinction in Thadou which have to coincide with different orders of an event and not with the time, measurable in the category of tense. Aspects with their markers are discussed below.

(1) *Perfective* has its range in all the three tenses. The perfective suffic -*tā* occurs immediately after the main verb in all the situations. It always takes the obligatory auxiliary -*è* which becomes -ɨ due to the tonal environment.

Present :

KĀ cie táɨ	=	'I have to go'
nĀ cie táɨ	=	'you have to go'

Past :

Ā-nĀ-cieɨ	=	'he went'
A-nĀ-cie-taɨ	=	'he had gone'
kĀ-nA-cieɨ	=	'I went'
kĀ-nA-cie--taɨ	=	'I had gone'
nĀ-nA-cieɨ	=	'you went'
nĀ-nĀ-cí e-tấɨ	=	'you had gone'

Future :

cie táŋė	=	'I will have to go' or 'I will be going'
cí e táŋ kĀtė	=	'I will have to go'

Go perfect future I emphatic.

n̄A cí e tấn nĀt	=	'you will to going' 'you will have to go'

(2) *Progressive* has two markes -lái-tà? and -pèt-tà? Both of them show the progress of the action both temporal and spatial with little difference of meaning. *-pèt-tà*? is used for the momentary action while *-lái-tà*? even for a long time and space, but both of them substitute each other. Both the progressive markers are followed by tha auxiliary -Ā*hi* and participate in all the tenses. Here *-lái-tà*? and *-pèt-tà*? are used inter-changeably.

kĀ-nė lȧi-tȧ? Ahi	=	'I am eating'
kĀ-n̄A nė lȧi-tȧ? Ahi	=	'I was eating'
nĀ-nė lȧi-tȧ? Ahi	=	'you are eating'
nĀ-n̄A-nė lȧi-tȧ? Ahi	=	'you were eating'
kA-nė diŋlȧi-ȧt? Ahi	=	'I will be eating'
A-né pėt-tȧ? Ahi	=	'he is eating'
A nĀ-né pėt-tȧ? Ahi	=	'he was eating'

(3) *Habitual* has been divided into two sub-categories on the basis of suffixes used after the main verb. Both the sub-categories are preceded by the main verb and necessarily followed by the:

(a) Habit. This sub-category shows that the actor performs a particular action as a habit which is always performed in the same way.

Suffix-*zi* is used for this sub-category :

kĀ-né zi è	=	'I habitual eat/I am used to eat/I always eat'.
kĀ-nĀ-né zi è	=	'I used to eat'
Ā-né zi è	=	'he always eats (see first)
Ā-nĀ-né zi è	=	'he used to eat'
nĀ-né zi è	=	'you always eat' (see first)
nĀ-nĀ-né zi è	=	'you used to eat'

(b) Usuality. Suffix for this category is *ziŋ* which shows the usuality of the action.

kĀ-né ziŋ-è = 'I usually eat'

kA-nA-né ziŋ-è = 'I usually ate'

A-né ziŋ-è = 'he usually eat'

Ā-nĀ-né ziŋ-è = 'he usually ate'

MOOD

Mood, tense and aspect are very much intermingled in Thadou, yet they can be separated by different affixes they take, and their place of occurrence in the predicate construction.

(1) *Declarative* is a simple statement without any suffix or prefix, except the auxiliary verb which is used after the main verb.

Ā-cí e-i = 'I usually eat'

mèi AsÀn-è = 'fire is red'

mȯl Ạlin-e = 'mountain is big', etc.

(2) *Imperative* is formed by adding suffixes to the main verb and can be devided into two sub-categories:

1. Command or instructions and
2. Request

(1) *-in* this suffix, when used, always indicates the first sub-category, *e.g.*,

bù?-nė-in = 'take (your) food'

lȯu-ā cie-in = 'go to (the) field'

bȯŋxÀt cȯin = 'purchase a cow'

tim (lòi) sí emin = 'form (a) team'

(2) *-mȯ* demonstrates request or the friendly expression.

bȯŋ cȯmȯ	=	'(please) buy a cow'
tīm siemȯ	=	'(please) form a team'

(3) *Subjunctive* is formed by adding the suffix -hilè after the main verb. The verb, in this case, is preceded by the personal marker. It forms the dependent clause.

bȯŋ kĀ-cȯ-hilè	=	'If I purchase a cow'
tīm kĀ-siem-hīlè	=	'If you form a team'
bù? Ā-nè-hīlè	=	'If he take food...'

NUMBER SUFFIXES

Thadou has a subject verb agreement which is denoted by different suffixes designated as number suffixes. These suffixes are different than the personal markers which occur as prefixes to the main verb. They are three in number and occur after the main verb in simple sentences but may change the place in Compound and Complex sentences. They are :

(1) Singular Suffix ϕ

The singular suffix is marked with zero (ϕ) *i.e.*, there is no number suffix for singular :

kĀ-hlèŋ-ŋè	=	'I choose'
nĀ-hlèŋ-ŋè	=	'you choose'
Ā-hlèŋ-ŋè	=	'he chooses'
kĀ-nĀ-hlèŋ-ŋè	=	'I chose'
Ā-hlèŋ-diŋ-Ahi	=	'you choose'

(2) Dual Suffix-hlȯn

kĀ-hlèŋ-hlȯn-e	=	'we two (excl.) choose'
nĀ-hleŋ hlòn-è	=	'you two choose'

Ā-hleŋ hlon-e = 'they two choose'

kĀ-nĀ-hleŋ hlȯn-e = 'we two (excl.) have to choose'

The 1st person dual inclusive does not take number suffix because of the fact that duality is expressed by the person suffix itself, as :

ihlèŋ-ŋè = 'we two (inclusive) choose'

(3) Plural Suffix -ū-

kĀ-hlèŋ-ū-wè = 'we (excl.) choose'

èi-hlèŋ ū-wè = 'we (incl.) choose'

nĀ-hlèŋ-ū-wè = 'you choose'

Ā-hlèŋ-ū-wè = 'they choose'

The tense marker *-diŋ* loses *-n* with the plural suffixes as:

èi-hlèŋ diu-Ahi = 'we (incl.) will choose'

kĀ-hlèŋ diu-Ahi = 'we (excl.) will choose'

nĀ-hlèŋ diu-Ahi = 'you (pl.) will choose'

INTERROGATION

Interrogatives are formed in two ways. One, by using suffix *-m* and the other by a completely different expression, *hái-mó*. The interrogative marker comes at the end of the utterance. The *hái-mó* is generally used by the Paite people and it seems, that Thadou has borrowed it from them.

(i) nĀ-cí e (h) Àm = 'do you go'

(ii) Ā-né diŋ (h) Àm = 'will he eat'

(iii) Ā-húŋ (h) ītám = 'has he come'

< Ā-húŋ Āhī-tá-hĀm

(ia) nĀ-cí e-hái mó = 'do you go'

(iia) Ā-né diŋ Āhi mó = 'will he eat'

(iii) Ā-húŋ tái-mó = 'has he come'

The *-mó* is equivalent to 'isn't it' in English and 'Ẽ nā' in Hidni.

The *h-* in *hÀm* and *hái* in *hái-mó* are the morphophonemic forms of the obligatory auxiliary *-Ahi*, and same is the case with *hi* in *hitám*. These are not separate morphemes.

SYNTAX

Syntax deals with the arrangement of morphenies, both segmental and intonational, in an utterance. Intonation which occurs in simultaneous with the segmental constituents has not been dealt with separetely in this study.

Immediate constituents of a construction may consists of a signle morpheme and/or a sequence of morphemes. The sequence of more than one morpheme can be taken as a syntactic phrase. The six phrase types are discussed below :

NOUN PHRASES

Noun phrases, which function as subjects in clause constructions are of two main types :

(i) Attributive noun phrases (ii) Co-ordinate noun phrases.

1. Attributive Noun Phrases

An attributive noun phrase consists of a noun head with one or more attributes. The attributive noun phrases can be attributes of larger noun phrases and function as subjects, objects, and topics. It can also be a single noun or may take the following attributes :

(1) Single Noun and Compounds

in-vá = (house-bird) 'sparrow'

thiŋ-phùŋ = (ginger-plant) 'ginger plant'

thèi-tùi = (fruit-water) 'fruit juice'

(2) Noun and Adjectives

lÀm-līa = (path-big) 'road, highway'

mī-ŋòl = (man-mad) 'mad man'

xō-lin = (village big) 'big village'

hùm pī Āhát = (tiger is strong) 'strong tiger'

(3) Noun and Demonstratives

In this kind of noun phrases the head is preceded by the demonstrative :

hīcē mī nòl... = 'this mad man'

cēxū in = 'that house'

(4) Noun and Numerals

bóŋ sĀgī (cow seven) 'seven cows'

cĀpÀŋ ŋá hó (chile five plural) 'five children'

(5) Noun and Post Position/Case

Adùŋ lĀŋā (river towards) 'towards the river'

cĀpÀŋpā tò? (child mail with) 'with (the) boy'

tēbĀl nói-yà (table below) 'below (the) table'

(6) Noun and Verb-Root

bù? né.... = (food eat) 'to take (the) food'

thiŋ tÀn diŋā = (wood cut for) 'to cut (the) tree'

Noun phrases of the above type are not very frequent and are a part of dependent clause.

CO-ORDINATE NOUN PHRASES

Co-ordinate noun phrases are those, any of whose immediate constituents can substitute syntactically for the entire constituent. They are of three types :

(1) Additive Noun Pharase

Additive noun pharse is made up of two or more nouns or attributive phrases by juxtaposing or joining the constituents with a conjunct :

bóŋ lĀ lōi = 'cow and buffalo'

bóŋ si el lĀ lōi = 'cow, mithun and buffalo'

hīcē bóŋ lĀ cēxū lói = 'this cow and that buffalo'

nūmèi pĀsĀl.... = 'man (and) woman'

gólhÀŋ nùŋà?.... = 'young man (and) young woman'

(2) Alternative Noun Phrase

In the alternative noun phrase the constituents are joined by a connective Ā*hi-lòu-lé* 'or' juxtaposed as in additive noun phrase :

Asōng Āhi-lòu-lĀ pĀtóng

'either Ashong or patong'

vò? xÀc A-hi-'óu-lĀ sí el xÀt

'either one pig or one mithun'

(3) Appositonal Noun Phrase

Appositional noun phrase is made of two nouns or noun phrases, both of them function as head as well as attribute :

milon kȧpngùl = Mr. kapngul

milum kȧpngùl kĀgú Al pā

'Mr. Kapngul, my friend'

ozĀ Ashóng = 'teacher Ashong'

thí em pū Tòngxōmȧng

'priest Tongkhomang'

The most common type of appositional phrases are the genetival phrases consists of one of the noun or noun phrase as possessor and the other constituent as possessed :

Mángī cĀnū	=	'Mangpi's daughter'
Āmáhó in	=	'their house'
kĀpā Ānāo nū	=	'my father's younger sister'

VERB PHRASES

A verb phrase consists of a verb head with certain other elements used as prefixes and suffixes. In spite of the elements shown on page 58 a verb can take the following suffixes discussed in the preceding pages, *(1)* Negative markers, *(2)* imperative suffix, *(3)* interrogative marker and *(4)* demonstratives which form a part of the noun phrase or serve as subject. The last one is discussed below as:

(1)	hīcē ka ból thèiè	=	'I can do this'
	hīcé ka cep-mè	=	'I suck this'
	xū:ē cùndò? è	=	'that this'

This kind of constructions in the language are not common because the verb generally takes the personal prefix to specify the doer of the action.

(2) Negative markers are three in number and are discussed in. Other elements of the verb phrase listed above can be referred with the relevant sections.

ADVERBIAL PHRASES

Adverbial phrases are the constituents, consist of a sequence of words substitutable for adverb, and single adverbs. Almost all the adverbs can enter into a construction and form the adverbial phrase with adverb as the head. Some of the examples of adverbial phrases are given below. For details *see* :

tū-lái-yin school ā kĀcí e zīŋè

'now a days I usually go to school'

ī-tī-phāt-na nĀhùŋ ham?

'at what time (when) did you come'

hī-lái-yā tÀu tÀŋó

'at this place sit down'

'(you) sit here'

nĀŋ zòŋ hùŋin

'you also come'

mùn-xÀt-nin cié ŋè

'I will go somewhere'

hòi ā nĀgĀváithām nĀhim

'where (in the world) had you gone'

In addition to the above constructions there is another suffix used with other grammatical catgory to make it function as an adverbial phrase.

vèi: The suffix shows the repetition and is used with the numerals. It gives the sense of Hindi 'bar' as in 'car-bar' 'four times' and so on.

nī vèi = 'two times'

sōm-vèi = 'ten times'

nī-le thùmvèi = 'two (or) three times'

NUMERAL PHRASES

Numeral phrases consists of a numeral or sequence of numerals as post-posed attribute (to function as specifier) preceded by a noun :

thèi-gá xÀt = 'one fruit'

lí eŋ thèi ŋále gup = 'five (or) six pineapples'

cÀpÀŋ giét = 'eight children'

The numerals can occur without following the noun if there is an earlier reference to the noun or noun-phrase concerned.

lī Āné tái = 'he has eaten four'

sĀgī piéŋé = 'I will given seven'

EMPHATIC PHRASES

The emphatic phrase is built by placing the emphatic particle just after the noun (head) in the noun phrase and at the end of the sentence in the predicate constructions. Given below are the emphatic particles and their functions :

(a) hi-: In a -*hī*- phrase the emphatic particle is placed after the noun or pronoun. This particle gives the sense of Hindi 'hi' as in 'ye-hi' *etc.*

hīcē lé-xĀ-bù hī

'this very book'

Āmá hī Ā-cie tá-i

'he himself has gone'

kèimá cóŋ hī

'my cow itself'

kĀból bi lóu

'I certainly do not do'

(2) -sè?-sè?: The *sè?-sè?-* phrase has a restricted occurrance. it gives the sense of English 'only' and Hindi 'kewAi.

nÀŋ sè?-sè? = 'you only'

cÀŋ sè?-sè? = 'all alone'

nÀŋ nī sè?-sè hlòh-nè = 'only you two are suning'

(3) -pī- : The *-pī-* phrase is formed by placing the particle at the end of the construction. It especially occurs with the negative predicates, but its occurrence with the statements cannot be overlooked. It gives the sense of English 'not at all' and Hindi 'bilku'.

kĀból lòu pī = 'I don't do at all'

nĀcíe lòu pī = 'you won't go at all'

kĀsèi tás-pī = 'I have told (you) emphatically'

(4) -cū : It sometimes happens that the definite article *-cū* gives the sense of an emphatic construction such as:

hīcē cĀpÀŋ cū = 'this very child'

xūcē in cū = 'that very house'

nĀpā cū Asèi tái = 'Your father himself has told'

VOCATIVE PHRASES

The vocative phrases are of three types made with a sequence of morphs both free and bound. They are :

(1) hieŋè~hiŋ 'yes'

hiŋ is the short form of *hieŋè* which serves as Hindi 'hã'.

Ān-hét~nÀm = 'do you follow'

híeŋè = 'yes'

(2) *xū-hái-tĀŋò~xūŋái-yin* = 'wait'

This type of vocative phrase serves as dependent clause after which something else is required to be told. It is the 2nd *sg.* imperative construction.

xūηái-tÀηó! kagei nÀt Ā ū́mè

'wait, I have something (to tell) you.'

xūηái-yin! kei zòη hùη táηè

'wait, I also have to come'

(3) hē 'O' is always followed by some interjection or a proper noun.

hé-kĀtè = 'Oh-o'

hē-pū = 'O! elder one'

hē-pā = 'O! father'

hē-ū = 'O! elder (brother or sister)'

hē-nā́o = 'O! younger (brother or sister)'

CLAUSES

Clauses are built up of a noun or noun phrase, or a verb or verb phrase, as a subject, followed by a verb or verb phrase as predicate. We have dealt here with two principal clause types: (1) main cluses and (2) subordinate clauses.

(1) Main Clauses

Main clauses consist of a complete verb phrase with one or more preceding phrases traditionally known as subject. It may also be built up of a form which do not contain a verb and can occur in isolation, thus they are a complete sentence. Some examples of main clauses are given below :

Ahùη diη Ahi = 'he will come'

A-hùη kit diη Ahi = 'he will come again'

Ahùη lē kèi tò? = 'he will come and stay with me'

Aùm diŋ Ahi

Amán pháiyā pÀt Ahùŋ	=	'he will come from Imphal and
le Shillong a zòtbā ā Delhi		go to Delhi through Shillong'.
lĀm Acie diŋ Ahi.		

(2) Subordinate Clauses

Subordinate clauses are built up of an incomplete verb phrase, preceded by subject or an incomplete verb phrase alone. A main clause can also be rendered to a subordinate clause by adding a subordinate conjunction at the end of the main clause.

mī Akihùŋ zòu-sâ?	=	'the man who came'
bù? Akiné {zòu - sà / cái - sà}	=	'the eaten food'
sā AkīthÀt zòu-sà?	=	'the killed animal'
in sà pū min	=	'while constructing the house'
nūi kōm-kōmin	=	'while caughing'
nūi pù-min Acie tái	=	'he has gone laughingly'

Main Clause to Subordinates Clause

When a main clause is rendered to a subordinate clause following conjunctions are employed :

(1) Āhī-lè		'If, provided, when'
Ahùŋ Ahi-lé	=	'if he come'
nĀné Ahi-lè	=	'provided you eat'
Ahán kÀinā Ahùŋ Ahi-lé	=	'if he come to my house'
(2) lèŋ		'if at al, after'

The conjunction occurs if a transitive verb is operating in the clause.

bù?né léŋ	=	'If at all (I) eat food'
nĀin ā cie léŋ	=	'after going to your house'/ 'If at all (I) go to your house'.
tùi dòhn léŋ kĀvá diŋ Ahi	=	'if I drink water I will be satisfied'

(3) *lē cùn* 'as soon as' the Hindi expression "jiõ hi"

nÀŋ gó-hĀŋ lē cùn	=	'as soon as you get young'
Àthlái lé cùm	=	'as soon as he runs'
kĀné lé cùŋ kĀlùp diŋ Ahi	=	'as soon as I eat I will go to sleep'

The subordinate clauses are also made by adding the interrogative adverbials in the beginning of the utterance

SENTENCES

A sentence consists of one or more clauses. They are of two main types (1) major sentences (2) minor sentences. A major sentence is any sentence which contains a main clause as one of its constituents or : the only constituent. The minor sentence does not contain a main clauses.

Major Sentences

Major sentences are further sub-divided into three types (1) simple (2) complex and (3) Compound.

(1) Simple Sentence. A simple sentence also known as kernel sentence is any sentence which contains only the main clause :

cie tāŋè	=	'I will go/may I go'
tī nĀóm tèi diŋ Ahi	=	'you must boil the water'

Anán sā, mé, lA Ā Àn - cÀŋ Ané diŋ Ahi	=	'he will eat meat, curry and rice'.

(2) Complex Sentences. A complex is any sentence which contains a main clause and at least one subordinate clause.

xūŋái - yin, kèizòŋ hùŋ diŋ Ahi.	=	'wait, I will also come'
hùmpī thá zòulè īné di - ū - wé	=	'after killing the tiger we will eat it'.
nÀŋ gólh Àŋlè cùn A-dèi diŋ Ahi	=	'as soon as you get young (man) she will like you'.

(3) Compound Sentences. A compound sentence is any sentence which contains at least two main clauses. It may also contain one or more subordinate clauses in addition to the main clauses.

kĀcā hī Ācie thèi hi? lái-yè túéi-yin Āvá thòi	=	'my child is not yet walking but still crawls'.
Ā in ā kĀcíe cùn hā uspūn thÀŋmÀn pón xÁt lē xūtaŋ xÀt èi nApéi	=	'when I went to his house the chief offered me a shawl and a woman's lion cloth.
xùl ā kón ā Ahùŋ pót dò? zòu-win cóŋthu iĀ Ālói hò ıııùnzòu sē? ā Avá? łe-e ù-we.	=	'after coming from the hole Chongthu and his friends moved every where.

(2) Minor Sentences

Minor Sentence is any sentence which does not contain a main clause. It may consist of any single word or syntactic phrase (except a complete verb phrase) which fulfils the sentence requirement or simultaneous occurrence with an intonation.

hiŋ	=	'yah'
ùm pói	=	'not present'

(ī-tī téŋ lē nÀci e = '(when are you going)'

cin hÀm) = 'ziŋ'.è' 'tomorrow'

kĀmin Tháŋxó máŋ = 'my name is Thangkhomang'

In the vowel system, long and short vowels listed by Hodsom are the contextual variations only and not separate phonemes. Some of the statements given in 'Thadou grammar' about modifications of consonants and vowels are quite dubious. The causative suffix *su*, 'faint sound of *w* after a' are not at all correct.

Though Hodson has contributed a few lines on tone (p. 5) but he over-looked the presence of tone in Thadou by saying "...there is no system of tonal modification, and the only emphasis is that which the natural exigencies of conversation demand".

So far as the grammer is concerned Hodson could do a bit justice with the language. Writing about article he writes "there are no definite articles..." While the language possesses it. He also mixes *-ho* plural suffix *-te* class suffix and even some adverbs together as plural markers. He records five cases namely, nominative, accusative, dative, genetive and agnetive mininterpreting the case markers with one another. Chapter on verb is quite confusing at places but can be helpful to compare the old language with the present form. The imperative suffix *-in* with verb base has been designated as verbal nouns by Hodson.

❐

8

Makers of Words

Philologists recognise a variety of processes by which new words are added to the stock of language. The process or deliberate creation of words is one of the important methods of he growth of vocabulary. Words are not born as if from no where; as L. P. Smith observes, they do not grow out of soil, nor do they fall from heaven. Some one invented them to cater to a need, to neme a new and unnamed object or to brand an old but badly named thing or idea. We may reasonably surmise that they were at first considered slang and at some point in the history of language, they met with popular favour, when people realised the utility of those words. Gradually they could elbow their way to the high pedastal of literary usage by way of colloquialism. Some learned words, however, first make their appearance in writing, and slowly gain popular currency or else they sink into oblivion until some other writer of a later generation revives and gives them a fresh lease of life. The study of such words is interesting in itself. It is all the more interesting because, those words like the coinage of a king, bear the unmistakable stamp of the personality of their creator, or they reflect the needs of mankind in different ages, when they were revived and popularised before they became part and parcel of language. It should, however, be borne in mind that it is not always the best masters of literary craft that can influence the vocabulary of language, but it is the most popular, albeit second rate, authors who enrich the vocabulary by introducing new words, by new application of old words or by giving wider currency to the words that are moribund.

The English language is fortunate in having a galaxy of word makers who made the language what it is to-day. The earliest I influence on the vocabulary of the English Language was the Bible and its translators. The influence of Chaucer on I English cannot, however, be overlooked. Chaucer gave ease and polish to the dialect he had chosen as his medium. He borrowed a large number of words from French and naturalized them in English. Some linguists claim for him the credit of giving curreney to a great deal of poetic vocabulary. Hardly any of his phrases became indispensable part of English vocabulary. His influence was more on learned and literary plane. Some important words like *attention, diffusion, fraction, duration* and *position* are traced back to his works.

Contribution of the Bible to the growth of English vocabulary can not be overestimated. Among the various translators of the Bible, Wyclif was almost a contemporary of Chaucer. Like Chaucer, he wrote in the East Midland dialect and like Chaucer, he had a genius for language. While Chaucer borrowed from French, for Wyc1if, the Latin of Vulgate's translation was the source of his adaptations. The importance of his contribution to the wealth of English vocabulary seems to have almost equalled that of Chaucer's but by the side of more powerful luminaries like 'Coverdale and Tindale, Wyclif is eclipsed.

While Chaucer and Wyclif were content with borrowing from foreign languages, Coverdale and Tindale began to form compound words freely from native resources. To Coverdale the English language owes some of its beautiful combinations like *Loving Kindness, Blood Guiltiness, Noonday, Morning Star, Kind Hearted.* In Tindale we find compounds like *long suffering, Peace maker, Broken Hearted.* Tindale is said to have used the word *beautiful* for the first time. He translated the Latin *Presbyter* in a native word of the same literal meaning. He called him a *senior* and as the word was unsatisfactory, he rebaptised him as *elder*. The word *Scape-goat* stands as an admirable illustration of his genius for word milking. It is said that the word originated in a misinterpretation of a hebrew proper name. Whatever might be the error that cropped it up, the word has become a valuable addition to the language. The phrases of Tindale have remained a part of the English language because, King lames's translators have taken them unchanged in their translation. In spite of many translations that had existed and disappeared earlier, it is the Authorised version that has remained a dominant influence on the English Language, on literary as well as colloquial plane. The chief contribution of the Authorised version to the English language was in the direction of reviving and preserving some of the archaic words which were already on the point of becoming obsolete. This was done perhaps with a conviction that the 'language of sacred-truths should be removed from the language of daily life. But then, the language of the people's book should not be different from the people's language. So King James's translators steered a course of compromise between the extreme pedantry of the early Roman Catholic translators and literalness and colloquialism of Tindale.

Some of the archaic words revived in the Authorised version now belong to elevated poetic diction. The words like *apparel* and *raiment* for dress; *quick* for *living, damsel* for young woman and *Firmament* synonymous with sky, do not form a part of the language of daily life. But many phrases have become English idioms and so inextricably woven in to the language of common man that they are often used with little consciousness of their origin. The phrases like *to cast pearls before swine, A labour of love, a howling wilderness, the shadow of death, the eleventh hour, to wash one's hands off the whole business, to hope against hope the burden and heat of the day, the powers that be, and eat, drink and be merry* (the last three Tindale's) belong to the stock of spoken language. As Henry Bradley observes, the Bible, being one of the widely read books, has given rise to some phrases through popular misunderstanding. The word *help mate* is a striking illustration of the Bible readers' blundering into excellence. The origin of this word was 'an help meet (suitable) for him'. People thought that it meant 'one who helps to make both ends meet'. The- second element in the mistaken compound, *help meet* was imagined to be synonymous with *mate*, and so a new compound was made; help mate meaning, partner in life.

Spenser's language stands aloof from that of his contemporaries, by its pseudo-archaic quality, artificiality, and provincialism. Ben

Jonson's remark that in trying to imitate his ancients. Spenser writ no language, is not wholly untrue. He deliberately invented words or revived the obsolete words. The literary vocabulary of the present day English bears a few marks of his influence. Spenser's vain-glorious knight in the *Faerie Queene* gave us the word Braggadocio. The phrase 'squire of dames', comes from the same source. *Blatant* and *elfin* seem to have been deliberately invented by Spenser. The story of *derring-do* is interesting. It is one of not a few words that originated in blunder. Chaucer characterised Troilus as one "dorring-do (in daring to do) that longeth to a knight". In Lydgate's Troy-Book the phrase was misprinted as derrynge-dce and later Spenser mistook for a substantive, meaning manhood and chivalry. Spenser owes *gride* to Lydgate which Spenser's friend E.K. explains as 'to pierce'. It was thought that the word was a child of scribal error for *gride* which means to smite. Many later poets who imitated Spenser used it in the sense of a passage of a sharp weapon through flesh. Shaley used it to express the notion of grating sound.

As in literature, Shakespeare is the greatest figure in the English language. In his immense interest in the English language, in his consciousness of its needs and in his experiment-s with all kinds of linguistic innovations, none can out Shakespeare. The freedom of the individual suggested by the Renaissance found its fullest expression in Shakespeare's use of language. His experiments with the language are startling. He rediculed and renounced stylistic fashions, linguistic snobbishness and pedantic equivocations among his contemporaries. But he was not tired of exeprimenting 'with the language to explore its potentialities to express every nuance of thought. He made the dramatic use of dialects, archaisms, provincialisms and 'Low class' wards and elevated same of them to literary status.

The greatness of Shakespeare's influence is in the abundance of campaund wards, which he had invented and added to the literary vacabulary, and also in the wealth of wards and phrases cained by him which are waven into the fabric of everyday language. The following phrases serve as samples; *tower of strength, full of sound and fury, yeoman service, the sere and yellow leaf, hoist with his own petard, moving accidents, a triton among the minnows, to wear one's heart upon one's sleeve, one's pound of flesh,* all these and hundreds mare have become part of the wealth of English idiomatic expressions.

Same phrases, however, are literary in nature. Shakespeare is supreme in ward making, when he writes in the glow and fire of emotion. Macbeth's hysteric cry, "No this my hand will rather the *multitudinous* seas incarnadine" is a testimony to the intensity .of Macbeth's emotion and the poet's audacity to invent unheard wards. Prospera's *Cloud capt* towers, and *the baseless fabric of this vision, Romeo's Yoke of inauspicious stars* are all happy literary expressians. Shakespeare surpassed all other poets in the extent and variety of his vacabulary. His contribution to the English language is in the creation of happy phrases and in bringing the archaic wards to life. With the French prefix en (or em) he made a large number of wards, such as, *endeared, enkindle, enmesh, embattle, empoison* and so on. He made free use of nouns and adjectives to make new verbs; *happy, safe, spaniel* were all used as verbs meaning *to make happy, to make safe, to follow like a spaniel* respectively. The verbs, *childed* and *fathered* are too well known to need any special mention. The interchange of functions of various parts of speech gave flexibility to the language of Shakespeare. The genius of Shakespeare is in moulding the language in such a way as to accommodate his thoughts, in providing the language with a wealth of idioms and proverbs, which act as models for further coinages.

The 16th century and the early half of the 17th century abound in eccentric word makers who seem to have invented new wards more for novelty than for necessity. Nevertheless, some important wards were cained during this period. By constant experiment with the language they stumble upon a few good words. Sir Thomas Brawn, for instance, created words that are characteristic of his scholarship and meditative temperament. *Insecurity, hallucination, retrogression, precarious, antediluvian* are some of the words that bear the stamp of his genius. While mast of his creations are literary in nature, some of them like, *medical, Literary, electricity* are quite indispensable in modern speech. During the same period, Cudworth created *dramatist* and *fatalism*. *Central, Circuitous, decorous, freakish* and *fortutous* are traced to Henry More. Evelyn imported and naturalized many foreign words that belong to the vocabulary of art; contour, *cascade, Opera, outline* and *attitude*. Boyle created mostly scientific words like *pendulum, intensity, pathological, essence, corpuscle*. Dryden can not be said to have added much of value to the English vocabulary. But his influence on English still remains great. He regarded himself as an improver of the language and as a member of the Royal Society, he tried to standardize the language. His influence, however, is more on stylistic plane. He aimed to bring the language of poetry closer to the language of conversation and he brought ease, clarity and simplicity to his prose.

Among the 17th century writers Milton stands out in many respects. In the realm of style, he is the delight and despair of the modern reader. He was immensely interested in matters of spelling, stress and pronunciation. In the realm of vocabulary, Milton is extremely latinate and shows how deeply he was influenced by the models of Latin prose and poetry. Nevertheless, Milton has left significant marks on the English language. *Gloom* in the sense of darkness, from the earlier *gloomy*, was invented by him. He created *anarch* to connote the personified chaos. From the Greek *Pan* (all) and *daimon* (devil), Milton created the word Pandemonium as a designation for the palace built in Hell by the devils. Some of his phrases are still widely used, at least in the literary sphere of the language. Here are some of them; *darkness visible, The human face divine, barbaric pearl and gold, precious bane, the bad eminence, the gorgeous east, confusion worse confounded, Pillar of State, to some appearances, a dim religious light, men of light and leading, the last infirmity of noble mind, writ large, fresh woods and pastures new.*

Dr. Johnson is yet another great influence on the English language. He added a considerable number of literary and learned words to the treasure of English vocabulary. *Literature, comic, irrascibility, acrimonious* are traced to Dr. Johnson. His greatest achievement, however, was the publication of a *Dictionary of the*

English language in 1755. It was a stupendous task of one man labouring without assistance, for a short period of seven years. With its ludicrous etymologies its capricious and discriminating definitions, his Dictionary is painfully inadequate, judged by modem standards of lexicography. But it has its virtues too. For the first time, the English vocabulary was exhibited much more fully than had ever been done before. Spelling was fixed, however arbitrarily, and in a way standardised. Dr. Johnson supplied innumerable quotations to illustrate the use of words where explanation is inadequate. It is claimed for him that he preserved the purity of language (whatever it may mean), ascertained the meaning of words and fixed the pronunciation and spelling. It can not be denied that he was an academy for his country. Coming down to later times, we may mention many writers who contributed to the English vocabulary by creating new words or reviving archaic words. Burke was one of those who had this faculty of minting new words.

With the rise of the romantic movement many obsolete words were revived. Walter Scot was the greatest of those who revived archaic words; *Raid, Foray, onslaught, gruesome, lodestar, bluff, glamour* are some of the words whose revival is attributed to Scot. Among many outlandish coinages of Coleridge we find the current words like *pessimism, Phenomenal, Elizabethan,* and *intensify*. The word *idealism* attributed to Shelley seems to be descriptive of his mind. Strangely Wordsworth has not contributed much to modern vocabulary. Keats, however, was a genuine maker or reviver of words. He created words like *auroream* and *beamly*. But his genius is greater in creating compound epithets, which are said to be miniature poems; *deep-masked, dew-dabbled, full-throated ease* and many more.

Like Keats, Tennyson possessed the faculty of making compound words like *evil-starred, green-glimmering, fire crowned moonlit* and *fairy tales*. Browning's creations are old and unpleasant, of his *crumblement, fabricity, darlingness, garnishness* and *artistry*, only the last one has some limited currency.

Among the victorians, Carlyle had the great audacity to create words bearing a stamp of his temperament. He made words like *Croakery, Dandiacal, bedlaism* and he introduced words like *Feckless, outcome*, and *lilt. Environment, dacadent* are the most useful of his coinages. Those who dislike economics as a subject will find a ready-made name in Carlyle, *dismal science*. Bentham formed the word *international*, Huxley made *agnostic* and *agnosticism*. A meterologist deliberately invented *cyclone*, to describe the phenomenon of circular winds and a few years later Sir Francis Galton created anti-cyclone, Macaulay is said to have apoloized for his creation of constituency. Whewell created *scientist*. In the 19th century *Eurasian, exogamy, folklore, hypnotism, telegraph, telephone, Photograph* were deliberately created.

Some proper names of fiction and drama attain a degree of currency and they deserve a place in the History of the English language. Bunyan's *Vanity Fair* and *slough of despond*. Swift's *Lilliputican, brobdignagian,* Sheridan's *Malapropism* from Mrs. Malaprop of the Rivals are only some of a host of such words in the language.

In modern period Journalism is steadily increasing its importance in making new words. The reporter has no time to think for the most idiomatic expression and the editor has no space enough to accommodate long and polysyllabic expressions. The head lines are often brief, not however to the point of obscurity or equivocation, and they are often striking, sometimes to the point of being sensational. The journalist tries to be interesting, racy and colloquial and in this effort, he is justified in creating phrase like *Sweet death* to describe the death due to excessive eating of sweet meats. In journalistic language winners of Nobel Prize are called Nobelity. Some of the phrases frequently seen on sport-page attain currency, gradually and imperceptibly. How many of us know that *Crest fallen, fight shy,* and *show the white feather* originally belong to cockfighting? The influence of journalism on the English language deserves a separate chapter. Thus, writers have been making new words or using old words to express new concepts, through ages. Often words are created out of unwholesome zeal for novelty and freshness and some times, to supply the genuine needs of the age.

CHANGES OF MEANING

Words are symbols of thoughts or things and they should mean the same thing to the speaker as they mean to the hearer. If the meaning of the hearer differs from that of the speaker, misunderstanding creeps in and the language fails to communicate. The primary function of language—to serve as a means of communication—depends on the three-fold relation between the speaker, hearer and the things that their talk symbolises. This relation is a matter of convention; words are collocation of sounds, which by usage and convention are made to signify certain objects, things or ideas. They have no natural or essential meaning which belongs to them more than any other. It is by convention that the sounds 'dog' signify a particular species of animal kingdom. There is no reason, excepting convention, why the word should not signify what is spoken of as 'cat'. That language is a convention, is also seen in what we call irony. Thus, when Mark Antony says, "Brutus is an honourable man", he conveys the opposite meaning without any difficulty. The intention of the speaker and the understanding of the hearer are all that do the trick. In intending to convey a meaning other than what is usually understood, we are trying to create a new convention in place of old. So, linguistic conventions undergo changes as new situations demand. To put it more plainly, the meaning of a word may be changed as a result of its repeated use; sometimes it extends its meaning and sometimes it narrows down its scope; it may be elevated in its meaning or it may also be degenerated. Some times in addition to its central meaning it may acquire a cluster of new shades of meaning. Many words have so changed their meanings in course of time that their present sense has either obscured or totally ousted the meaning which they formerly had. There are quite a good number of words which have acquired emotive values from their dull intellectual associations of earlier days. The study of the forces operating on this plane of meaning is called semantics. The best way to study semantics is to classify the operating forces and examine the meaning of a few words under each head.

1. Generalisation. This is a semantic process by which a word which at one time had specialised or restricted meaning comes, in course of time, to have a wider application; that is to say, the word can be applied to everything in general and not anything in particular. In the words of Greenough and Kittredge, "a term that can be applied to everything means nothing, as a man who is equally intimate with everybody has no real friends." A few striking examples of Generalisation may now be considered. "Religion' seems to have originally signified a "scrupulous regard for omens, portents and other divine intimations". Christianity has broadened and deepened its meaning. In the Middle Ages, "Religious' monks, friars, nuns and so on were members of Holy Order. A pious layman was not qualified to be called religious. But in modern usage the word has taken all types of devout, pious and god fearing persons into its fold. The word 'box' is another striking example of the process of Generalisation. Originally it was the name of a tree and wood from that tree (box-tree). Being rare and expensive, box-wood was used for making luxury-articles like small caskets to put the jewellary in and so the caskets were called boxes. At a later stage any I wooden box of small dimensions was called by the name.

Similarly with the words 'Journey' and 'Journal'; the root meaning of 'Journey' is a day's walk or ride, and a 'Journal' originally a daily record of events. The sense of the *Journal* is still retained when it is used to mean a book in which daily transactions are recorded. In both these words the restricted meaning denoting a *day's work* has been lost and we can speak, without any hesitation, of "Journey of several days" and "a fortnightly or monthly Journal".

A few other examples of Generalisation may be briefly indicated; *Companion* originally meant "one who shares bread with another person, and *comrade* literally means "one who shares room". In modern usage the root meaning has been totally lost and emphasis has shifted from "sharing bread or room" to "intimate" nature of such relation. In more recent times, the word *Comrade*, however, has been running the risk of acquiring some political colour, especially, since it is being used as a prefix of respect among all Communists. *Tragedy* till recently had a strict dramatic sense, but now has come to mean any event of sorrow and great calamity. *Crisis* is no longer applied to the turning point in the course of events, but has been used in the more general sense of "serious situation" as in "crisis in conscience" or similar situations. The word *virtue* meant manliness accompanied by courage and "prowess in war" . Later the word was made more comprehensive including any excellent quality: moral, mental or physical. But when the word is applied to women it acquires a specialised sense of "chastity". Paper was originally a substitute for parchment and was manufactured from the Papyrus plant.

2. Specialisation. This is more frequent and more effective than generalisation. By this process a word which at one time had general significance has, today, a specialised significance. When this special application gains currency, the word, in many cases loses its earlier meaning. Thus, the word *liquor* means in Latin any liquid. But in English it often connotes what are called "ardent spirits". Again, the word *fowl*, in Chaucer and in the Bible, was used for any bird. But in Middle English bird also existed and had the same meaning as *fowl*. But gradually *fowl* took a specialised meaning, while bird continued its general application. And similarly *deer* meant any wild animal and now it signifies a particular species of animals. In Old English, any kind of pledge or promise was called *wedlock*, but now the word is restricted in application to mean only matrimonial pledge, that is, to mean marriage. But it was borrowed into English in its specialised sense and its literal meaning has been lost in English. The word *prohibition* has acquired specialised meaning in this century. It actually means "the act of forbidding something".

Kittredge in his "Words and Their Ways" observes, "the manner in which a word may carry numerous specialised senses along with its more general meaning, and let no confusion arise among them all, appears almost miraculous when one takes the word by itself, as an isolated phenomenon. But words are not used by themselves. It is their combination in different contexts or circumstances that enables the same term to symbolize so many different things". We can study this phonomenon in our own experience. Every man is said to be his own specialiser and special meanings of words depend on our business, and on our outlook on life. *Pump* suggests one picture to a country boy and another to a water-works engineer and yet another to a cycle-shop-keeper. *Stone* calls up one picture in the mind of the dealer in Jewels. But it suggests various other things to the mason, the maker of tombstones, the workman on a road and the police trying to control the stonethrowing crowd. *Cataract* means one thing to the Geographer, another to the Occulist and yet another to the Poet. One more example of this process. To the mechanic *play* means rapid movement as in phrases "play of the valve", "the piston-rod does not play freely". By natural shift, the word specialised the meaning of 'sport' or 'game'. Again, even in this sense, it suggests several things to several people. By *play* children understand a 'game', a gambler understands it to mean a different sort of game. So also the musician, the base-ball player, cricketer and the actor, all have different games in view when they speak of play. The word is generally used in the actor's sense of 'drama'.

3. Radiation. Words, as Kittredge says, seem to have mastered the magician's trick of being in more than one place, at the same time. That is to say, in different places they exist in the same form, but in different specialised meanings. The difference between specialisation and Radiation is chiefly this. In Specialisation the word loses its original meaning, or its specialised sense acquires wider currency. But in radiation, the word does not lose its original meaning. On the other hand, the original meaning acts as the basic meaning or nucleus from which several other meanings spring up. The basic meaning is like the hub, the centre of a wheel, and the divergent growth of new meanings is like the emergence of spokes from the hub. For example, the primary or basic meaning of *Power* is "ability to do". Clinging to this basic meaning, the word has developed prop-meanings spreading in different directions. Thus, the word signifies:

(a) control over one's subordinates as in "the power of the king";

(b) delegated authority as in "the collector exceeded his powers";

(c) mechanical energy as in "water-power" or "steam-power";

(d) physical strength as in "the power of his muscles";

(e) a person of great influence;

(f) a great nation of the world;

(g) moral or intellectual force;

(h) a mathematical concept as in "three to the power of four";

(i) an effective quality of expressing through writing, art or oratory.

It can be noticed that all the divergent meanings here have equally close relation with the primary meaning of the word, though each of them is independent of the other.

4. Concatenation. This is closely akin to specialisation and radiation, but different from both. In this process a word shifts gradually away from its primary meaning until it reaches finally a highly specialised sense. There is not a shadow of relation between the primary meaning and the final specialised sense. The successive changes in meaning are like the links of a chain. Each succeeding stage has partial relation with its proceeding stage. The development of meaning of cardinal serves as an example. The word meant "pertaining to a hinge", before it was borrowed into English. Now let us follow the successive steps in the change of this primary meaning:

(a) (A) Pertaining to a hinge.

(b) (A) + (B) : as fundamental and important as a hinge (cardinal virtues).

(c) (B) : A church dignitary connected with one of the *cardinal* or Parich churches of Rome.

(d) (B) + (C) : One of the seventy ecclesiastics who constitute the Pope's Council and wear scarlet robes.

(e) (C) : Scarlet dress and Scarlet colour.

(f) (C) + (D) : bird with scarlet plumage.

Now, each stage in the evolution of final meaning is linked with its preceeding stage, thereby giving a chain-like appearance. The final meaning is so far removed from the primary meaning, that it is difficult to relate them without some knowledge of the history of the word. Similarly with the word *treacle* which originally meant "pertaining to wild beast". In modified sense, it meant in the second stage "remedy for wild beast's bite". In the third stage it acquired general applicability to any antidote or remedy. In the fourth stage it has specialised in its meaning, remedy in the form of syrup. In the fifth stage it meant any syrup in general and finally now it means sugary syrup. It can be noticed here that the word has acquired its last meaning in successive steps of generalisation followed by specialisation. Words like *candidate, cheater, squire, person, pen, pencil* and so on are other interesting examples of thi!; semantic phenomenon.

5. Degeneration of Meaning. "Descent is easy", observes: Kittredge, "and words, like people, show a propensity to fall away from their better selves". Respectful terms have become terms of extreme contempt and reprobation. It is difficult to say when a word starts on its downward journey. The word *villain* is a striking example of this process. It was derived from the Latin *villa*, 'farm-house', and signified a 'farm-labourer' in the beginning. That is, the word was descriptive of a particular station in life. Soon it came to signify one who did not belong to gentry. Thus, gradually *villain* was applied to a *low fellow* and villainy to low form of conduct. In modern English class distinction has been lost. A king or a beggar can be called a *villain* if he is morally wicked. *Knave* had a similar history. It meant originally 'boy'. Since servants were often addressed as boys, the word was applied to servants and men of inferior station in life. Since such inferior classes were supposed to have no moral values, the word acquired its final meaning of moral worthlessness. *Fellow* is another word which had seen better days. It was derived from the Old English *feologa* "one who laid down his property" and, therefore, a partner, and then a companion. Since each partner has a tendency to accuse the other of idleness and so on, the word has arrived at the slighting modern sense. The original meaning, however, is preserved in combinations like *fellow-ship, fellow-feeling, fellow-countryman*. There are many words in English which have suffered this downward tendency in their meanings. *Lust, simple silly, innocent, crafty* were all at one time good and commendatory words but "they have not remained so in the corrupted currents of this world".

It is said that the English have a well-developed talent for discovering moral obliquity in others, and it may be that the frequent occurrence of degeneration in English words is the result of such a propensity. *Lewd* originally meant "not in holy orders". Later it came to signify "the untaught" and remained a term of a sort of contempt. This contemptuous sense has been specialised into modern sense "lascivious" or "unchaste". *Cunning* was nothing but the present participle of *can*, which meant "to know, to be able". Sly once meant only 'skilful' without any modern associations.

6. Elevation of Meaning. It is a form of specialisation, like degeneration and is seen in a good number of English words. The word fellow which has been given as an example of degeneration, can also be made to illustrate this process. *Fellow* in its academic sense is certainly an elevation from its earlier business associations. From the fifteenth century, *fellow* was the name given to a member of a college or any learned society. Today a *Fellow* of the Royal Society is the highest academic distinction attainable. While *knave* is (which meant boy in Old English) an example of deterioration in meaning, its Old English synonym *knight* tells us the story of elevation of its meaning. Similarly fame meant originally "report" or "talk", neither good nor bad, but now the word has specialised in its good sense. Its older meaning is preserved in a phrase like a *house of ill-fame*. *Luxury* is another word which has undergone elevation. The change in this case is perhaps due to our attitude to life. In its early sense it was a word of strong blame; *luxury* was then what is *lust* today, one of the seven deadly sins. From the seventeenth century the word came to signify any indulgence (not necessarily blameworthy), in anything choice or costly.

7. Euphemism and Prudery. Euphemism is a process of semantic change and Prudery is the cause of euphemism. Prudery is the result of a certain false sense of delicacy and refinement and implies an element of social snobbery and affectation. This process of semantic change is chiefly due to our reluctance to call spade a spade. Otherwise there is no reason why *legs* should be called limbs, *dirty* is described by a negative term like *untidy* or *unclean*. It is because of this habit of calling unpleasant things by superficially pleasant names that we use *passing away* for *death, insane* for *mad* and *executed* for *hanged*. The blatant fact that "you lie" is given a verbal veneer in various circumlocutions, like "you are somewhat distorting the facts" or "you make inaccurate statement". A courteous Elizabethan would prefer to say, "I fear you have done yourself some wrong". In the language of a Parliamentarian, "you are guilty of terminological inexactitude". It is due to similar semantic process that a *boarder* is called a *paying guest*. Unscrupulous and exorbitant moneylenders are stylishly called *financiers*. In the language of Euphemism and Prudery butchers are *meat-purveyors*, plumbers are *sanitary engineers* and *undertaker* (at least in America) are *morticians*. The nineteenth century abounds in such snobbish expressions. Simple *spitting* was made to sound high in *expectoration*. The words *guts* and *belly* were regarded as so vulgar that they were not mentioned in polite circles. Certain words in common use today have originated as euphemisms. *Lavatory*, for example literally a washing place", is called "an office" by the auctioneer; public authorities call it "convenience" and strangely Americans call it 'toilet'. Since Ben Jonson's word *muckinder* sounds gross, the *hand-kerchief* (literally hand-head-covering), though a contradiction in terms has been introduced. For the sake of refinement *dung* was replaced by *manure* and in recent times *manure* has begun to be replaced by *fertiliser* or *chemical*.

❐